UFO's and the Complete Evidence from Space

The Truth About Venus, Mars, and the Moon

by Daniel Ross

Pintado Publishing
P.O. Box 3033, Walnut Creek, Ca. 94598

Printed in the United States of America

Times such as ours have always bred defeatism and despair. But there remain, nonetheless, some few among us who believe man has within him the capacity to meet and overcome even the greatest challenges of this time. If we want to avoid defeat, we must wish to know the truth and be courageous enough to act upon it. If we get to know the truth and have the courage, we need not despair.

- Albert Einstein

Acknowledgements

The author wishes to express his appreciation to Adrianne Brown for the cover painting, and a sincere dedication to Pamela Ross for her immeasurable assistance and valuable contributions during the preparation of this book.

Special thanks and acknowledgement to GAF International Publishers for permission to quote from the books of George Adamski.

CONTENTS

Illustrations

> *Plates 1 to 16 follow page 58.*
>
> *Plates 17 to 31 follow page 154.*

Chapter 1
Defining the Mystery

Few people today have not heard the term UFO. Used as an abbreviation for sightings of Unidentified Flying Objects, the term has been in general acceptance for many years. Implicit in the term is the belief by most people, that many unidentified flying objects are space vehicles of extraterrestrial origin. Though its usage has been commonly accepted, few people today know the truth behind the very real existence of UFOs.

It should not be a mystery at the present time; yet, for a number of reasons the subject has been promoted as such, in order to protect certain vested interests. This book will categorically dispel the confusion, and present the real truth behind the interplanetary space vehicles that have been seen in our skies and reported world-wide for four decades. The evidence and interpretation will be presented on a solid-ground basis. Regarding the subject of UFOs, any presentations of a mystical basis are false, and therefore are not a part of this book's content.

These visiting spaceships, which have maintained an ongoing rendezvous with our planet, have home planets that are equally as habitable as our Earth. There is no mystery about UFOs once their origin is learned and understood. Their origin is the other planets of our solar system, and the space travelers are human in every respect.

Intelligence departments within the U.S. government, such as the National Security Agency, the Central Intelligence Agency, and special military departments, have had this information for many years. High-ranking administrators within the National Aeronautics and Space Administration (NASA) have had full knowledge of the situation. But during the last twenty years, an entirely false picture of space findings and planetary conditions was promoted and publicized. Orthodox scientific thinking was determinedly propped up, and as a direct consequence, the subject of UFOs became more controversial - and a seemingly unsolvable mystery to the public.

The main part of this book will therefore explain the actual planetary conditions on Mars, Venus, and the Moon, along with the recent history of UFOs. The two subjects are completely related. In short, this work is an up-to-date presentation on space science.

The reader may be interested to learn how I first got started in this field. My research in the subject began in 1974, following a well-documented UFO sighting in upstate New York. Prior to that time, I was not familiar with the subject of UFOs, nor was I interested in space research. I had been involved in scientific learning though, in a natural way, ever since my early years of education.

Like many students, I had studied all the college preparatory courses in chemistry, biology, physics, and mathematics. About a year after high school, I decided to enter the U.S. Navy and join the submarine service. I looked forward to an adventurous tour of duty on nuclear subs. So early in 1966 I enlisted, and boarded a train for "boot camp" at Great Lakes, Illinois. While at basic training, I qualified for the Navy's electronic school, and the nuclear power training program for reactor operators.

After completing the 38-week course in electronics, I headed to San Diego for temporary duty on board a submarine tender. In 1968, I began my nuclear power training at the Navy's school in California. It was a full educational program of nuclear physics, reactor plant technology, chemistry, radiation principles, and fluid mechanics. To complete the 12-month program, I received my prototype training at the Naval Reactors Testing Site in Idaho. Then following a short school in Connecticut, I was assigned to a fast attack submarine in San Diego. A surprise set of orders came for me one day, to transfer to a submarine under new construction at Mare Island Shipyard in California.

The submarine was the U.S.S. Pintado (SSN 672). During the lengthy construction period, the ship's crew was completely trained for each phase of operational testing of the reactor's primary and secondary power plants. Every step of the way towards completion involved rigorous learning and application of new knowledge by the ship's crew. There are no short-cuts to bringing a new submarine into the fleet, and that ship's crew becomes highly qualified in the process. Following the sub's commissioning, we received the highest performance evaluation on the Operational Reactor Safeguards Examination, - an exam given annually to each nuclear-powered ship in the Navy.

As a new ship of the Pacific fleet, we set out for naval ports along the western coast. We went to Canada and Hawaii, before returning to homeport San Diego. The submarine experience was a combination of hard work and adventure. It seemed like a good time to be in the Navy.

My three years of duty on the Pintado was up in 1972, and then I went to the PME school in Colorado for an advanced course in electronics. My last 16 months in the service were spent on another submarine, that was homeported at the naval subase in Groton, Connecticut. While attached to that boat, our operations took us to ports on the eastern coast, and down to the Virgin Islands. On a separate two-month trip, we traveled past the Arctic Circle, around northern Scandinavia, and into the White Sea.

In retrospect, I can now see that while serving in the Navy, I was very unaware of anything else going on in the world, let alone what was going on in space. It had been an educational adventure on the finest technological machine ever built by man, and I was absorbed in the challenging work. Consequently, I never found time to pursue other interests, or read up on much. And regarding space, I only knew that we had made it to the Moon and back.

My tour of duty, and enlistment, ended in June, 1974. It

had been a "full" eight years. Many of the guys with whom I had served went off to work at nuclear power plants around the country, but I was in no hurry to follow that occupational route. Reactor physics and technology had been a good experience, but I wanted to extend my education, and explore other fields of knowledge at college. It was an easy decision for me to return to San Diego, California, where eventually I completed three years at San Diego State University. I studied courses offered by many departments - from humanities to natural sciences, philosophy to engineering, cultural history to psychology, along with studies in upper division experimental courses.

But during that time, I was doing more personal study and research in other fields outside of college work, than I was at the university. Part of my efforts required a lot of time and money seeking hard-to-find books, journals, and little-known publications. I was on a quest for knowledge beyond that of any single profession. This new and limitless field was space science and space age philosophy. Yet it had very little to do with any national space program. Rather it was a self-learned and self-directed search for fundamental truths, which then could integrate knowledge from many fields for a fuller understanding of life. Something took place shortly after my discharge from the service, that prompted my search in this new direction.

I had been in upstate New York briefly, before my move to San Diego, California. In fact, I was staying in the town where I was born and grew up - Glens Falls. And on the evening of August 20, 1974, one of the best UFO cases on record occurred over our small city. For several hours, hundreds of residents watched as a fleet of brightly illuminated spaceships hovered and flew in various directions across the sky at low altitudes. I first heard of the sightings when radio station WWSC of Glens Falls scrapped its regular programming in order to air the phone calls coming into the station by excited residents. I went outside with the rest of my family and kept the transistor radio tuned to the broadcast. Then we learned that several hundred people had gathered near the radio station to watch the sightings. Since I had a good view from where I was, I decided not to drive the mile or so to where the crowd was gathering. Traffic and parking would consume too much valuable time, and while driving my view would be obscured. And I didn't know when the objects might fly off for good. I heard that both the state and local police were on the scene directing traffic and asking the large crowd to move down to the nearby recreational park.

I scanned the sky trying to find the objects. Being unaccustomed to looking at the night sky, I first sighted what turned out to be a cluster of bright stars. But after several minutes, I suddenly saw a brightly illuminated orange object speed across my view. It came to a complete stop and hovered briefly, before reversing its direction and flying back to join a group of fainter objects. Its speed was incredible. Then all of the objects slowly moved to another area of the sky.

It was an impressive and beautiful moment for me, and I would imagine for most of the people who saw these luminescent objects in the sky. The ships moved in close frequently during the night, radiating beautiful luminescent colors. The feeling is hard to describe, but suddenly so many thoughts or impressions were passing through my mind. There was no question that these were intelligently controlled ships. Wherefrom I couldn't be certain, but there was an absolute feeling of a close relationship somehow, between Earth and their home. Many feelings really couldn't be put into words, and there didn't seem to be any reason to do so at the time. It was simply a feeling of awe, wonder, and illumination. The sighting I was witnessing, was convincing proof to me that we are not alone. It was a tremendous realization, and a peaceful feeling, that words seem inadequate to convey.

That evening a lot of people came into the area to find out what all the excitement was about after hearing the radio reports. Perhaps some remained skeptical. The sightings varied in duration and were unpredictable. But the majority of people who were patient, caught glimpses of the ships in several localities during the evening. Many people sensed that the impressive event was an undeniable display of extraterrestrial spacecraft. The origin of the ships certainly couldn't be determined from just seeing the objects, and many people probably had their own guesses or theories. But there was a predominant feeling of tremendous significance behind the reality of what we were seeing.

The radio station did a very fine effort in coordinating the information and making it possible for the people in our area to share the excitement of the sightings. Also, the Glens Falls Post Star newspaper did a good write-up on the eventful night in their August 22nd edition, mentioning that several hundred residents witnessed a stunning display by airborn objects.

That is the event as I had witnessed it. However, later I found out that there had been more sightings earlier in the evening, by residents who lived closer to Albany, which is the capital of New York. In fact, the UFO sightings of August 20, 1974, has become one of the best documented cases on record, because it involved the state police, county sheriffs, and the Federal Aviation control tower at the Albany Airport, in addition to hundreds of citizens as already mentioned.

At about 8 pm, residents near the farming community of Round Lake called the state police to report numerous lights in the sky. Trooper Michael Morgan was dispatched to the area to investigate. After arriving there, he and another officer watched as a large blimp-shaped object moved slowly out over Saratoga Lake. The immense object glowed with a reddish, pulsating luminescence. Then the police noticed two small white objects at a height of about 1500 feet fly down and apparently enter the large glowing blimp. The police called the airport, and Supervisor Robert King confirmed that he and several air traffic controllers on duty were able to track the huge object on all four radar screens. Suddenly the two small objects reappeared and flew off in the direction from where they had come.

The cigar shaped blimp turned slowly and moved towards the nearby police barracks. Then it accelerated in a tremendous burst of speed towards Albany. An Air Force pilot on a training flight in the area excitedly called in that a brilliant object had just flown across his flightpath towards the airport.

In the control tower, the men watched the radar screens and calculated the speed of the craft to be 3,600 miles per hour. The flight of the ship was also seen by Warren Johnson, a state trooper who happened to be parked on the route 87 highway near Albany.

Shortly after this incident, other brilliant lights were seen and reported. It was then that the Civil Air Patrol at Albany sent up planes to investigate. One pilot was flying at 8,000 feet when he saw a silent object pass his plane at an unbelievable speed. The traffic controllers turned on another radarscope and spotted the speeding object on the screen. By using the anti-clutter device, they confirmed once again that they were tracking a solid object. Its speed increased from 3000 to 5000 miles per hour as it vanished from the Albany area.

Prior to August 1974, I had no personal reason to research space science. Then I happened to be at the right place to witness an event that was proof to me and hundreds of other people, that UFOs exist. My scientific background and worldly education were not complete enough to explain it. That was obvious. But I wanted to know the answers. I would never be satisfied with a mystery. What point is there in just knowing that UFOs exist? These spaceships were alerting us to life beyond the Earth for a reason, or purpose. And I did not believe that the visitors would leave us in endless confusion by only allowing our civilization to speculate. Since traveling space definitely equates to intelligence, then they would have used some down-to-earth means of contact with reliable and credible people.

The excitement of the sightings lasted a few days among the residents, but for my wife and I, it was time to drive our car and our belongings across the country to San Diego. Soon I was enjoying my first months as a civilian, and especially so, being in this beautiful area of southern California. The beaches, the weather, the parks, and the city nights were what we had been looking forward to. We took short trips along the coast, and north to Palomar Mountain, then south to Mexico. Another day we went down to the navy submarine pier where my old ships were homeported. We found some time to go camping in the mountains that lay east of the city. At our new home in San Diego, the future looked bright and promising.

Shortly after we settled into our new environment, I picked up a small paperback book. The topic was on archaeological puzzles and other unsolved mysteries on Earth, along with a brief discussion concerning theories about extraterrestrial visitors in the past. The book was only somewhat interesting, but strictly speaking, it was essentially meaningless. My interest quickly subsided and I soon forgot all about it. That is the way many UFO and ancient mystery books go. There is little if anything definitive, amid a barrage of speculation and guesses. There is the chance that a little of the information is true, but the significance cannot be understood until the reader (or that book's author) is familiar with the best books on UFOs and related space sciences.

Writing now years later, I can personally attest to the fact, that there is an extremely long distance between a simple curiosity or belief, and the real knowledge behind what is happening in space concerning the evidence of interplanetary spaceships. One can not fill that gap with simply his own speculations, or with someone else's speculations, and claim to be knowledgeable about UFOs. The truth is not subjected to man's wishful thinking, ever.

While reading the newspaper, I spotted an announcement that a course was being taught on UFOs, on Wednesday evenings at a local school. The sighting in New York had occurred but a month before, and therefore I did not hesitate to check out the class. More than a hundred people showed up the first night of the 10- week course.

The man teaching was a very energetic person, very fluent in his discussions, and he spoke with a good measure of enthusiasm. He obviously enjoyed introducing this subject to others, and he talked about everything in a very down-to-earth way. Yet he was not there wasting his time or anyone else's. There were some definite "knowns" on this subject, and solid evidence regarding numerous sightings of UFOs. He showed slides and various 8-mm movie clips taken by independent witnesses in recent years. Most pictures were of bell-shaped scoutcraft. The instructor also showed the class a semi-documentary film based on Air Force records.

The man gained my respect early. He never talked down to anyone, nor did he speak as an intellectual defending some professional status. He encouraged people to express their thoughts, as numerous people had had sightings of their own. They had seen something 3-dimensional and physical in the Earth's atmosphere. And in the case of two young men, a large object was seen quite close to the ground, before it slowly rose and shot up into the night sky. There were no "mental experiences" or nonsense psychic talk among the people in this class. They had real visual sightings as I had had, and they wanted to know what was the real knowledge about UFO sightings. Or in other words, who are they, and why are they here?

The instructor spoke knowledgeably about the whole spectrum of UFO evidence, but his most thorough discussions were on the work of George Adamski - a man who had authored three books on flying saucers, and who had gained world-wide recognition for his presentations on the subject of interplanetary visitations. It took me about a week to find a copy of his first book, *Flying Saucers Have Landed*. We could obtain the paperback editions of Adamski's two other books from the instructor, though later I found both of these in their original hardcover editions through used bookstores.

The teacher handed out a suggested reading list, which was a bibliography of about twenty books. Few were then currently in print, but eventually I traced all of them down through my wanderings in used bookstores in San Diego and Los Angeles. But by that time, I had picked up another 150 books on this subject and related fields. Science, archaeology, cultural history, astronomy, astrophysics, meteorology, mythology, philosophy, important biographies, and countless obscure publications. Also, many books and articles on the Moon. I studied science magazines and started filing articles from them, along with newspaper clippings. Most of the valuable books I obtained cannot be found in libraries, or in current bookstores. One has to build up his own library. I did make good use of public libraries also, and photocopied what I needed. But this type of research slowly developed over a few years' time. My new interest in space sciences began quite naturally, after reading the books written by George Adamski.

George Adamski's account in *Flying Saucers Have Landed* is an honest and straightforward discussion. His story intelligently broke ground in a new subject, that by 1953, had intrigued a global population concerning flying saucer reports. Adamski recounted his five-year-long efforts to photograph these space objects, an effort that actually began with a request by the U.S. military laboratory at San Diego, California. After hundreds of nights at his telescope watching the heavens from his Mt. Palomar home, Adamski had obtained at least a dozen photographs which were good enough to show that these craft maneuvering in our skies and near the moon were not of earth origin.

By 1952, he had heard a number of reports that the saucers were frequently being seen near our military sites, and at times, making brief landings in remote desert areas. Adamski loaded his camera equipment and 6-inch telescope, and made several trips to these out-of-the-way spots. He had no success in seeing the objects at close range until a fateful day late in the year.

It was in November, when on short notice, Adamski left his Palomar home with two assistants to meet a group of four acquaintances for a drive to an area near California's Mojave Desert. After reaching the city of Blythe, they decided to drive back to a small town called Desert Centre, and from there continued driving about 11 miles down Parker Highway. The small group chose to stop at a location not far from an old abandoned military site. It was not a sandy desert area. The ground was rocky, and covered with sparse desert scrub. Just a few miles distant stood a ridge of mountains.

After eating a light lunch which had been packed for this trip, the small party of men and women took in a little survey of the area on foot. Around noontime a solitary plane flew overhead, breaking the stillness of the desert air. Within minutes of seeing this conventional airplane, the group simultaneously spotted a gigantic cigar-shaped object flying higher, and silently, across the distant mountain range. Slowly it turned towards their direction, and then it stopped - hovering motionless. Passing around two pairs of binoculars, the excited witnesses realized that this was a spaceship.

Adamski quickly reasoned that any chance of personal contact might be lost if they remained at a spot close to the highway, since they would naturally attract the curiosity of passing motorists. He and two of his companions drove one of the cars along a rough road on the abandoned target range, stopping about a half mile from the originally chosen spot. All the while, they kept the large spaceship in sight. While setting up his camera equipment, Adamski requested that his two friends get back to the others, and for all of them to watch closely should something take place. Adamski had a definite feeling that something would happen, but just then the big spaceship turned and went in the opposite direction. Several military planes suddenly flew across the sky, apparently trying to circle and identify the huge ship, but very quickly it turned upward, and "shot out into space, leaving our planes circling -nothing."

Another five minutes elapsed, when Adamski suddenly noticed a flash in the sky. A beautiful small craft was slowly drifting down towards a cove between two nearby mountain peaks. He quickly took a few chance snapshots with the camera that was attached to his portable telescope. Then as he picked up his other hand-held camera and snapped a picture, the craft disappeared behind some prominent hills. Adamski was awed at seeing a ship so close, and he wondered what to do next as several minutes passed by.

Then suddenly, he saw a man standing near a ravine between two low hills, who motioned to Adamski to come towards him. Adamski was uncertain as to where the man had come from - was he a prospector of the area? Maybe a stranger who had also sighted the little ship. Or maybe someone who needed help. The man was about a quarter of a mile away, so it was impossible to tell. Adamski decided to walk towards the man, while making sure that he was in full sight of his friends back near the road.

As he approached, he saw that the man was smiling in a friendly way. He appeared to be young, and his clothing was somewhat different. It looked like a one-piece garment with ski-type trousers. As Adamski got close, the man took a few steps forward until they were within an arm's length of each other.

At that moment, and without a word being spoken, Adamski fully realized that he was in the presence of a man from space - a human being from another world. The visitor immediately impressed him with a feeling of infinite understanding and kindness. And by then the slightest trace of caution had left Adamski completely.

Adamski was so taken with the visitor's pleasant and noble features, that he did not think to inquire about the ship at first. Adamski relates:

> He extended his hand in a gesture towards shaking hands. I responded in our customary manner. But he rejected this with a smile and a slight shake of his head. Instead of grasping hands as we on Earth do, he placed the palm of his hand against the palm of my hand, just touching it but not too firmly. I took this to be the sign of friendship.
>
> He was about five feet, six inches in height, and weighed according to our standards about 135 pounds. And I would estimate him to be about 28 years of age, although he could have been much older.
>
> He was round faced with an extremely high forehead; large, but calm, grey-green eyes, slightly

aslant at the outer corners; with slightly higher cheek bones than an Occidental, but not so high as an Indian or an Oriental; a finely chiselled nose, not conspicuously large; and an average size mouth with beautiful white teeth that shone when he smiled or spoke.

The space man's hair was long, reaching to his shoulders, sandy in color and blowing slightly in the wind. Adamski described his skin as beautiful, and similar to the color of a medium suntan. It did not appear that he ever had to shave, for there was no more hair on his face than on a child's.

Adamski described the man's clothing as a one-piece garment of very fine woven material, with long sleeves and pant legs. It was chocolate brown except for a golden brown band that circled his waist. It appeared to be a very comfortable uniform for space travel. Adamski did not see any zippers, buttons, or buckles, and noticed that the man wore no ring, watch, or other ornament. The shoes were like leather, but soft and flexible, and the toes were blunt.

While collecting his thoughts on the man's appearance, Adamski put forth his first question, asking the man where he came from. But the visitor didn't seem to understand the spoken words. So Adamski attempted to express his thoughts by using gestures, signs, and by means of natural telepathy. This is a natural form of expression where thoughts and mental pictures can be communicated through the cardinal sense of feeling. Adamski had studied along these lines, and had taught this as fact for more than 30 years.

(This is a natural, inherent ability in man, and in all forms of life. But the mind must be freed from its usual personal thoughts, emotional conflicts, and everyday anxieties. While in the exhilarating freedom of space, and with their minds temporarily unburdened from everyday uncertainties, our own astronauts all of a sudden sensed this natural ability. James Irwin (Apollo 15) recalls in his book, *To Rule the Night*, "Everybody felt...more efficient in space than on earth, that they had achieved a feeling of mental power. We all thought with a new clarity, almost a clairvoyance. I could almost anticipate what Dave Scott was going to say, and I felt I knew what he was thinking.")

Telepathy is natural. It has nothing to do with psychic promotions, extra-sensory perception (ESP), or other forms of wishful thinking. It is not "extra-sensory," because it is a natural feeling aligned with the senses. In other words, it is a natural ability to communicate thoughts. Our astronauts stumbled upon this awareness while in space, whereas Adamski had self-learned and developed this inherent ability on his own.

Along with corresponding gestures, and occasionally a repeated word, Adamski and the space visitor had little difficulty understanding the thought that each other wished to convey. The spaceman affirmed that he had come from Venus, the second planet in orbit around the sun. He repeated the answer, and actually confirmed it by saying the word, Venus.

To Adamski's question of why they were coming to Earth, the man indicated that they were concerned with the radiations going out into space as a result of our experimentation with atomic bombs in the atmosphere. Yet Adamski was made to understand that their coming was friendly. In all that the man conveyed during this contact, there was no trace of resentment or judgement on his face. "His expression was one of understanding, and great compassion - as one would have toward a much loved child who had erred through ignorance and lack of understanding." This feeling was impressed upon Adamski throughout the meeting.

Adamski was successful in getting responses to several topics, ranging from answers on their basic methods of space travel, to reasons why the visitors were alerting us to life beyond the Earth. One point that the space man was emphatic in making clear to our earthly representative, was that the human form is universal throughout the solar system and the cosmos. All planets that have civilizations are inhabited by human beings, as is the Earth, and all space travelers are human beings, men and women. Adamski was more than assured that the space visitor knew exactly what he was talking about. There are no weird occupants, strange aliens, or other imaginations, such as has been suggested by small minds and unknowledgeable "experts."

The meeting had lasted about thirty minutes, when the man indicated that it was time for him to return to his ship. He motioned to Adamski to come with him. Together they walked about 100 yards towards a nearby hill, where a small scoutcraft was hovering just a few feet above the ground. Adamski caught a fleeting glance of another person within the ship - apparently it was the pilot of the little spacecraft awaiting the return of the Venusian visitor.

Adamski was both thrilled and speechless to be so close to one of these beautiful spacecraft. He described it as more bell-shaped than a saucer, and there was a translucent quality to the metallic body, which reflected the sunlight in beautiful prismatic colors. In his written account, he related in detail the general features of the small ship - the domed top, with portholes and a magnetic power coil at its base, and a solid flange that extended beyond the three-ball landing gear.

Adamski asked if he could go inside the ship but the request was denied, since the visitor indicated that he had to be going and no time remained. But the man indicated that he would like to take one of the photographic plates which Adamski had been carrying in his pockets. He made Adamski understand that he would return it at a later time. Then he stepped up to an entrance around the side and entered the ship.

It slowly rose and flew silently toward the crest of the mountains in the distance, finally taking altitude and disappearing up into space. From his earlier discussion with the visitor, Adamski realized that the little spacecraft would return to its large interplanetary mothership that was waiting in an orbit above the Earth's atmosphere. He signalled to his friends who had been watching from their waiting point. They had been able to witness the entire contact, and had seen the scoutship's departure. They raced down to talk with Adamski, and began firing all sorts of questions. Together they all walked back to the spot where the contact had taken place. It was here that the visitor had purposely left behind distinct footprints, before returning to his ship with Adamski. He had indicated that there was importance in the markings left behind in the imprints, and Adamski surmised that the visitor had worn specially embossed shoes for the purposes of this contact. There were several strange symbols and markings contained in the neat impressions. Adamski's group made sketches, photographs, and then plaster casts of the two sets of footprints, before gathering up all the equipment and camera gear and packing everything in the cars.

They spent an hour or two absorbed in the tremendous realization of what had taken place, while waiting for the plaster casts to sufficiently dry. They made a few markers of the location with stones, should someone want to come out and investigate the site in the near future. Then Adamski and his companions drove back the ten miles to Desert Centre, and there they spent the evening recounting the eventful experience over dinner.

This is how the historic contact took place on November 20, 1952. Within a few days of the incident, the story was given to newspaper reporters in Arizona and California. After a careful check into the details, photos, and accounts given by the witnesses, two newspapers gave a full report of the amazing contact.When Adamski's book was published the following year, it quickly became the first widely-accepted account of a meeting with a visitor from another planet.

Included within his book were close-up telescopic photos of the Venusian scoutship that made a return visit on December 13, 1952. At his Palomar Gardens home, Adamski had kept himself constantly alerted for such a possibility, since the spaceman had indicated that he would return the borrowed photoplate. Twenty-three days after that initial contact, the promise was fulfilled.

Because he had heard some jets flying overhead,

Adamski stationed himself out by his telescope. It was early morning around 9 o'clock. Shortly after the sky was clear of our planes, he saw a flash in the sky. Quickly he set his telescope on it. Adjusting his focus as the object flew silently towards his property, Adamski could clearly see the bell-shaped craft reflecting its brilliant colors in the morning sun. At about 1000 yards from him, it suddenly stopped, and hovered in mid-air 500 feet above the valley. Adamski believed that the pilot knew he was there at his telescope, and he quickly took two shots with his camera. Then he turned the camera on the eyepiece and took another picture. A fourth picture was taken just as the ship began to move again.

When it had approached to within 100 feet of Adamski, a porthole opened slightly and a hand went out, dropping the previously borrowed photoplate to the ground. The scoutcraft did not stop, but moved quickly over the property and headed east, fast disappearing in the brilliant sky. A few days later the photoplate was developed, revealing that a symbolic message had been superimposed on the film. Much later it was determined that there were two distinct aspects to the symbolic characters and writing, establishing a link to ancient records on Earth, along with symbols relating to present methods of space travel by interplanetary civilizations.

After the full discussion of his flying saucer research and the November 20 contact, Adamski concluded his first book by stating:

"The truth about flying saucers does exist. There are space visitors in our midst. And they are here for a purpose. We may as well search out and acquaint ourselves with this truth and address ourselves to its challenges and ultimatums...A deep analysis of events of the past makes me firmly believe that these people from other planets are our friends. I am convinced that their desire and their object is to help us and perhaps to protect us from even ourselves; as well as that, they mean to insure the safety and balance of the other planets in our system."

Much of Adamski's later information will be discussed throughout the text.

Many books have detailed the early years of UFO sightings. Kenneth Arnold made the first public report on June 24, 1947. While flying his private plane over the Mount Rainier area of Washington State, he suddenly noticed a formation of nine bright objects off to his left. They were flying very close to the mountain tops, and traveling on a line that would make them pass directly in front of his airplane. All of the objects were disc-shaped and appeared to be 45 to 50 feet in size. The objects traversed the mountainous terrain, in a manner that Arnold compared to a saucer skipping across the surface of water. It was on hearing this description, that newspaper reporters coined a phrase to describe the oval objects that Kenneth Arnold had seen - flying saucers. His report was the beginning of thousands of sightings world-wide.

During the next few months, many sighting reports were made by military and civilian airline pilots. The pilots were taken by surprise to see unknown airborn objects pacing their aircraft and making stunning maneuvers and accelerations. There were numerous reports of saucer sightings near military bases. The Air Force began its investigation at top levels, while newspapers carried frequent sightings from the civilian population.

Within three months, a secret memo was drafted and forwarded to the Commanding General of the Air Force, stating that flying saucers were real and intelligently controlled. But no real answers were given to the public, as the number of sightings continued to stack up month after month. A number of stock explanations were bandied out to the press - misidentification of known objects, high flying birds or balloons, hoaxes, mirages, and delusions.

But the Air Technical Intelligence Center for the Air Force drew up a top secret report in August 1948, called the "Estimate of the Situation." It concluded that UFOs were interplanetary spaceships. From then on the UFO security lid was down tight at government levels. The Air Force was forced into a burdensome public relations role for the next several years - conducting studies and investigating reports, but publicly claiming that no absolute proof existed. Quoting scientific advisors from the conservative ranks added weight and prestige to the government's position. The Air Force also decided that the term flying saucer was too suggestive of a space vehicle, and preferred instead to emphasize the more official term - Unidentified Flying Object. That designation would help perpetuate the idea of an "unknown" and undefined phenomena.

Despite the official position that nothing was known for certain regarding the reports of outer space vehicles, the public was steadily learning to accept the idea that life existed beyond the Earth, as the real UFOs constantly made their presence known. Edward Ruppelt, who authored *The Report on Unidentified Flying Objects* after heading the Air Force Project Blue Book investigations, wrote that during a six-month period in 1952 alone, 16,000 news items on UFOs were carried by the one hundred major newspapers in the country. That averages out to 160 news reports per newspaper. These were only the public reports. At the same time during this period, the military office at Project Blue Book was getting "frantic phonecalls from intelligence officers all over the United States, as every Air Force installation in the U.S. was being swamped with UFO reports. (Ruppelt) told the intelligence officers to send in the ones that sounded the best."

There are two types of spacecraft that have been sighted since the late 1940's. The smaller vehicles have been described as saucers, ovals, disks, globes, and bell-shaped scoutcraft, depending on the object's distance from the observer, or its position in the sky relative to the observer. Descriptions also vary due to the general seeing conditions night or day, and because the energy field surrounding the spacecraft can change in intensity, causing varying luminescence effects. These saucer-type spacecraft range in size, from 30 feet to 150 feet in diameter. This type of space vehicle can be piloted to a landing on Earth, and this has been reported in numerous UFO incidences over the years.

The interplanetary ships are large cigar-shaped craft. These carrier ships seldom venture below our upper atmosphere, and the much smaller scoutcraft disembark and return to these ships. The large interplanetary carriers, or mother-ships as they are called, are several hundred feet in length, at a minimum. Some gigantic ones are much longer. Both carrier ships and scoutcraft derive their operating power by harnessing the natural electromagnetic energy fields in space.

All spacecraft can send out small scanning disks. These are remotely-controlled little spheres, ranging from tennis ball size to basketball size. All UFOs are of metallic construction. The saucer-type scoutcraft and the scanning disks have brightly reflective surfaces. They are often intensely luminescent, particularly in the nighttime sky. This is an effect caused by the electromagnetic frequencies of their propulsive energy. The presence of this energy causes ionization of the air immediately around the spaceship, or around the disk, giving the appearance of a brilliantly colored object.

There is a third type of spacecraft which can plunge into seas and travel underwater, as well as travel through space. It is shaped like a submarine. There have been more than a few incidents recorded in the logbooks of ocean-going ships, whose crews have witnessed occurrences related to this type of extraterrestrial spacecraft. I have read of several cases, which were reported in well-researched books.

In 1975 I got to hear a first-hand account by a civilian engineer. The witness was a middle-aged man, who was professionally employed as a nuclear engineer. He told a group of us about an experience that he had kept silent about for 13 years. During the fall of 1962, he had gone on a fishing trip off the New England coast with two of his co-workers. When they were several miles from shore that afternoon, they suddenly noticed that the water near the boat was turbulent and frothy. One of the men thought they were in the middle of a large school of fish, and he went rushing for some nets. Another fellow yelled that he was sure they were dangerously close to a submarine preparing to surface. Their moment of panic and confusion was suddenly interrupted when a gigantic craft rose from beneath the surface and hovered noiselessly 25 feet above the ocean. What had appeared was a cigar-shaped ship not more than 150 yards from their little boat. It was close enough that they could see water drip off back into the ocean. The men all watched in stunned amazement for several seconds as the nose of the craft became encircled by a brilliant blue glow, and then the front end tilted up. The ship made a slight increase in altitude, and then shot up into space. In scarcely a moment, it was but a barely visible dot in the sky.

It had all happened right before their eyes. That much they were sure of. But what it was, they didn't know what to believe. Before any discussion or jumping to conclusions, they decided to each write down his own account of what had happened.

The engineer who told us of the experience is very conservative, and by his own admission, keeps to the orthodox views of science. Yet he knew he had seen something that was beyond our technological achievements. And it wasn't until he came across a photograph that looked identical to his sighting, that he decided to tell his experience. The photograph was one taken by George Adamski, showing this type of submarine-spacecraft.

Chapter 2
Important Case Sightings

According to a Gallup poll in 1973, half of the adult population in the U.S. believes that UFOs are real. Eleven percent of the people surveyed said that they had seen a UFO. This high percentage meant that a projected 15 million people in the U.S. had had a sighting.[1] Another poll was taken by MENSA International (an organization of people with high IQs), and its survey showed that 64 percent of its highly educated members believe that UFOs are "spaceships from other planets," and that the spaceships "are carrying passengers who are studying our behavior."

Former astronaut Gordon Cooper appeared as a guest on the nationally broadcast "Mike Douglas TV Show" in January 1977. During this program, Cooper described in detail a sighting he witnessed in Europe when he was a pilot with an Air Force fighter squadron in the early 1950's. High flying objects had been spotted maneuvering through the sky, generally from east to west, at an altitude greater than 50,000 feet. It was estimated that several hundred objects were seen passing over the area, during a period of two days. At one time or another, nearly all the pilots attached to the fighter squadron took a plane up as high as they could get, in order to see the UFOs. On one of the days, the whole squadron of Air Force jets took out after the UFOs. Mike Douglas asked Gordon Cooper to describe what they looked like.

Cooper: "Well, it's difficult to say other than they were sort of the typical, classical double saucer shape, metallic looking, no wings."

Douglas: "Were they revolving or actually spinning or

what?"

Cooper: "Not that you could see, no. But you couldn't see any propulsion trails behind them either."

Douglas: "How many men saw them?"

Cooper: "Probably a total of a hundred."

Douglas: "And didn't you chase them one day?"

Cooper: "Well one of those days; there really wasn't much chasing to it, because they were so much higher than us. They had us outclassed."

"There was another particular case where two friends of mine actually pulled up along side one, and at a lower altitude, on the airways here in the U.S. The UFO just tipped up at a sharp angle and climbed straight out."

Douglas: "Could they describe the speed?"

Cooper: "Well, it was accelerating pretty rapidly and they were in a jet."

As one of the original seven astronauts chosen by NASA, Gordon Cooper made his first orbital flight with the Mercury 9 spacecraft in 1963. Two years later he was the commander of the eight-day Gemini 5 mission. Curiously enough, Cooper never got to fly an Apollo mission, even though he was considered to be one of our most skilled space pilots. There were many in the space agency who think NASA removed him from the Apollo flights that would eventually land men on the Moon, because he had already seen too much in space, and his nature was such that he wanted to talk about it.[2] That knowledge was closed to anybody outside NASA until several years later.

It was in August 1976 that Gordon Cooper made these statements to the press during an interview in Los Angeles. "Intelligent beings from other planets regularly visit our world in an effort to enter into contact with us. I have encountered various ships during my space voyages. NASA and the American government know this and possess a great deal of evidence. Nevertheless, they remain silent in order to not alarm the people."[3]

Another significant statement was made by the former astronaut in 1978, when he appeared as a guest on the "Merv

Griffin TV Show." In response to a question on what the space visitors look like, Cooper answered that it is known from all the reliable accounts, that the UFO occupants do not look any different than we do. He indicated that he knew there had been genuine cases of contact. But with subsequent interviews, the former astronaut did not add any further information, and it was unclear whether or not he knew where the UFOs were coming from.

During an investigation into the Albany, New York, sightings of August 1974, (discussed in the previous chapter), Margaret Sachs learned of an interesting case of a scoutship landing, and wrote about it in her book, *Celestial Passengers.* This particular incident had occurred in the nearby town of Altamont, close to the time of the Albany sightings. The details of the case became available only after a local police detective contacted Sachs' co-researcher, Ernest Jahn, and suggested that he arrange to meet with one of the witnesses - a Mrs. Ruth Currie.

Mrs. Currie was the director of the Nash Nursing Home, and although she had been reluctant to discuss this incident previously, Mrs. Currie agreed to meet with UFO investigator Ernest Jahn. The sighting had occurred on or about April 30. That night, both she and her daughter noticed a strange light sitting on the road not far from the nursing home. Together they went outside in order to see what it could possibly be. They walked to within 200 feet of it, and found themselves staring in amazement at a large oval spacecraft that gave off a soft golden glow. It was resting on the road, and through a large round window there appeared to be a person walking back and forth within the craft, - apparently checking controls or working on something.

By this time, another woman from the rest home had joined them. Being quite unprepared for a sighting of this nature, the women decided within a few minutes to return to the house and call someone on the phone. Then, just as they turned to leave, they heard a soft whistling sound, and watched in awe as the spacecraft lifted up and quickly disappeared into the sky.

An employee's husband had been on his way to the nursing home at the time. He too had witnessed the craft leaving, and after stopping his car, watched as the craft gained altitude. He noticed that it gave off a pulsating glow, before it accelerated out of sight. The following morning, all of the witnesses went up the road and located the spot where the craft had been seen the previous evening. There were landing gear markings shaped like half-moons within a scorched, circular patch about 75 feet in diameter.[4]

Cases like this are not as rare as one might initially think. Over the years, they have typically happened to sincere and honest people who were unfamiliar with anything regarding UFOs. The witnesses usually were reluctant to tell anyone outside of their own family. In many cases, the witness felt that it was a personal and very profound experience, and therefore had no desire to seek believers or to allow the press to sensationalize it. So it was rare for researchers to discover the genuine accounts of very close sightings and actual landings. Now and then, the pilots or occupants of the scoutcraft have been seen briefly, in or outside of the ship. The visitors are always described as human in the authentic cases, if of course, they can be seen well enough.

One further note on similar cases should be mentioned. There have been actual incidents, after which an honest witness, with no intention to deceive, reported strange details. Often, the witness only saw the landed spacecraft and its occupants from a distance, and he did not wish to venture closer. His own ideas (and most people have them subconsciously as a carryover from fictional movie themes) then filled in the details. In other cases, the witness' fear of the unknown led to a complete misinterpretation of what he encountered. And when a person is too frightened, the space people would rather get in their ship and leave, because proper communication would be impossible.

In October 1954, Mrs. Jennie Roestenberg and her family watched as a domed scoutship hovered briefly, just above the roof of her home in England. Two men within the ship stood momentarily at the dome compartment windows, and looked down at the amazed family. Mrs. Roestenberg could see that the men were wearing blue clothing that resembled ski-suits, and a kind of transparent helmet. They had shoulder-length hair and high foreheads, and their skin appeared light. While surveying the little group of watchers below, the space pilots had unsmiling, but seemingly compassionate expressions on their faces. She said they looked like Earth men.

By their large numbers of ships, the space visitors from other planets have allowed millions of people to witness their presence in our skies - as the phenomena of UFO sightings has now spanned four decades - in order to stimulate our awareness to the degree that we accept. There was a sequential purpose to their visitations, that in the beginning, included frequent landings to make open contact with people.

During the decade of the 1950's, there were perhaps a few hundred cases worldwide, of landings and genuine contact with human visitors, though many incidents received little or no publicity due to the prevailing attitudes back then. Not only did the general public and the press have a disbelieving attitude, but the main investigative groups of the time were restricting UFO data to sightings and sighting reports. Additionally, there was some understandable reluctance by the witness to tell of his account and face hostile skepticism.

Yet despite the lack of coordination on our part, the varied incidents of close contact served their purpose, just as the large numbers of sighting reports were stimulating people's awareness to the reality of UFOs. The public was gradually learning to accept that the visitors were human, and not really different from us. Only when this was accepted by an individual, and by society, would the individual or that society be able to learn what lay behind this field. To know, in other words, what the actual truth was, as opposed to all the speculation. Because the truth has been brought here by human beings from other planets, and by making contact with reliable individuals, the interplanetary visitors did make known the true reasons for their coming.

The acceptance was, in large part, left up to society, since the space people would never force our thinking. If we wished to ignore or disregard the evidence, that was our choice. However, learning by our own way (as the Earth travels along its errant path of war) would be slow, difficult, and confusing. And our civilization's rightful progress may never come, due to the threat of nuclear annihilation.

I will take a moment here to explain the following. There was a lot of fraud and false claims also, in the early years of the UFO controversy, both in the reports of weird encounters and purported contactee claims. The same is going on today, and even though it has taken on a new dimension which is often supported by self–appointed "UFO experts," it is still nonsense. There are no non-human visitors, or "entities,"or "E.T." variants, or bizarre humanoids. And there is no truth whatsoever in psychic contact. These ideas about UFO occupants have been generated by man's imagination, and for the most part *fostered* - by years of absurd discussions and hypotheses of the so-called UFO experts, who lecture, publish, and circulate these ideas through the media. Where else would today's crop of alleged witnesses get their ideas? All the false stories are variants of the same fiction: an abduction, blackout, missing time, examination table, strange humanoid with no mouth, post-memory only through hypnosis, etc. It's a strange circle - the experts give credibility to wild and bizarre stories, publicly discuss them, and soon hear more of the same.

It needs to be re-established firmly, that the space civilizations coming our way are human in every respect - even more so, since their understanding of life is far greater than ours. People are no different anywhere in the cosmos, except for mental development and society growth. In other words, the only differences lie in their understanding of the true nature of life, and in the scientific technology of that civilization.

The reason for personal contact through landings in the early years was to open communication. The reports of genuine contact - whether or not immediately accepted by our civilization - would begin to stimulate our society's thinking towards space. This was a natural prerequisite leading towards peaceful space research and developments on our planet. And yet at the same time, the truth about life on the other planets of our solar system was established near the beginning of the UFO visitations through those same contacts. As we made some progress into our own space age, the world-wide UFO sightings continued. But genuine cases of personal contact by the space visitors has been relatively infrequent since the 1950's and early 1960's. It is of monumental importance to note this fact.

After the truth behind their existence was established by open contact in the 1950's, our society was left to its own space developments. UFO sightings have continued throughout all these years, right up to the present. But there will be no new revelations or "breakthroughs" in the 1980's regarding the identity or the origin of the space visitors, as some people would have you believe. The truth remains the same today, and can only be learned by understanding what was established by peaceful open contact on the part of the space visitors in the 1950's.

George Adamski was the most important individual having contacts, and his contributions on the subject of space visitations and space knowledge became world known. His work will be discussed throughout this book. In comparison, many individuals had seemingly personal experiences, yet the publicity of the genuine cases played an important role in getting society to think. A number of contacts looked at individually might seem to be minor incidents, but taken together amounted to an impressive amount of evidence. And the incidents were occurring in many different countries; therefore many more people were beginning to learn that space visitors were in our midst. Publicity regarding any true contact, regardless how minor, did alert part of that society. The space civilizations coming our way did make hundreds of landings and isolated contacts throughout the 1950's.

Making contact was a very important gesture on their

part, and it wasn't done indiscriminately. The best candidates for contact here, as you might expect, exhibit a basic integrity in their natural thought patterns. Occupation in life is irrelevant. It only matters that the earth person possess a balanced state of mental alertness and sincerity in their daily living. This can be registered beforehand by the space people's frequency instruments, a device briefly referred to in Adamski's *Inside the Spaceships*.

This particular instrument simply registers the type of thought vibrations relative to a person's thinking. In this way the space visitors would know before making a contact, who would prove friendly and receptive. By the same way, they could avoid the hostile and arrogant, and those whose curiosity lacked humility. Those who have a tendency to be unduly frightened at anything they do not understand, could usually be screened out too, though there is always a certain unpredictability in the human make-up. It should be understood by now, that our friends from other worlds were not here to harm or frighten anyone. They do not bring that type of feeling.

Those are the cases of pre-planned contact. Yet there are a number of reports when accidental meetings occurred. The witness was unknowingly in the vicinity of a landed scoutship and happened to see it. Depending on the person, some chose to observe the craft from a distance, while others, according to their reports, went closer for a better look. Sometimes it was possible to see pilots or crew within the ship through the glass portholes; or on occasion, occupants were found to be outside the ship for some reason. The witness or witnesses, caught off guard by such an unworldly experience, would usually do one of two things - either run away, or decide to stay around and see what happened.

On the other hand, the occupants of the spacecraft would have a similar choice if they saw the earthly witness. They could choose to make a friendly greeting because of the chance encounter, or they might simply leave in their ship if they did not have the time or the inclination to converse with the earthperson. So in those cases of accidental meetings, the degree of contact varied, depending on the actions of both the witness and the space visitors.

Though contacts are rare today, this does not mean that there are no new developments. But the *full* truth of the UFO visitations is best understood by knowing what was brought forward at the beginning - most notably, the work of George Adamski's. Shortly after the world had grown accustomed to reports of flying saucers, the space visitors established the truth behind their coming right then, at the beginning. They knew that it would take some time and society development, before full confirmation and world acceptance. That it has not come about is not their fault, but our own, and those reasons remain to be discussed in this present work.

In the book, *UFOlogy - New Insights from Science and Common Sense*, author James McCampbell states that between 1952 and 1968, there were 83 reported incidents where witnesses saw normal-sized UFO pilots near their landed spacecraft. During some of these reported incidents, the witnesses were able to converse by spoken language with the space visitor. McCampbell credits Adamski as being the first to publicize his experience, after meeting the Venusian pilot of a landed saucer in 1952.

Another case cited happened the following year in Mexico. Salvador Villanueva, a self-employed chauffeur, was hired to drive two men to the U.S. border. But after his car broke down about 60 miles outside of Mexico City, his clients took their baggage and hired another car, leaving Salvador alone to contend with the problem. He was stranded and it was raining.

When the rain stopped, Salvador crawled under the car to inspect the damage. Soon after, he heard someone walk up to the car. Salvador stood up to see two men about 4 feet-6 inches tall, clothed in one-piece aviator suits, and carrying helmets under their arms. They had pleasant expressions on their faces, and then one man smiled and asked the driver if he was having trouble.

Salvador responded to the man's question, and a casual conversation developed. Noticing that only one man was speaking, Salvador asked the man if his friend spoke Spanish too. To which he learned that the other man did not, but that he was able to understand what was being said. The conversation continued inside the car after it began to rain again, and Mr. Villanueva began to realize that his new acquaintance knew far too much for an ordinary man. So he asked him where they were from. The man answered that they were not of this planet.

Villanueva was not ready to believe them until they asked if he would like to see their ship. Leaving the car, he followed them across a muddy marsh, to a clearing about half a kilometer from the road. But the manner in which the two men walked across the rain-soaked marsh stunned Villanueva. Their feet never quite came in contact with the muddy pools. An invisible force seemed to repel the mud away from their feet - an effect seemingly related to lights glowing on the perforated belt each was wearing. Villanueva's boots were caked in mud.

When they all reached the clearing, there stood the ship from another world. The shiny craft was about forty feet across, and above the rim was a shallow dome with portholes. It was resting on three giant metal spheres or landing balls. A panel opened, forming a short staircase to the interior. The two space men climbed up to the opening, turned and asked their friend if he would like to come on board.

It had all happened too fast for Villanueva. He was suddenly a little afraid of all the things that had added up to an event somewhat beyond his understanding. He decided not to, and ran back towards his car. Reaching the road, he glanced back and watched the ship rise above the bushes. After hovering a moment, it gained altitude by a pendulum motion in reverse. At several hundred feet altitude, it suddenly glowed brighter, and then shot up vertically with incredible speed.[5]

It was several months before Villanueva decided to tell others of his experience. He related it simply, from his perspective as a practical working man. The press picked it up, and eventually he was called to speak before the Mexican

Government. The case was recognized as genuine, and received wide publicity.

Dr. Joao de Freitas Guimaraes, a respected lawyer and authority on ancient Roman Law, who in his own words admitted that he had never given a thought to the idea of flying saucers and therefore knew virtually nothing about the subject, had a most unexpected contact in Brazil in the summer of 1957. At a coastal town on the Atlantic Ocean, the doctor had gone for an evening stroll along the beach after dinner. While sitting near the shore and watching the rolling waves, he noticed a disturbance on the ocean's surface. Suddenly a "high-bellied craft" surfaced and slowly flew into shore, where it gently set down on spherical landing gear. After a brief moment, two men stepped out of the craft and walked towards Mr. Guimaraes.

Though slightly startled, Mr. Guimaraes gained his composure and asked in Portuguese (that being his native tongue) if there was anything wrong with their craft, and why they had landed. Knowing many languages, the doctor repeated the questions in French, English, and Italian, but received no reply to any of his questions. He could see that the visitors were completely human, had long fair hair and light skin, and stood about 5 feet, 10 inches in height.

Even though his visitors were not speaking, the doctor received a distinct impression that they were inviting him aboard their craft. And while they had not spoken, the men's presence radiated a feeling of peace and tranquility. Realizing that he would indeed like to see the interior of their spaceship, Mr. Guimaraes unhesitatingly accepted the opportunity. He walked with them to the craft. After getting inside he met a third man, and soon the craft left the ground for a short ride into space. While on board, he was surprised to learn that his friends employed telepathy, in addition to occasional words.

Anxious to learn all that he could, Guimaraes observed everything around him in the compartment. He was told that a circular instrument showing vibratory readings was actually measuring the magnetic forces in Space. This force was utilized to propel their ship. Looking out through the compartment's portholes, he was astonished at the splendid beauty of outer space. Certain regions in the atmosphere appeared as bright-colored violet, and other areas were intensely black, allowing a picturesque view of the stars. Another zone showed innumerable points of light, and brilliantly shining bodies, cascading through a rainbow of colors. After viewing these spectacles, the craft travelled outside the atmosphere. The total trip lasted about 30 to 40 minutes.

Later in his hotel, the doctor had a desire to shout and tell everyone about the wonderful experience, but refrained after a little thinking about it. For more than a year afterwards, he told no one except for his wife. Subsequently, he related details of the event to his close colleagues, and eventually an account of the story was published in several newspapers. The public was quite impressed, and there were great demands on him to speak concerning the experience.

Guimaraes did not hesitate to state that the space visitors were friendly, and that they were engaged in a task of investigating the inhabitants of our planet. More importantly, they were studying the conditions brought about by man's experimentation with atomic energy. The doctor had learned a great deal during his short trip in space. And he concluded that the indiscriminate manner in which scientists and politicians explode their nuclear tests was having a great effect in destroying the protective layers of our atmosphere. Eventually, we would all suffer from serious consequences of these frivolous explosions. From his experience on the ship, Mr. Guimaraes was certain that the visitors from other planets were here to alert us regarding this dangerous experimentation.[6]

In this chapter, we have reviewed but a few of the cases on record. Many more incidents have been publicized over the years. As in the representative cases already discussed, reports ranged from seeing a human form through the porthole of a distant craft, to those reports of a brief encounter on the ground, to the very rare cases like Dr. Guimaraes, where the witness was invited aboard and given pertinent information along with a view of space.

Their existence was on record through the thousands of sightings worldwide. But beyond that, we would have to accept the truth of why they were here on their terms. The space people would only bring out the truth behind their coming through face-to-face contact with individuals on Earth. Of course, not everyone who reported they had had a contact was telling the truth. It was left up to our society to separate the wheat from the chaff, the truth from the speculation.

Still, it must be recognized that most accounts of contact were little more than a friendly greeting with the space visitor. Those reports simply support the fact that the visitors are human. George Adamski, on the other hand, became the space people's main representative in bringing forward the full truth of the visitations from a cosmic understanding, because he had the capabilities to do so. His three books were widely recognized as definitive accounts about the interplanetary spaceships and the people coming our way. The books were translated into at least 18 world languages.

It was mentioned earlier that there was a definite purpose and sequence in their visitations. Although there were frequent landings of scoutcraft in the 1950's and 60's to allow contact to take place, there have been very few authentic cases of contact since that time. This is basically the reason why. By around 1965, the space people had completed a gradual awakening of our civilization to the knowledge that life existed beyond the Earth. This generally coincided with our own progress in technology, as now the Earth's superpowers (U.S. and Russia) were on the verge of exploring space. Also by 1965, the complete truth behind the UFOs, and a program for putting that knowledge to work, had been given.

The spaceships maintained surveillance - they will always be in our skies in large numbers as long as our planet is stockpiling its nuclear weapons and arming nations towards a day of total destruction. The only way this threat of nuclear annihilation can be averted is by making our economy based on space instead of war. What this means, is *an economy based on our becoming a space civilization,* as the other planets in our system are. Brotherhood between nations would replace the need for maintaining a war economy. This change must come by the collective will of society. It is our responsibility. The space people cannot force us to change.

Our neighboring planets had brought their spaceships into our atmosphere, and by showing their presence through 18 years of sighting reports, had stimulated our development towards space. By 1965, society as a whole had not accepted the truth behind the UFOs. The space people were well aware of that fact, but now it was time for man to learn in the only other way he could. So man was allowed his rightful chance to use his own methods of finding out about space...solve the so-called mystery on his own.

The space people had done all they could do earlier. Through open contact, their information had been brought out completely - who they were, why they were here. There was no point in continuing repetitiously after so many years. Now that man was on the verge of obtaining information directly through a space program, it would be an opportunity for scientists to work out the details towards man's progress and understanding. But as it turned out, the science establishment's lack of objectivity in studying the UFO mystery earlier, carried right on in its total lack of objectivity with space findings. So mankind did not advance towards constructive and worthy space knowledge.

The interplanetary visitors watched all our space developments, and particularly our trips to the Moon. Sightings of their spacecraft in our skies was frequent enough, but open landing and contact with individuals on Earth virtually ceased. The U.S. was not particularly inclined towards space during much of the time anyway, because of all the social changes and social unrest - the struggle for civil and human rights, the tensions surrounding the assassinations, the growing opposition to the Vietnam War. But as our spaceprobes struck out for Mars and Venus in the early seventies, the space people put in a lot of UFO sightings to let us know they were still here. In fact, the 1973-74 wave of sightings worldwide surpassed all previous periods of UFO activity in numbers of reports, and brought out a resurgence of public interest.

The controversy over UFOs picked up where it had left off. New books were published - short on meaningful documentation, but long on speculation. As if to reaffirm what was the truth of the recent past, the spaceships often came in to photographic range. One of the best examples happened in October 1973, near Lima, Peru. An architect took an extraordinary photograph of a scoutship from only 50 yards away.

Hugo Vega had taken a client to the Lima countryside in search of a home site. While surveying an area along the Rimac River, he and his client saw a shining object in the bottom of the valley, that was slowly advancing towards them. Mr. Vega quickly ran to his car to get his Polaroid camera. In a matter of seconds he returned, and when the object was less than 50 yards away and 20 yards off the ground (making it about eye level for the witnesses who were on a rise above the valley floor), he took a picture. Then suddenly, the object changed its direction to avoid some high tension wires, increased its speed and disappeared from view.

Mr. Vega said "the object was shaped like an overturned soup plate with a cupola on the top. At the very top of the cupola, there was a round object giving off a fixed sky-blue light. Lower on the cupola, we could see a row of small windows like portholes in a ship."

The spacecraft itself was the color of burnished silver. From the underside of the flange in the middle, a reddish light pulsated and appeared to be due to the propulsive force of the object. Also in the undercarriage, he saw "protuberances like half-eggs." They saw the object for about 30 seconds before it disappeared.

"I never thought I would see a flying saucer, much less photograph one," said Hugo Vega. "I think, using the finest camera equipment in the world, I would never be able to do it again without the same extraordinary luck that I had last Friday. In the middle of the three-by-four-inch photograph, we could see the flying saucer, even the row of rounded windows. After this experience, I am convinced that flying saucers really exist. So is my client."[7]

The photo and story was published by the press in many parts of the world. His picture and description are identical to the Adamski Venusian scoutship.

A Japanese high school student obtained pictures of low flying spacecraft near his home in Onomichi, Hiroshima Prefectura, Japan. On the morning of October 11, 1974, young Kazuhiko Fujimatsu looked out his bedroom window and saw a giant cigar-shaped object flying toward the northwest. At the same time, a bell-shaped saucer was coming slowly towards his house from the opposite direction. The witness ran out into the yard with his camera and quickly took pictures of the spacecraft. Three of his pictures clearly showed a bell-shaped saucer flying over nearby homes, and two additional photographs showed a remarkably close mothership.

Captain Lawrence Coyne was commander of the 316th Medivac unit based at Cleveland Hopkins International Airport. On October 18, 1973, he was flying an Army helicopter en route to Cleveland with three aviators on board. The helicopter was flying at about 2,500 feet altitude when one of the crew spotted a red light in the distance, and within a few seconds it appeared that the moving light was coming straight at the helicopter. Capt. Coyne thought it was a fighter plane, and to avoid collision he immediately put his helicopter into a fast dive. But even after dropping to 1800 feet, it appeared that the object was still closing in on a collision course, and the men braced for impact.

As the helicopter reached 1500 feet, the approaching craft came to a stop about 500 feet above the helicopter, and banked to one side. Captain Coyne and his crew looked out to see a cigar-shaped craft with a glowing red light on its leading edge and a softer green light coming from the aft section. With the helicopter still headed downward and the controls still set on dive, Capt. Coyne was completely startled while looking at his instrument panel. The altimeter showed that his helicopter was rising from 1500 feet to 3800 feet. This sudden rise in altitude took just a few seconds, and none of the crew members felt the gravitational pull usually experienced when a helicopter rises. The helicopter then stopped at 3800 feet with a slight bounce, and the crew watched as the other craft took off to the northeast and disappeared from view. Arriving at their base airport thirty minutes later, Capt. Coyne and his crew reported their extraordinary flight experience.

This had been much more than a UFO sighting. It became a rescue mission, after the UFO's flightpath had inadvertently caused panic on board the low-flying helicopter. The craft physically demonstrated its capabilities, by pulling the helicopter out of its dangerous dive, and lifting it to a safe altitude. Then after gently releasing the helicopter from the craft's gravity forcefield, the spacecraft continued on its way. The visitors are not here to harm, frighten, or generate disturbance. But every kind of peaceful incident or sighting serves in a way to make us think a little.

Together with the thousands of regular UFO sighting reports, these first-hand accounts established the solid case that there is a close relationship between the Earth and the visiting space civilizations. But where is the origin of the friendly visitors riding those spaceships? It has never changed since they first made their appearance in large numbers during the 1940's and 1950's. It was widely believed and logically accepted back then that Venus and Mars were the likely home planets, even before there had been any known personal contact with the space visitors. Adamski was the first to bring forward his account of personal contact, after meeting a man from Venus who piloted a small scoutship to a landing in the California desert. Less than a year and a half later, a scoutcraft from Mars made a similar landing on the coast of Scotland, and this account was well documented in a book by Cedric Allingham. Although there had been much speculation regarding UFOs prior to these two incidents, and much more controversy to follow, both of these accounts had established a reasonable basis for habitability on Venus and Mars. And both cases are still the only two *contact* cases that are substantiated by clear, close-up, daytime photographs of the visiting spaceships.

This type of introduction seriously challenged our orthodox scientific theories at the time, but in the more intelligent circles of scientific thinkers, the evidence was at least debated with healthy skepticism and reasonable arguments. As the sightings increased in the succeeding years, to the point where the evidence could no longer be ignored, the scientific community as a whole gradually came to accept UFOs as a real phenomenon. But as the credibility of visiting spaceships slowly gained acceptance and came into favor, all thinking about the possibility of life on our neighboring planets was losing favor. Mankind was actually becoming more confused as time went on, instead of less. Organized science is not to be blamed by itself. It was the censoring of true planetary findings by government agencies during the 1960's and 1970's that deepened the mystery behind the space visitations.

Venus and Mars are the home of the spaceships, along with other planets of this solar system. Of course, that is one of the premises of this book, and this will be fully established from a scientific standpoint as I bring the space science record up to date in the succeeding chapters. But let's first review how the public received its first introduction to Mars and the UFO connection, by recounting the experience of Cedric Allingham. His book, *Flying Saucer From Mars*, was published in London in October 1954, and the American edition came out in the following year.

Cedric Allingham had a studious background, both as a writer and a trained scientific observer. Allingham owned a 10-inch reflecting telescope and he became a competent amateur astronomer. He had first heard of flying saucer reports in 1947, but he did not immediately accept them as proof of spaceships. However, Allingham thought that it was a possibility, since he knew from his own specialist reading and studies that there was no real evidence to disprove the existence of advanced beings on either Venus or Mars. Within a few years though, evidence of the saucers was steadily increasing, with numerous reports and photographs being publicized around the world. Then in 1953, Leslie and Adamski's *Flying Saucers Have Landed* was published, and Allingham's own reaction to the first contact was described as: "Well, it has happened at last." He had felt that it was bound to happen sooner or later with all the sighting reports on record, and he added that Adamski had taken some convincing spaceship photographs which had passed examination by experts.

However, in February 1954, Cedric Allingham was not thinking of the saucers or of the recent accounts. He had been in London on business for several weeks, and he was looking forward to a restful vacation away from the city. That is how Mr. Allingham happened to be traveling through Scotland early that year.

It was on the morning of February 18, as Allingham was walking along Scotland's northern coast absorbed in his own thoughts, when he first saw a shining speck of light in the sky. He quickly focused his binoculars, and then realized he had sighted a metallic spaceship glinting in the sunlight. Through the high power magnification of his binoculars, Allingham thought he could make out the craft's rounded dome and the spherical landing gear. Then he took three photographs of the object before it sailed beyond the clouds.

After remaining on the spot and scanning the heavens for at least half an hour, Allingham sat down to eat his lunch before continuing his walk along the ocean. He fervently hoped that he would catch another glimpse of the spaceship, and therefore kept his attention fixed on the sky. A little more than two hours later, he saw it again, momentarily. The little craft was higher up and moving more rapidly, before drifting clouds obscured the view once again. For the first time that afternoon, Allingham felt that there was a slight chance of making contact.

At about 3:45, he heard a swishing sound, and turned to see the saucer coming in across the sea. He knew that it was going to land, and quickly took a couple photographs as the craft made its final descent. From a distance of fifty yards, Allingham watched the spaceship hover for a few seconds, as its whole metallic body cast a soft glowing light. Then the spacecraft landed. Allingham estimated it to be fifty feet in diameter and twenty feet high. It was bell-shaped, with a dome, three-ball landing gear, and at least two groups of portholes around a central wall. Allingham walked towards the magnificent craft.

A sliding door opened, and a man alighted from the ship. The two men waved and approached each other. Allingham was not surprised to see that the visitor was completely human, and in fact, he stated that the spaceman would not have had any difficulty in passing for an Earthman, had he been dressed in terrestrial clothes. The man looked to be about 32 years old, stood about 6 feet tall, and his skin color was like a deep tan.

The first essential point to find out was where the man came from. With pencil, pad, and gestures, Allingham succeeded in learning that the visitor was from the closest planet outside the orbit of Earth - the planet Mars. Allingham felt that this answer was most important, and succeeded in confirming the answer beyond a doubt. And he noted that during the friendly meeting, the spaceman smiled pleasantly, both with his eyes as well as his lips.

Allingham gave an interesting account of how they were able to communicate fairly well, despite not having a common language. He successfully established that the Martians and Venusians do cooperate in certain activities in space, including stopping off on the Moon. To another question, the visitor indicated that he himself had been to Venus. When the same question was asked in regard to Mercury, the visitor said no. It would seem logical to conclude that the Martian himself had not been to the planet Mercury, but Allingham unexplainably interpreted the answer to mean, "No, because the planet is uninhabitable."

(We will discuss the question of Mercury in chapter 11.)

The man from Mars posed a few questions of his own. He wanted to know if people on the Earth were about to start another war, and if we were making plans to fly to the Moon. (Remember that this was in 1954). Allingham could not answer the first, but gave an affirmative reply to the second. The spaceman looked rather serious. Allingham reasoned to himself that the idea of our learning spaceflight in order to visit the Moon and other planets would not be enthusiastically welcomed by our peaceful visitors. Allingham allowed that since we had not yet proved ourselves fit to rule our own planet, they would not want us out in space with our same attitude, and perhaps try to influence or threaten their affairs.

Their conversation had to end when the Martian indicated that time was running short. Allingham photographed the scoutship, which was resting about twenty yards away from them, and as the spaceman walked back towards his ship, Allingham took a quick photo of the man. It is unlikely that the Martian would have allowed any frontal picture anyway, so it was lucky that Allingham managed getting as much of a full profile view as he did.

The pilot got back into his saucer, and a moment later, a soft humming noise could be heard as the spaceship gently lifted itself into the air. Slowly it glided to an altitude of about forty feet, then it shot upwards at a tremendous speed, disappearing into the sky in just a few seconds. The arrival, meeting, and departure had lasted but half an hour. Yet the written account of it startled a skeptical world. Allingham knew that he had learned things which scientists had been trying to learn ever since the days of Aristotle - proof that our neighboring worlds were inhabited by advanced and compassionate human people.

Allingham collected his thoughts and his camera gear, and started back towards the town. While reflecting on his privileged experience, he encountered a local fisherman, who from a distance of about five hundred yards, had seen the last few minutes of Allingham's meeting, and the subsequent take off of the Saucer. He offered his evidence in a signed statement.

Allingham stayed in northern Scotland for a week or so, and then returned to London. When he had developed the film, he knew that he had to write the book. But rather than rushing his account into print, he felt that he should conduct some further researches, and then present the complete facts in a properly scientific way. Allingham explained that the real duty was to wait until he was prepared to present his discoveries to the world in a form that would be of permanent value.

Cedric Allingham's *Flying Saucer From Mars* is a remarkable and insightful document, considering the event and the times. The book was written in 1954, which was years before the space age. He respectfully balanced his extraordinary experience (which he knew to be absolutely true), with the known astronomical science of the day (which he knew was in its infancy, and at best, only educated guesses). Being a trained scientific observer, Allingham had done his researches well, and the result was a clear and understandable book. He had spent a good deal of effort in order to present his case simply.

As Waveney Girvan wrote shortly after Allingham's book came out, "*Flying Saucer From Mars* presents a truly formidable challenge to scientific opinion. If Allingham is telling the truth, his account following so soon upon Adamski's amounts to final proof of the existence of flying saucers." Girvan's was a rare open-minded opinion among professional speakers, at the time.

Chapter 3
A Planetary Mission

Bertrand Russell once wrote a one-sentence history of the human race: "Since Adam and Eve ate the apple, man has never refrained from any folly of which he was capable. The End."

A dictionary defines folly as "a costly undertaking having an absurd or ruinous outcome." The ultimate folly of man exists today as a gigantic stockpile of nuclear weapons. To defend his ignorance, man has always sought to complicate everything around him, to the point now that he has threatened the very existence of life on this planet. He could have everything much simpler, but he will not let it be so. Greed has become the dominate force in man's thinking, to the point that peaceful and harmonious co-existence has been utterly ruled out. Hence the folly of man's ways.

All the talk and argument against the madness of nuclear weapons has not changed a thing. We are still building the deadly bombs every day. The only thing that could begin to change this obsessive and mindless course to nuclear annihilation, is if the people were given the truth about space, and the truth about the advanced space civilizations in this solar system. Then the people would not elect or follow leaders who spearhead trillion-dollar budgets to arm the world with nuclear weapons in order to make the world safe for hypocrisy.

It has been said, we are in those days: "For we wrestle not against flesh and blood, but against principalities, against powers, against the rulers of the darkness of this world, against spiritual wickedness in high places." We cannot ignore what is happening in these days and call ourselves intelligent.

Commenting on the course of world events, Albert Schweitzer said: "We must muster the insight...and the courage to leave folly and face reality." The same attitude must be applied today to our understanding of space and UFOs. Society has been too long complacent with the nonsense that has been promoted, and indifferent to the reality behind the visitations. At the same time, powerful forces have used every means available to them, to confuse the public on space, and to complicate the subject of UFOs in order to hide the reality. For a very long time - too long - it has been charged that there is a cover-up. It is time to expose this cover-up, and exactly what it is that has been covered up. Rather than more complications, we need less. We're out to simplify things. The truth is not complicated - it only becomes so with man's interference. We need to remove the interference. The truth by itself can be understood by anyone.

It has been said that ignorance is bliss. But in no way is it freedom. Ignorance does not allow freedom from all the sophistry that misguides mankind in this century. There is knowledge and truth that transcends all the petty political quarrels, preaching, and materialistic doctrines of this war-torn world. But man (and society) must make an effort to find out about this knowledge, before he can escape the ruts of materialistic doctrines.

It has been conservatively estimated, that there is an average of one hundred sightings every day, of interplanetary spaceships in the skies around the world. No one needs to ask some skeptical authority whether or not these things exist. The ships are here. The questions that need answering are concerned with what lies behind this evidence from space.

A scientific approach to the study of UFO reports led to the publication of *UFOlogy - New Insights from Science and Common Sense* in 1973. The book was written by James McCampbell, a man whose diversified background of accomplishments in science and engineering had earned him recognition in *American Men of Science* and the *International Who's Who In Atoms*. His methodology and competent research for *UFOlogy* provided exacting and convincing proof, that the observed physical effects of airborn and earth-proximity UFOs were consistent with our present understanding of scientific knowledge, and could be explained by such. What this means in simplified terms is that the UFOs are solid, 3-dimensional, physical spacecraft operating in our atmosphere. The only difference is that they utilize advanced methods of propulsion by harnessing the natural electromagnetic energy in space, whereas we use artificial methods to fight gravity.

Though uncertain as to the wide range of reported contacts, McCampbell's analysis of UFO landings and near-landing cases led him to the conclusion that there are two distinct categories of humans occupying the visiting UFOs. There are space people having the same height and size as our average population. Then there are those who are notably more than a foot shorter than our average height. McCampbell observes that these two different types of UFO occupants generally travel about the Earth independently, though he believes that they are cooperating in their ventures and are probably coming from the same place. (This book defines that place as this solar system).

There have been advanced cultures on our own planet, whose geographical inhabitants were separate and distinct races of little people. They existed in different parts of the world before our current period of civilization of the last 10,000 years. Archaeological discoveries of their stone structures and buildings found that entries, steps, passageways, and ceilings were built for a community of small stature adults - under four feet tall. Their handling and construction of megalithic stonework suggests that they had rediscovered one of the lost arts, or a form of power, to overcome gravitation. There are many legends among Asiatic, Polynesian, and Central American Indians, of the little people who existed prior to the world's great flood.

A very detailed study of this evidence was discussed by

M.K. Jessup in his book, *The Expanding Case for the UFO.*
The brief paragraph above is only a fragmentary hint of his
extensive and original research. He found that separate,
small races existed on the Earth for millenia, and some
connection may even exist to today's pygmy man. Jessup
came to the conclusion that since separated cultures of little
people have existed on our planet in recent geological times,
we should expect that another planetary civilization might
have a distinct size variation among its present inhabitants.
Carrying this further, we should expect that interplanetary
visitors coming from the same place would show this distinct
variance. This is what McCampbell points out - many
accounts report normal-size humans piloting the spacecraft,
but there are others indicating visitors of a smaller stature.
Yet they can still be from the same planetary civilization.

It should be introduced at this time, that the most
important reason why the interplanetary ships are visiting
our planet is purely of a scientific nature. They are not here
primarily to observe us. They know who we are. But they are
watching, and studying with their scientific instruments, the
natural changes taking place in the Earth's atmosphere, and
in the spatial regions around the planetary body. Magnetic
pole shifts, magnetic and gravitational fields - these all
change in direct relationship to the constant activity of the
Sun's electromagnetic fields. There is an intricate balanced
relationship between the Sun and all the planets of the solar
system.

Also of primary importance for them to watch is how man
has been disturbing his natural planetary environment -
rampant pollution into the Earth's atmosphere, and
unnatural stresses and pressures in the planet's crust from
continual nuclear tests. The space people are keeping a
constant vigil on our "progress." These facts will shed some
light on the following discussion.

Most all cases of landings and reported contacts (in the
years of those events) were described as meetings with
normal-sized human visitors, generally between five and
six feet tall, although we can include Salvador Villaneuva's

visitors, who happened to be about four feet, six inches in height. Our authorities knew also that another group, probably from the same planet(s), but shorter in height, was scouting our planet also, and that this group apparently did not have plans for making contact with individuals here. It would seem that their ventures were primarily coordinated for the scientific study and observation activity, and that they left the landings and whatever contact deemed necessary for the other group to conduct. Frank Scully's book, *Behind the Flying Saucers*, introduced the first evidence that this smaller group was involved with the scientific study of our planet, - a study that was conducted in earnest by our interplanetary visitors after the U.S. began testing atomic explosions in the atmosphere.

In separate incidents during the late 1940's, three disabled spacecraft came down in the southwestern United States. In each case the U.S. military at nearby testing grounds immediately cordoned off the area, and flew out top specialists who were under government contract in scientific research. The crews of each ship were found dead, although the ships did not crash, but apparently landed gently by some automatic guidance system of their instruments. Geophysical scientists employed in magnetic research were flown in to inspect and help dismantle the ships. It was with some of these men that Scully learned the full story of the incidents in 1949.

The first ship that was recovered came down on a ranch twelve miles east of Aztec, New Mexico. A group of eight specialists were called in to assist the Air Force in studying the ship and breaking it down so that it could be moved to a government testing laboratory. Upon finding a way to get inside, the scientists found a crew of 16 small-sized men on board. Their bodies were between three and four feet in height, and human in every respect, but some unknown catastrophe had caused severe charring of the skin. One of the contributing factors to the fatal accident could have been a sudden decompression in the cabin pressure, since one of the ship's portholes had a pencil-sized hole in it. More on the cause of death will be discussed shortly.

All of the instruments and articles on board were studied. The outside of the ship was aluminum colored, and the appearance did resemble a huge saucer. The outside measurements were carefully taken, and it was determined that the ship was built on a system of 9's. The disk was 99.9 feet in diameter, with a central cabin 18 feet across and 72 inches in height. Seated in the bottom of the saucer, the cabin's vertical dimension lay 27 inches below, and 45 inches above, the outer rim of the craft.

The second ship that was recovered came down in Arizona. The conditions were similar to the first, except that this ship was 72 feet in diameter. The crew of sixteen had died only a few hours before the craft was found with its door open. It was initially reasoned that a sudden change in atmospheric pressure was responsible for the fate of the crew, and in this incidence nothing had caused any burning of the skin. They were perfectly normal human beings from a medical viewpoint. It was noted that their teeth were perfect - no cavities or fillings were found in any mouth. The men were fair-skinned, had normal lungs and blood type, and were judged to be in their thirties according to our standards of age.

The third spacecraft to come down intact was a small one, 36 feet in diameter, manned by a crew of two. It appears that this was the same type as the Venusian scoutship photographed by Adamski, for the scientist described the ingenious operation of the three ball landing gear to Frank Scully. This ship was recovered outside Phoenix, in an area called Paradise Valley, and was examined extensively before being shipped to Wright Patterson AFB in Dayton, Ohio.

Another notable incident happened two years after the publication of Scully's book. Persons living in Spitzbergen (a territory seven hundred miles north of the Arctic Circle) reported seeing a mysterious object fall from the sky and crash in a remote area. The year was 1952. Norwegian authorities immediately sent their military out to locate the site of the accident. The wrecked spacecraft was found and transported to Oslo, Norway, where it was positively determined that the ship was not made on Earth. U.S. and British experts were flown in to examine the finding, and to instruct the Norwegian authorities on the need for strict public censorship.

But in May 1955, this story was leaked to the British press by a high ranking cabinet official. The official told Dorothy Kilgallen, a prominent journalist based in London, that British scientists had examined the wreckage of a mysterious flying ship. He stated that the spaceship recovery was proof positive that sightings of these aerial objects were not optical illusions or Soviet inventions, but that they were actually flying saucers that come from another planet.

According to Scully's book, it was thought that the ships came down because they encountered magnetic fault zones high in our atmosphere. These unnatural conditions in our atmosphere were suspected to be there as a result of our atomic experimentation with bombs. After examining the three recovered ships, the scientists were certain that these spaceships derived their motive power from the magnetic lines of force around a planet and in space.

After those early crashes, it appeared that the visitors learned how to detect our disturbed magnetic fields, and solved a way to conduct flight safely through these zones. As if to demonstrate that they had overcome the cause of these early failures where three of their ships had fallen, the space visitors came out in full force on March 17, 1950. More than half the townspeople of Farmington, New Mexico, watched as hundreds of the saucer spaceships zoomed through the skies over their town. They flew at every conceivable angle and direction at incredible speeds, played tag, and remained in the sky for over an hour. The spaceships demonstrated their far-superior maneuverability to our aircraft, and to dispel any other doubts, they came in close enough so that the observers could easily see the silvery, saucer-shaped craft. The following day's newspaper carried the front-page headline: "Huge Saucer Armada Jolts Farmington." In nearby Las Vegas, a newspaper headlined: "Space Ships Cause Sensation."

As in the thousands of previous sightings reported in the period of 1947-50, the public's curiosity was being prompted - and this time quite dramatically. But with the earlier recovery of spacecraft that had landed in the southwest United States, intelligence agencies for our government and the military knew that life existed beyond the Earth, and knew that flying saucers were real. The only question was, which planets were they coming from? Those involved with the investigation of these early crashes reasoned that Venus or Mars, or both, were likely to be inhabited. And indeed, those planets were sending their spaceships in large numbers at that time, giving rise to all the flying saucer reports.

Not knowing all the facts, a few outspoken critics denounced *Behind the Flying Saucers*, and then fabricated information in order to refute the book. Fully aware of the controversy his book would generate, Scully steadfastly maintained that his facts were accurate. He personally knew two of the scientists involved, and he had been introduced to others. He had seen a few items recovered from one of the ships - a pocket-size radio device, small gears, and little disks of an unknown metal alloy. And Scully had been shown a filmclip of the disabled saucer on the ground. The film had been taken by one of the magnetic scientists before the Air Force had tightened security on the project.

In the case of the large spaceships, it was the scientists' opinion at the time, that the crews were found dead in both due to a rapid decompression when their cabins were inadvertently open to our atmosphere. One ship had been found with an access door open, and the other had a small break in one of its portholes. It was thought that the spaceships were observing the areas near our atomic proving sites, before malfunctions led to the mishaps.

At that time, the U.S. was testing atomic bombs in the atmosphere. With every explosion, vast amounts of radiation were released upwards in our atmosphere. With time, these radiation clouds were gradually dispersed by atmospheric winds, and varying amounts of fallout was spread around the earth. Fallout contamination was serious, but no doubt paled in comparison to the lethal radiation clouds that remained for days in the atmosphere over test sites. Spacecraft from other planets encountered these unnatural conditions.

George Adamski had this to say about Frank Scully's *Behind the Flying Saucers:* "Although one of the first books written on this subject of spacecraft, and bitterly denied by the opposition who feared the acceptance of such facts even in those days, this book stands as one that has never been disproved. Of the hundreds of books written regarding space visitors and their ships, this remains one of the comparatively few authentic treatments of the subject."

In a booklet printed in 1957, Adamski explained the following information which he received directly from his space contacts. "The early crashes were caused when the radiation in our atmosphere was taken into their craft through a process similar to our air conditioning systems. The crews became ill and lost control of their ships, resulting in fatal crashes. After a number of these fatalities had taken place, the crews on other ships began studying conditions and seeking ways to avoid such disasters. Now they have succeeded.

"They have perfected a small object which each crew member carries on his person while their ship is moving through our atmosphere. A similar object on a much larger scale is used to purify the atmosphere within their craft. No space person ever comes to Earth without one of these for protection to help him withstand the radiation present not only in our atmosphere, but in our food and water as well."

The smaller UFO occupants traveled about the Earth independently, but coordinated their activities with the main group of space visitors. It was from this latter group that landings were initiated for the purposes of contact in the early years. Frequently, some of these space people were brought to Earth specifically to work for a period of time amongst our civilization. Having no outward differences in appearance from us, they could easily pass through society with their true identity remaining unknown. In fact, they would never reveal their identity and origin, knowing our lack of understanding. Many obtained the necessary papers (and usual forms of identification) to temporarily establish their earthly "identity," and in this way many worked in various industries, including those of science and technology, - yet easily remained unrecognized as space travelers. Some even worked through government programs in different countries.

There was a very noble purpose to their living among our society, and thousands of space travelers were engaged in this type of earthly activity throughout the world, during our brief transition towards becoming a space-oriented society. Adamski later explained it this way: "The space travelers are as interested in us, our ways of thinking and acting, as any humanitarian would be...(They) endeavor to help us unfold intellectually. They do not impose themselves upon us, nor do they take a superior attitude toward us. Rather, realizing that we do not understand the laws involved in our thoughts and acts, they live amongst us, hoping that, by their example of harmonious living, they can instill in us a desire to do the same... While they never advise a fellowman, they have an inexplicable ability of passing thoughts to another in such a way that he (the earth person) believes them to be his own. Thus he is free to accept and follow them, or discard them without the thought that someone else advised him. (This is the manner in which the space people could elevate progress through their various positions in industry, government, and scientific development. -author) Furthermore, through casual conversations they could awaken sleeping minds to a vaster concept of life and the Cosmos."

One thing should not be misconstrued. The space people do not "know everything." They are learning all the time, just as we are, even during their time spent on Earth. But they do know things about life that we have yet to acknowledge, and they do know the directions that need to be taken if man is ever to progress towards a civilized and peaceful future.

While serving in this capacity, the space people often made a friendly and noticeable impression on a few people in their surroundings, be it in industry, government, or day-to-day society. Their work was not hampered by the interference which would develop should their identity be revealed. Naturally, society would not suspect, or believe, that certain people were from another planet, because society has not been taught along these lines. Yet many numbers of people did meet and come in various contact with space travelers without recognizing them as such.

Very occasionally, an identity could be revealed to a person known to be trustworthy, and if a better purpose could be served from that knowledge. Naturally, there was an inward recognition as well on the part of the earth person. Following his initial face-to-face meeting with the Venusian pilot of a landed scoutcraft in 1952, George Adamski was accorded more contact with the space travelers. He had proven his reliability, his concern for his fellowman, and his capacity to bring out the truth after that initial contact. Quite naturally then, Adamski was a person whom the spacepeople felt could be entrusted to promote further understanding about the space civilizations coming our way.

During 1953 and 1954, he was contacted more directly by a few space persons working and living in the California area, and then by being driven by car to a remote area away from the city, he was able to be picked up by a small scoutship for short excursions on board their spacecraft. When taken to the large mothership, Adamski learned much about space, our atmosphere, and the operation of their ships. Equally important is what he learned about the people themselves - their life on other planets, their philosophy as advanced space civilizations, their understanding of our solar system. The men and women on these interplanetary spaceships were from our neighboring planets - Venus, Mars, and Saturn.

These experiences led to the publication of Adamski's second book, in 1955. *Inside the Spaceships* was recognized by many people as having established the truth about the visiting spaceships. However, many in society were not yet receptive to the idea that flying saucers were visiting our planet. And an even larger majority wanted to believe in the traditional scientific theories that denied life could exist on other solar system planets. Man was unsure of what he would find himself when he got out into space, and the evidence of flying saucer reports was not yet proof to his understanding.

The space people came at the time our world started to develop atomic and hydrogen warheads. This development was an ominous threat to the future of civilization on Earth. By alerting mankind towards space and life beyond the Earth, it was hoped that in the following years man would use his free will to change away from his old destructive paths. At first his curiosity was questioning the reports of thousands of flying saucer sightings. How would he know the truth about space? It would not be decided by argument, since we knew nothing with certainty about space conditions beyond our planet at that time. The truth was in the philosophy. That is contained in Adamski's books, - their philosophy and understanding of life. To Adamski's credit, he was capable of putting that knowledge into print for the understanding of his fellow man.

Adamski's in-depth information preceded our nation's entry into the space age, which did not begin until a few years later. So at the time, it stood as a challenge to traditional thinking and prevalent attitudes about space. It still does challenge our present and common understanding of planetary environments, - because it is still the definitive book on UFOs, that fully establishes the truth about the visiting spacecraft. The present work will document how our own space developments were co-opted by worldly interests, in order to perpetuate the Earth's self-imposed isolation from life elsewhere.

It was after reading Adamski's books in 1974, that I read up a little on astronomy, and then I turned to a rigorous pursuit of space sciences proper. It was imperative for me to know precisely what our common theories and recent space findings were based on. I felt that all statements about space could be respectfully questioned in a search for the truth.

The research gradually developed over time, because initially I was setting out on an uncharted course. But I knew that the subject of UFOs and the field of space sciences were intrinsically related. The truth of one would be contained in the other, and vice versa. Therefore, I read all types of books, magazines, and journals having to do with planetary studies and space. I collected and studied the literature detailing our space probe data. I carefully filed various articles and news clippings. Nothing was too insignificant in the search for clues and patterns regarding our space age developments.

In the beginning, I was not aware of all the public distortion in reference to space findings. Back then, I had naively thought that as soon as one of our space probes radioed back signals indicating earthlike conditions on the neighboring planets, our officials would announce it to the world. But one soon discovers that many "official" statements regarding space findings are devoid of real credibility since the data behind them are so meaningless or inconclusive. The statements are basically the wishes and viewpoint of the status quo, entrenched in its professional dogma. NASA also provided a lot of distorted double-talk, so as not to undermine the faulty structure of orthodoxy, and so-called "national security."

A lot of theoretical nonsense about space has become very rigid, and accepted without question. And scientists whose secure positions are dependent on either liberal grants or salary from the government cannot be expected to question official statements. In my independent study, I was out to question everything. I have never subscribed to mass thinking, or ever accepted anything in life just because "that's the way everybody thinks." I have to learn and evaluate something for myself, if it is to have any meaning for me. And just as there were no short-cuts to qualifying in the navy's nuclear submarine program and bringing a new submarine into the fleet, I knew that there would be no short-cuts in researching this field. But I felt certain that my previous scientific background would help enable me to sift out the truth of space science and planetary findings, and remove it from the outdated dogma of the scientific establishment.

In the past, many researchers have made the statement that it was time the government opened its full files on UFOs to the public. That could help establish a good part of the picture, but it would still leave a lot open to speculation.

I say that what we really want, is for the government, i.e. NASA, the Pentagon, and the National Security Agency, to completely open their secret files on space knowledge regarding the planets, and publicize the full findings on Venus, Mars, and the Moon.

The following chapters will explain in detail, the planetary conditions on the home planets of our interplanetary space visitors. First will be a discussion of Mars, followed by the Moon, and then Venus. Also, there will be a chapter covering the rest of the solar system. While establishing the proper space findings and planetary conditions, the text will include relevant information on the UFO field. The purpose of this book is to provide a complete and comprehensive background on the truth of space, so that having read this book, the reader can go directly to the accounts and writings of George Adamski, and read with certainty. His information remains the most important in this field, for he was truly - our first ambassador to outer space. And as the trusted representative of his space friends, Adamski not only established the truth of flying saucers, but also the truth of man.

Chapter 4
Mars - The Telescopic
Evidence

Our space exploration program focused mainly on the three bodies closest to our planet - the Moon, Mars, and Venus. In order to better understand the origin and purpose behind today's space visitations, we should acquaint ourselves with the relative positions of these planetary bodies, along with the other planets of our solar system. The Earth and its large companion Moon are in the third orbit from the sun. Mercury and Venus are nearer to the sun, while the orbital path of Mars occupies the fourth position. Beyond Mars is the next group of four planets, orbiting at successively greater distances. They are Jupiter, Saturn, Uranus, and Neptune. Still further out lie Pluto and another three planets, making a total of twelve planets in our solar system. See Plate 29. Recent information on the planets beyond Pluto will be discussed in chapter 11.

We know that the sun's energy is not transmitted in the form of heat and light, but as an invisible spectrum of electromagnetic energy. The sun's electromagnetic energy does not manifest itself as heat and light until it penetrates a planetary atmosphere. And since this radiation from the sun is not appreciably reduced in its travel through outer space, the four inner planets receive similar amounts of energy in their respective orbits. The surface conditions on each planet would be dependent on the atmospheric shell, and the gravitational and magnetic fields surrounding the planet, and not on its relative distance from the sun.

When the spaceships appeared in the late 1940's, and

George Adamski
(1891-1965)

Plate 1. The world-famous books authored by George Adamski,
which were published in eighteen different world languages.

Plate 2. Adamski with his 6-inch reflecting telescope at Palomar Gardens in the early 1950's.

Plate 3. The famous picture of a Venusian Scoutship, taken by Adamski in 1952.

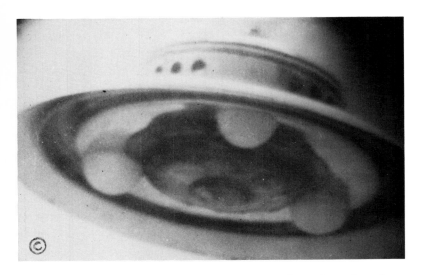

Plate 4. Another view of the spaceship from Venus. The craft was hovering above the valley near Adamski's Palomar Gardens home.

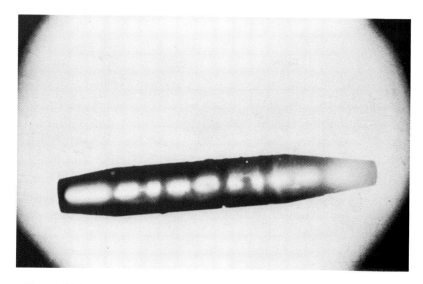

Plate 5. Telescopic photo of a giant carrier ship, taken by Adamski in May 1952. These interplanetary spaceships transport the smaller scoutcraft.

Plate 6. One of Adamski's famous series of photographs showing a "mothership" releasing several small scoutcraft.

Plate 7. UPI photo of a Polaroid picture taken by Hugo Vega near Lima, Peru on October 19, 1973. The original, and his description, clearly matched an Adamski-type UFO.

Plate 8.
Cedric Allingham, author of *Flying Saucer From Mars*. Plate 9 (below) shows the Saucer, moments before its actual landing on the Scottish coast on February 18, 1954. Shortly afterwards, the pilot alighted from the craft and conversed with the witness, Cedric Allingham.

Plate 10. First Viking photograph transmitted from the Martian surface in July 1976, showing a blue sky.

Plate 11. Extensive cloud cover and foliage near the summit of Olympus Mons - an area on Mars photographed in detail during the Viking mission.

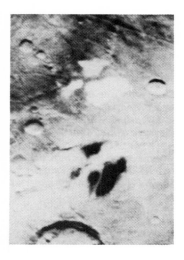

Plate 12. Thick clouds in the northern latitudes of Mars, casting distinct shadows on the ground.

Plate 13. Standard textbook and magazine photo of Mars, showing a false image of the planet's color.

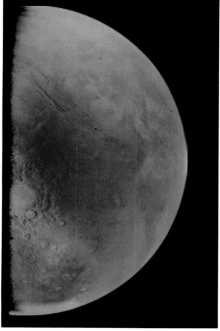

Plate 14. The planet Mars in true color. Photographed by the Viking 1 spacecraft as it neared the completion of its journey to Mars. The picture was taken by color television cameras on board Viking 1, at a distance of 336,000 miles.

Plate 15. Notable books on the Moon, which document
lunar activity and the true lunar environment.

Plate 16. Brown and rich Moon soil at the Apollo 17 landing site. Back on
Earth, laboratory tests found that some terrestrial plants grew "greener
and hardier" in lunar soil than in earth soil.

sighting reports began to number in the thousands, scientific specialists advising government and military authorities believed that Venus and Mars were the origin of the spacecraft. They were more certain after recovering a few ships that had crashed near our atomic test sites. Then an almost impenetrable security lid came down, to censor any evidence from official sources that life existed beyond the earth. A Silence Group, working for those in entrenched worldly positions, infiltrated secret departments and intelligence agencies to insure that confirmation would never come from official sources or government. Public or private institutions, being generally conservative in matters of science, were unlikely to speculate on the UFO evidence, but in any event, those institutions would not have the means to confirm the origin of the visiting spaceships.

Complete, uncontestable confirmation was strictly the domain of a government space agency, and the official results of any achievements in space exploration were under the sole control of the National Security Agency. Public disclosures regarding planetary environments were carefully slanted to coincide with long-held orthodox views, and with theories that had become rigid and dogmatic with the scientific establishment. That Venus and Mars have not been shown as having earthlike environments, is not due to a lack of technology in our space probe exploration, but due to secretive censoring by intelligence agencies directing operations from behind the scenes. So many false ideas on space have been promoted through official channels, and then become solidified in scientific journalism, that one may reasonably wonder if in today's world it can ever be straightened out.

There is no grand conspiracy by science writers to deceive, nor by scientific spokesmen with their speculations on space conditions. They actually believe what they write or say, because these are widely-shared and firmly held perceptions which have been taught for a long time. Their ideas have also been reinforced by the false disclosures publicized through the media by those in control of past space ventures. It is hoped that some of the discussions in this book will help the professional community in re-evaluating their scientific questions on space.

Likewise, this book is not in direct opposition to general astronomy. In fact, a lot of information in this present work is based on the observations and lifetime work of expert astronomers. But in establishing the truth about our solar system, it will be noted that there is little agreement with orthodox thinking in the astronomical field. And if one were to restrict himself to one field - any field - one would have very limited knowledge. Determining the reality behind UFOs requires a complete study involving the whole scope of space sciences.

The problem with all planetary research and common speculation to date, must be defined here at the beginning. It is this: Official presentations regarding planetary space conditions have been made to coincide with (complement) the long standing suppression, and censorship, of the real UFO evidence by our government. This is why the truth about Mars has never become known, publicized, or accepted, up to the present. Yet it is an important correlation, that eighteen years of UFO sightings, with reports numbering into the thousands, predated the first U.S. space probe to reach Mars on a flyby in July, 1965. Of course, it was never officially admitted that UFOs were a major stimulus for us to investigate the planet. Now, in this present work, it will be established that the Martian environment is very similar to earthly conditions, by a review of the early telescopic record, and then through a logical analysis of the more recent space probe developments.

The early history of telescopic observation of Mars has been recounted in numerous books. It began in 1877, when Giovanni Schiaparelli observed through his 8.75 inch reflecting telescope, a number of long lines on the Martian surface that connected up to larger dark areas. He described the lines as "canali," which in his native language meant channels. But the translation quickly became "canals," and his discovery of them led to the idea that intelligent beings on

Mars must have constructed artificial waterways. While Schiaparelli didn't publicly suggest that conclusion himself, he didn't really discourage others who were promoting the idea, because he had found 113 different canali that were long, straight, and neatly defined. He intricately mapped the planet from years of observation. His maps were the standard for many years, and he gave ancient names from Biblical and classical mythology, along with names from the old geography of the Middle East, to the large surface areas and distinct markings of the planet. The names he gave to the surface features are still existent on maps today.

A distinguished American astronomer, Percival Lowell, decided to dedicate his life to studying Mars. In 1894, he built the Flagstaff Observatory in Arizona, which housed a 24-inch refracting telescope. By 1915, he and his staff had charted nearly 700 canals - a precise network of large-scale construction on Mars that channeled water from the polar ice caps. They were straight, narrow, sometimes parallel, and at numerous locations the canals intersected geometrically. These latter areas were noted to become seasonally dark, and Lowell named them oases, indicating that vegetation and crop growing were abundant. He naturally concluded that there would be attendant cities for the Martian people at these oases.

Lowell understood that the actual waterways could not be seen from Earth, if it were not for the broad areas of seasonal growth lining both sides. It was the combination of both factors that made it possible to see the network of geometric lines on Mars' surface with clarity. Some of the channels were approximately 3000 miles long, and from 15 to 25 miles wide.[1] In 1915 Lowell stated to the scientific world, "Mars is inhabited, and we have absolute proof." He proclaimed that the Martian civilization had an intricate and highly advanced irrigation system that could be seen and photographed through Earth-based telescopes. A few pictures had been taken as early as 1907. Lowell's position was so revolutionary to the orthodox views of the scientific establishment, that it received harsh contempt from many, and went virtually ignored by others.

Once every 26 months, Earth and Mars are at their closest distance from each other in their orbits around the sun, and in astronomy this is called being in opposition. But because the orbits are elliptical, the most favorable opposition occurs only once every 15 to 17 years, and at this time the two planets are at their closest, about 35 million miles distant. To view the extensive canals and markings, an astronomer had to have unlimited patience and determination, and more importantly, an open mind. Like the establishment scientists today, Lowell's contemporaries often lacked such traits. Studying the distant features on Mars through the telescope was difficult and tricky, and could only be done at the large observatories when the local atmospheric conditions and other visibility factors were exceptionally coordinated. But even during the brief periods of favorable opposition, the disk-like image showed a blurring of detail almost continuously, due to the ever-present atmospheric turbulence around both the Earth and Mars.

Our atmosphere is constantly in molecular motion due to thermal activity. To the naked eye, the sky might seem so clear and calm, that a person would assume there is perfect seeing conditions. For looking at stars and nebulae, that would be true, but it's not the same when we view our neighboring planets with a large telescope. Through the high power magnification of a telescope, the barely perceptible dynamics of heat (wind) movement in the atmosphere causes a slight shimmering effect, and while the broad features of a planetary image may be easily recognizable, any fine detail is lost in an almost continual slight blurring. Ever so momentarily, our atmospheric unsteadiness will cease for a second or two. At that precise moment an astute telescopic observer will have a perfect seeing condition, and be able to see in fine detail the planetary image 35 million miles away. Yet these views last but a few seconds, making it extremely difficult to obtain a distinct photograph. Furthermore, the only way that the photographic evidence of the canals can be obtained is when the planet is viewed directly overhead at perihelion. These observations must be made from the best suitable locations in our southern hemisphere.

Lowell made a special expedition to Chile in 1907 and obtained the first photographic evidence of the canals. His successor, Dr. E.C. Slipher, had better success in later years with observations from South Africa, when camera equipment had improved considerably. The Martian canals are seen on plates VI and XLVII in the book, *The Photographic Story of Mars*, by E.C. Slipher. The edition I obtained was published by Northland Press, Flagstaff, Arizona, in 1962.

The quality of photographs can always be debated by the establishment scientist who denies everything he has not seen for himself. In reality, the eye is superior in viewing telescopic images in detail, compared to the photographic results when taking telescopic pictures of a planet 35 million miles distant. Dr. Slipher stated in 1962, "The history of the canal problem shows that every skilled observer who goes to the best available site for his observations has had no great difficulty of seeing and convincing himself of the reality of the canals. I am not aware of a single exception to this." A fellow astronomer, Dr. Pettit, confirmed this visual documentation, by reporting in 1953 that "there are moments when the whole canal pattern can be seen on Mars."

Today's literature never fails to mention that the early Mariner probes during the 1960's proved that the canals are non-existent, and that the controversy over the Schiaparelli and Lowell evidence has been laid to rest. It is true that no actual evidence of canals was released by NASA, but it should be realized, that if the picture-taking cameras on those early probes did photograph certain areas showing canals with sufficient clarity, the evidence would not have been released anyway. The fact is, that until Mariner 9, only a very small and unrepresentative fraction of the Martian surface was photographed, and most of that, very poorly. Mariners 4, 6, and 7 never even found the huge 2300 mile-long Valles Marineus canyon on Mars, which is a natural formation. The fuzzy black and white photos that were released to the public lacked any clarity whatsoever. We can get better telescopic photographs of the Moon 240,000 miles away, than those camera pictures taken only a few thousand miles from Mars. An important point to realize is that the probes carried cameras, not telescopes. Even NASA admitted that the cameras aboard the Mariners could not have provided evidence of a Martian civilization from their photographic distance. However, the publicly-released photos were quickly interpreted as disproving the canal controversy.

What are space photographs in reality? The "picture" is relayed back to Earth in the form of numerous dots, contained within a radio signal. The picture has to be reconstructed from this electronic message, by computer imaging each dot into a shade of gray. The first image processing is considered the raw picture, and is basically a washed-out, blurry gradation of gray. Then the imaging team can reassign the gray levels by computer, in order to better distinguish any identifiable spots or features on the raw picture. A slightly improved image is given to the public.

American astronauts have said that the only visible man-made construction on Earth that they could see from their high orbit around our planet was the Great Wall of China. If there were a Great Wall on Mars and it turned up on one of the photographs, the space agency could still release the picture, but without the slightest trace of a wall. With computer imaging, it is easy to fade out features and erase contrast, to the point of an unidentifiable gray blotch. By starting with the original raw, washed-out picture, it is only a matter of re-assigning the gray levels so that the wall never appears during processing. On the other hand, if another photograph shows a natural landmark or feature, that picture can be electronically sharpened and focussed to show great detail. We have reached a new state of the art: we can increase or decrease picture quality by subtle electronic brushing.

Now to clarify the situation regarding the canal evidence first discovered by Schiaparelli and Lowell through their telescopic studies. It was only "laid to rest" because authorities withheld official confirmation. Mariner 4 did photograph some straight-line canals, and this was finally admitted some time later by Dr. William Pickering, the head of Jet Propulsion Laboratory.[2] (JPL conducts all the planetary projects for NASA.) Dr. Clyde Tombaugh, the scientist who discovered Pluto, also confirmed that the canals were photographed by the 1965 probe. But officially, this type of evidence has never been released. The public was shown computer-enhanced photographs, but the detailed originals were in the hands of the authorities. And if the canals were filmed by that first probe, it is a certainty that they were filmed by later Mariner and Viking probes, yet that information has always been withheld. We'll discuss the censoring aspect relative to the later space missions thoroughly, but first let's continue with the telescopic record.

Early in this century, expert astronomers recorded several anomalies during their observations of Mars. On one occasion, a long series of blinking lights lasting 70 minutes was observed, leading one observatory director to describe the incident as "absolutely inexplicable."[3] In 1937 and again in 1949, Japanese experts witnessed a brilliant glow on the surface of Mars, that was as bright as a 6th magnitude star. To be visible from the Earth, these "flares" had to be tremendous. Any type of volcanic activity couldn't possibly be seen from our distance, and so the cause of the brightness remained a mystery. Other strange lights were seen on different occasions.

There was a cloud-like object observed and photographed in 1954, that was in the perfect shape of a W, or an M if we consider that a telescope inverts an image. It was 1100 miles across and remained in a fixed position above the planet for more than a month. (Natural atmospheric clouds will change shape and dissipate within a few days). At the three intersections of the W, were intense bright spots, or "knobs." Speculation was running high, even at the Carnegie Institution at Washington. It was such a rigid and unusual shape, that there was a strong suggestion of artificial origin.

Throughout the 1920's and 30's, recurring radio signals

were picked up coming from the direction of Mars. The spacing and pattern of the radio waves ruled out the possibility that these cryptic signals were random radio noise or electrical disturbances in space, because there was an intelligent coding system to these radio waves. That much was certain, even though they remained undecipherable on our end. Even the famous scientist Marconi, the man who invented the "wireless," picked up these interplanetary radio waves with his advanced experimental equipment in 1921, and later stated that he believed he had intercepted messages from Mars. He emphasized that the transmission wavelength of the coded signals was 150 kilometers, whereas the maximum wavelength used by our transmitting stations at the time was about 14 kilometers.[4]

Many others had come to the same conclusion over the next few years when intercepting these signals, especially when Mars was in orbital proximity to Earth. And speaking to the British Association for the Advancement of Science in 1931, the late Bishop Barnes stated his belief that many other inhabited worlds exist, and that many must certainly be able to propagate interplanetary radio communication. It was such messages that were being picked up now he said. And when these interplanetary signals were recognized and acknowledged by our Earth, it would be the dawn of a new era for humanity. But at this new beginning, he added, there would be opposition between those who welcome the new knowledge and those who deem it dangerous for that information to be known and accepted. And is this not what happened two decades later, when UFOs demonstrated the very existence of life on other worlds? Was it not the beginning of an era of opposition between those who were open and accepting of the new knowledge about space, and those who worked to prevent the truth from coming out?

Along with the later observations of mysterious clouds and lights, the cryptic radio signals led some independent astronomers to conclude that we were being given rudimentary signals from Mars to challenge our thinking about life beyond the Earth. Regarding habitability, there was even more scientific certainty in other telescopic studies. As early as 1926, photographs were taken in ultraviolet light that clearly showed a substantial atmosphere on Mars. Compared with infrared photographs taken at the same time, the pictures proved that there is a dense atmosphere, possibly 40 miles in depth. There are undoubtedly more rarified layers above this altitude, much like the upper, tenuous atmosphere around the Earth, that would be too thin to be recorded by photography. It has been suggested that the top of the Martian atmosphere might reach 400 miles, by the British scientist-writer Earl Nelson, author of *There Is Life On Mars* (1956).

The early photographs showing the Martian atmosphere were taken by G.E. Hale of the Mount Palomar Observatory and are reproduced in Nelson's book. There are two immediate and important conclusions that can be drawn from those observations. The surface gravity on Mars must be substantially higher than has been taught, for a low gravity would not be sufficient to retain such a sizeable atmosphere. Secondly, with such a dense atmosphere, the sun's energy would interact much differently than orthodox theories suggested, and the temperatures on Mars would be considerably warmer, more moderate, and more Earth-like.

Although the length of the Martian year is nearly double our 365-day year, the seasons on Mars vary and alternate just like on Earth. When the northern hemisphere is in its summer cycle, the southern hemisphere has its winter. The length of the Martian day is 24 hours and 37 minutes, and the inclination of its axis is 25°, which is very close to Earth's 23°.

Both the northern and southern polar caps extend nearly half way to the Martian equator during their respective winters. With the onset of spring in either hemisphere, its ice cap recedes and a wave of darkening over broad areas spreads slowly towards the equator. This cyclic surface darkening was widely considered to be seasonal vegetation growth as water was liberated from the polar caps. Each polar cap will shrink considerably during its respective summer cycle. Sometimes the southern polar cap melts completely.

The broad areas near the equator, such as Mare Serpentis, Mare Sirenium, and Syrtis Major, change from their winter shade of brown, to light green and then to dark green. This latter stage has often been described as a dark blue-green. Astronomers also noted that as the seasons changed to autumn, the colors would gradually turn to yellow and gold, finally returning to brown in the winter. (The surface color of Mars is not dark red, as I will prove later).

The parade of colorful seasons was interpreted by open-minded astronomers as the seasonal growth and ripening of vegetation. Cyclic growth coincided regularly with the natural climatic changes on the planet, just as we have here on Earth. I am not discussing the canals and their irrigation for crop growing, at the moment. These seasonal changes showing cyclic plant life would be taking place even if man were not there on Mars.

The presence of vegetation on Mars was held to be a certainty in some quarters, but hotly debated by others. But the way to end all argument was to prove the existence of carbon dioxide, oxygen, and the water in the Martian environment, which would indicate that photosynthesis (the life process) of plants was in fact taking place. Carbon dioxide was there in abundance - even conservative scientists agreed on that, for it was commonly speculated that the atmosphere's chief constituent was carbon dioxide. Oxygen seemed likely, though it could not be detected in the atmosphere from earth-based studies. The evidence for oxygen was indicated by some regional soil colors, which indicated that certain areas contained a large amount of ferrous oxide, or limonite. We have some tropical regions on Earth where the soil is reddish-brown limonite, and two things are necessary for its formation: abundant oxygen and extreme humidity in the air. Apparently, oxygen was in the atmosphere of Mars, as the natural product of plant photosynthesis.

To briefly explain photosynthesis, it is the biological process by which green plants containing chlorophyll use the energy of sunlight to synthesize carbohydrates from carbon dioxide and water. Six molecules of water and six molecules of carbon dioxide are transformed with the aid of solar energy into one molecule of glucose and six molecules of oxygen. The oxygen is then liberated into the atmosphere. We breathe in oxygen and exhale carbon dioxide, which in turn the green plants use in photosynthesis, and oxygen is returned to the atmosphere. This is Nature's perfect cycle. If all the green plants were suddenly removed from the Earth, all human and animal life would die, because the oxygen we breathe would not be replenished.

The last thing that needed to be confirmed in order to prove the seasonal vegetation on Mars, was the existence of water. For this evidence it is easiest to jump ahead for a moment to the U.S. Viking project of 1976. The Viking I orbiter photographed extensive ground fog, mists, and cloud cover in the northern hemisphere, and from readings taken by sensitive instruments on the orbiting probe, it was proven once and for all, that the polar caps were frozen water.[5] That it is ice! If the polar caps were completely melted, it was estimated that the water produced would cover the entire planet to a depth of about 20 feet.

Along with the early ultraviolet photographs showing a substantial atmosphere, it has been shown that the environmental constituents for life exists on Mars. The three basic parameters are carbon dioxide, water, and oxygen - the ferrous oxide soil being the indirect evidence for oxygen. It is necessary to point to the indirect evidence for oxygen, since NASA refuses to confirm the presence of oxygen in the Martian atmosphere. That is the single remaining ace in their hand. And they keep it, because they know that only the process of photosynthesis by living plants can account for the presence of oxygen in any planet's atmosphere. During the Viking mission, NASA admitted finding nitrogen, argon, carbon dioxide, and water vapor, although they kept the relative percentages and overall density out of proportion to the true conditions. But NASA is holding out on the oxygen and will not admit finding it with the Viking probes, because *atmospheric oxygen* would be recognized by scientists as positive proof that life exists on Mars. But the remaining evidence to be discussed will prove the case.

Before the space agency came into existence on October 1, 1958, scientific astronomers at the large observatories were still the experts and authorities on the planets. It seems as though it was preordained in the heavens that the independent thinkers would have one last chance to probe the mystery of our neighboring planet, as Mars swung by in favorable opposition in 1954 and 1956. In its first approach, Mars came within a distance of 39,800,000 miles. The second time, in 1956, the planet was only 35,120,000 miles away. It would not be that close again until 1971, when planetary exploration and pronouncements were in the hands of NASA.

But in 1954 excitement ran high in astronomical circles, because an international Mars Committee had been formed, to plan an around the world "Mars patrol." Prominent scientists from 17 countries would be coordinating telescopic studies from the world's largest observatories, as Mars made its closest approach in July. Some of the countries involved included the United States, France, Italy, Turkey, India, Japan, Australia, South Africa, Java, Egypt, and Argentina.[6]

The international team of scientists was headed by the world's greatest Mars expert, Dr. E.C. Slipher, then the Director of the Lowell Observatory. He and most of the committee members were well aware of all the previous astronomical records - the mysterious clouds, flares, markings, radio signals, and the evidence for canals and vegetation. Some privately believed there was an intelligent civilization on Mars, for in 1938, it had been announced that the Lowell Observatory found evidence of changes in the canal system, and the changes appeared to have been altered by design. This 1954 Mars "expedition" was primarily planned to settle the question. It is quite possible that some members linked the numerous flying saucer sightings that had been widely reported since 1947, to the renewed and intense interest in Mars.

Because the government was heavily guarding the UFO evidence, the National Security Agency made it a top priority to use its influence to keep check on the developments of the

Mars patrol study. It was imperative that planetary speculations and press statements be kept in a totally ambiguous light. The censors were especially concerned about the Mars patrol because of the caliber of open-minded men who were involved with the project. They included Dr. Seymour Hess, a meteorology expert who was on record as having sighted a UFO; Dr. Harold C. Urey, a prominent astrophysicist who was genuinely curious about life on other planets; and Dr. Slipher, who was following in the footsteps of the pioneer Percival Lowell. Dr. Slipher assigned himself to make observations from the best location possible - the Lamont Hussey Observatory in South Africa. It had the largest refracting telescope in the southern hemisphere, and Mars would be passing directly overhead each night during opposition. And before the project got underway, Slipher publicly stated that if he found proof of life on Mars, he would announce it to the world.

The Mars Expedition took 20,000 photographs and confirmed the presence of both the canals and vegetation. The canals did not meander at all like a river would; they followed great-circle courses, which are the shortest distance between two points on a globe. Many planetary astronomers had speculated previously, that if photographs showed that the canals were along great circle paths, it could be concluded that they were the work of intelligent beings. The scientists were getting exceptional pictures also, because the Lowell Observatory was using a new electronic camera that could amplify faint markings, and photograph in 1/10 of a second to prevent atmospheric turbulence from blurring the details. One canal was found to run straight as an arrow for 1500 miles, something that no natural water channel could do.

Dr. Slipher brought enough photographs back from South Africa to prove that the canals were real, and man-made. While providing abundant vegetation growth alongside their straight-line courses, the canals also proved to be the common link between the green oases. An intricate pumping system seemed to be the only explanation when considering the distances involved. More than 40 canals and 15 oases were photographed in the first week.[7] But the Mars Committee reports never became public, and they were therefore unknown outside a very limited part of the astronomy community. The new findings were privately logged at the observatories, and sparing details were barely covered in only a few astronomical journals. But everything was kept out of the newspapers.

The government's intelligence agency had succeeded in blocking the Committee's early plans for public reports and press conferences. Then they firmly executed their plans for a blackout of real information about Mars. The government keeps itself in control by keeping world-wide opinion in control, especially with regard to sensitive and dramatic issues. Allowing an announcement by an international team of scientists suggesting that Mars was inhabited, would be tantamount to the government confirming that UFOs are visiting our planet. So the censors knew what they had to do.

Pressure was put on those who headed the project to furnish no reports to the public press. Though the astronomers studied Mars for 5 months, only one little statement was given to the public at the beginning. Dr. Slipher had announced that some new and interesting changes were observed on Mars with their photographic study. Following that report, there was only silence. All plans for further publicity were blocked, and no worthy Mars Patrol bulletins were ever released.[8] The excuses given out were in the category of "difficulties in communication and coordination, disagreement as to what had been seen and photographed, months of studies and review were necessary to properly analyze, and so on."

How can any silencing agency of the government achieve such suppression of this, or any other, kind of dramatic information? It is difficult to determine for each case just what methods are employed, but their forceful persuasion does escalate until the cooperation is achieved. Presumably, they start out with the position that such information is related to the national security, and that the government is the entrusted agency to best handle the social implications of confirmed announcements. They imply that the public isn't quite ready for this information, that the world isn't ready for this information. That the economy isn't prepared for this type of information. They fear that there would be an upheaval in thinking, (although I am certain that it would be an "upliftment" in thinking, and this is the real problem that threatens the censors).

They will say that the public might panic, or they could offer the excuse that there might be an attack from Mars. The possibilities for persuasive argument are endless, but the only end requirement is that planetary evidence be shown as inconclusive, vague, and debatable. It has always been maintained officially, that known life does not exist beyond the Earth, unless possibly it is light years away from us in another part of the galaxy. In which case, the distance is so great that our civilizations will never meet.

After being persuaded to withhold the significant findings, including the discovery of the great-circle paths of the canals, the Mars Committee only issued a simple press release. Dr. Slipher made a statement to the effect that Mars is alive. That certainly satisfied the censors' insistence in keeping things nebulous. (Alive - how? Geologically with volcanos, dust storms, and polar cap shrinkage? Or alive in the sense of intelligent constructions?) He noted that there were color changes in the Martian geography that were more interesting than in his previous observations over the years. But the tiny report was essentially meaningless, and obviously did not affect public or scientific opinion. The question of Mars might have still been left open, but the orthodox theories of inhabitability were not threatened in the least.

It was not until eight years afterwards that notable documentation of the 1954 Mars observations was published, in a book titled *The Photographic Story of Mars*. Recently, I obtained a copy of this book, and it appears that the publication had a relatively small printing, and was mainly published to be a reference type of book for science libraries. Certainly, few in the public would have been inclined to buy such a costly book, and take it on their own to study an involved scientific text. Yet the answers are there if one wishes to read through complex analyses and carefully worded discussions. The book was written by Dr. Slipher in 1962, and the full text is based on fifty years of telescopic studies, and thousands of photographic images taken at the world's largest observatories. The conclusions also referenced the last major finding by astronomy regarding the Martian environment.

During the November 1958 opposition, Dr. William Sinton conducted studies at the Smithsonian Astrophysical Observatory. The scientist-astronomer performed careful infrared scans of the bright desert areas and the dark green oases, and found that the sun's energy was absorbed in certain wavelengths over the dark areas, but not over the desert regions. The absorption wavelengths were at 3.43, 3.56, and 3.67 microns, and these are exactly the same wavelengths absorbed by hydrocarbon compounds. His study proved that there is green plant life on the broad oases of Mars, and that it is organically composed of carbon-hydrogen compounds, the same as our own terrestrial vegetation. In other words, his scientific evidence showed that Martian plant life is based on the same carbon cycle as we find on Earth.

But new experimental evidence is never accepted that quickly. It is always challenged, and subject to much debate, because old established theories are very hard to change. The old theories had predicted that there was no appreciable water or atmosphere on Mars, and that the surface temperatures were too extreme for vegetation life. (The canal evidence also, carried too many implications to be considered acceptable, and was rejected outright as incompatible with respected establishment theories.) Dr. Sinton's experiments with infrared scans were viewed as inconclusive, and any such results would have to be confirmed over and over before conservative science would budge. The scientific community much rather preferred to wait until future space probes settled the questions about Mars. The scientific arguments lingered in limbo, until the government formed a space age bureaucracy, called NASA, that could preempt all discussions on matters of space. The days of independent astronomy speculating on planetary conditions were soon over. While representing the government in its authoritative role, NASA's position was unassailable - almost.

Initially, NASA had three functions:

1 - To launch artificial satellites into orbit around the Earth.
2 - To put men into space.
3 - To explore the other planetary members of our solar system, including the Moon, with remotely controlled space probes.

The first two they did admirably well, and mankind was on the threshold of becoming a space civilization. But with the third, NASA did not advance our knowledge towards an age of enlightenment. In fact, there is a bitter irony to our space age developments, in that our authorities led thinking back to the Dark Ages, through distortion and suppression of actual space findings.

Long ago, Earth was isolated from the rest of the system, through its ignorance and superstitious thinking. By the 20th century, man's intelligence had progressed to where he could rationally understand and accept, that advanced civilizations do travel space and have home planets similar to our Earth. Space visitors traveling in ships which we have termed UFOs, were making their existence known at the same time we were reaching technological crossroads in science. But the men of war and all their institutions denied it, and the censors would not allow the confirmation of life beyond the Earth, whether in spaceships or on planets. The doors were kept shut by the silence group and vested interests opposed to the truth, and NASA then turned out the lights. NASA made out space to be an uninteresting wasteland, devoid of life or recognizable purpose. The end result was that mankind on Earth reverted back to an extreme thinking of self-importance, alone in his own egotistical sphere of a world.

Had our authorities left a few questions open for balanced speculation, it would be easier to be less critical. But instead, they determinedly set out to present a completely negative picture of the planet. A living environment was totally negated without qualification, in order to complement the suppression of UFO evidence. It was apparent that our planetary probing was not conducted with any objectivity, right from the start. *Being a government bureaucracy*, NASA had no choice but to serve the hands of the most powerful economic interests of our present-day world. NASA censors cooperated with the corporate interests that demanded the continual coverup and suppression regarding UFOs and their origins, and therefore publicly presented an unrealistic picture of the planets.

The first official flyby of Mars was achieved by Mariner 4 in July 1965. The probe radioed back 22 pictures of the Martian surface, and NASA initially claimed that there were no canals. Lifetimes of telescopic studies were casually obliterated with that one statement. A radar occultation reading provided a basis for NASA to declare that the atmosphere density on Mars was less than 1% of Earth's, and another type of signal allowed experts to suggest that the planet had no magnetosphere. At its closest distance, Mariner 4 was 6000 miles from the planet, yet NASA spokesmen claimed readings showing that the average surface temperature on Mars was -170°F.

The censors may have had a tough time back in the Mars Patrol days curbing speculation, but this was a brand new ballgame. NASA was the perfect vehicle to paint a lifeless picture beyond the Earth. Who could possibly challenge statements coming from the U.S. space program? Telescopes or not. UFOs or not. Anybody who still wanted to claim intelligent life existed on Mars would be considered a lunatic.

The Mariner 4 flyby did not have the capability to realistically confirm habitability. That much can be conceded. But likewise, the space probe could not realistically confirm those alleged planetary conditions that were put out as flat statements by the authorities, either. With future planetary probes, it became apparent how the censorship was being orchestrated, and by whom.

The real problem this book confronts is not with NASA specifically. The space agency had practically no choice but to follow the dictates of the powerful economic interests that control governments and their subordinate agencies. It is these international cartels that have been behind all censorship regarding planetary space. NASA has only been the publicly-identifiable distorter, regarding space pronouncements.

So NASA can be partly excused for not being in a position to objectively conduct space probe explorations. But false values can never be changed by anything but truth. And we are at the critical crossroad of time. Either we become a space civilization, or we will be a nuclear extinction. Therefore NASA has to be held more accountable for its past actions, and for its lack of presenting realistic evidence. But we can give the space agency a small bit of credit, for by accident or design, they have leaked a few clues about the truth of the neighboring planetary environments. And we can be thankful that some strong members of our society put their creative ideas and efforts into a space program, and caused some truths to be discovered.

The next chapter will therefore be an objective look at the planetary evidence given out by NASA during its exploration of Mars by the Mariner and Viking space probes. Some patterns may be seen as to how the space agency sought to confirm the early telescopic studies done by astronomers. Despite widespread belief to the contrary, the 1976 Viking project did reveal some very tangible evidence showing that the Martian environment is indeed Earth-like.

Chapter 5
Mars - The Mariner and Viking Missions

In the summer of 1969, two more space probes flew by Mars. Mariner 6 and 7 were each equipped with two television cameras. One camera had a wide angle lens, and the other had a close up lens. A total of 202 pictures were taken from distances of one million miles down to the closest approach of 2000 miles. The photographs allowed scientists to conclude that there were 3 general types of Martian terrain:

1 - large regions dotted with flat smooth craters.
2 - desert areas that are crater-free, such as the Hellas Plain.
3 - mountainous areas with apparently dry river beds and gorges.

By comparing infrared and ultraviolet surveys, project scientists still insisted that the atmosphere and polar caps were almost fully composed of carbon dioxide. But the Viking probes disproved this fallacy seven years later, although there was scant emphasis publicly, to that effect.

The first probe to successfully orbit any planet was Mariner 9, which reached Mars in November 1971. From a high orbit it sent back thousands of pictures. NASA still wasn't using color cameras, but that was in the space agency's favor. Whereas the earlier Mariners were only momentary flybys, this probe would be photographing the entire planet. And if color cameras were used, the wide, darker irrigation plains along the canals charted by Lowell, and later photographed by the 1954 Mars Expedition study, would be seen in clear contrast to the surrounding areas. The official decision makers knew the full facts behind the UFO evidence, and that a good percentage of the interplanetary spaceships were from Mars. They knew it was imperative to prevent showing any indication of a habitable planet.

The decision was to make the planet appear lifeless, unnatural, and barren. This was accomplished by photographing in black and white, and computer processing the pictures into a non-distinct, drab gray. Broad areas simply resolved into shadows and blurs without any apparent surface features, except for a few pictures of deserted badlands and canyons. The majority of photos released were pointless to look at, because they were nothing more than shades of gray, with no detail. The routine sampling that was handed out to the scientific community led to the automatic conclusion that the latest pictures proved the non-existence of the canals. But the photographic quality and resolution was so artificially poor, that the Mariner 9 photographic results could not have proved anything, (and the censors knew it.)

Although Mariner 9 had reached Mars in November 1971, the probe reportedly wasn't able to start photographing until early in 1972 because of an alleged planetary-wide dust storm on arrival, along with winds of 200 mph on the Martian surface. This is where the contradictions start. NASA claims that there is an extremely rarified atmosphere of about 7 mb pressure at the surface, compared to 1000 mb on Earth. Wind is a movement of air. If there is virtually no air, what is whipping around at 200 mph? And if there is only a negligible atmosphere, what is supporting tons of dust particles?

There could be 200 mph winds on Mars, but they are not near the surface any more than they are on Earth. I was flying into California a few years back, and the pilot made a routine announcement over the intercom that we were flying at 37,000 feet and the wind was from some direction at a speed of 170 mph. And the jet streams we hear about reach speeds of up to 300 mph. So I do not accept that the reported 200 mph wind on Mars was a surface wind. The later Viking 1 lander radioed back information from the surface from 1976 to 1983, and there were no reports of high winds.

Understanding the recent history of the telescopic study of Mars helps to dispel this Mariner 9 report of a planet-wide dust storm, because the evidence shows that the Martian seasons are exactly earth-like. At any given time, one hemisphere is always in its fertile spring or summer season, and many large green areas of 200,000 square miles or more are easily viewed from Earth when Mars is at opposition. So while there may be some dry dusty areas in the opposite winter hemisphere, the vegetation cycle in the summer hemisphere would preclude anything but local, isolated dust storms there. In other words, an alleged planet-wide dust storm would have no viable scientific explanation.

There could be a rational explanation for some partial obscuration of the summer hemisphere. If there were a violent volcanic eruption, immense quantities of very fine ash would be hurled into the atmosphere, and winds in the upper layers of the atmosphere could carry the ash to scattered regions. Having been schooled in the theory that Mars has a very thin atmosphere, scientists observing the evidence of some type of obscuration would erroneously conclude that there were surface dust storms.

Other natural explanations may provide partial answers, also. It could be possible that there is an atmospheric layer which reflects a certain wavelength of color in the sun's energy. Perhaps a shade of yellow. If there were normal cloud patterns near the Martian surface, and by normal I mean water vapor clouds, then this particular atmospheric layer could make the clouds appear as yellowish fog or haze, that would in turn obscure the broad surface features. This may be a partial answer, because astronomers studying Mars through telescopes have sometimes reported seeing luminous yellow clouds, 700 miles in diameter or more. But they never have seen anything approaching a "planet-wide" condition lasting three months.

It's not out of the realm of possibility that the "3 month-long dust storm" report was a calculated ploy by NASA, in order to secretly study and photograph the planet with a low-orbiting Mariner 9. Then having completed that, the probe was placed up into a high orbit again, and the fake dust storm subsided. At that point, NASA could begin the transmission of the dull, gray, low-resolution pictures that were released to the public. Bureaucratic institutions have a long history of pulling the wool over the public's eye, in sensitive matters on space which are always covered by the blanket of "national security."

The Mariner mission was orbiting Mars during the time of the Vietnam War. Political, social, and economic forces play the most dominant role in keeping scientific revelations in check. On the national corporate front, the most important question in 1972 wasn't whether there was life on Mars, but how to keep the public backing the disgraceful disaster in Vietnam. The American government was pumping $1.5 billion every week into the war effort, and that translated into huge profits for the armament manufacturers. In short, the economy was rolling along. What if suddenly, photographic proof of life and habitable conditions on Mars were presented to the world? Everyone's attention would shift in wonderment towards the stars, and the futility of our war games would rise to the surface of our public consciousness. The slaughter on the battlefields in Vietnam would cease, as would the war profits. Nobody would care who had the biggest arsenal of bombs. Mankind would want to be human again, - not pawns of political ideologies.

Although the Mariner 9 evidence is rather dated today, and the originally publicized findings reflected little - if anything - definitive about the planet, I have reviewed that mission in its proper perspective for the following reason. It has always been cited as the mission that unequivocally disproved the canal evidence and habitability. Yet what really happened is this: that what the censors wanted the public to see, also became what the scientists wanted to see, and everything regarding Mars has been seen through tunnel vision ever since.

For an illuminating comparison, one should read the definitive astronomical book, *The Photographic Story of*

Mars, published in 1962 by Dr. E.C. Slipher of the Lowell Observatory. This masterpiece document readily proves that commonly published articles on Mars, which are based on the government's "official" evidence, are little more than nonsense. The Lowell Observatory book is based on 200,000 photographic images taken over 50 years, which proved that Mars has a deep atmosphere that supports water vapor clouds, that the polar caps are composed of frozen water, and that the Martian surface is covered with canals, oases, and cyclic vegetation. Dr. Slipher did not go so far as to state human habitation on Mars (he left that implicit in the canal evidence), but how could NASA possibly miss all the natural environmental features of a habitable planet with Mariner 9?

It is hard to assess how the relatively scant findings were doled out over several months. It can be safely stated that project scientists were given relatively little to go on. In fact, a lot of Moon pictures look like an inviting landscape, when compared to the Mariner 9 photo album handed out to the scientific community. There was perhaps only one picture released that caused a little excitement or speculation. In a regional photograph of the Elysium plateau, stands a group of four distinct pyramids. The two larger ones are nearly identical in size, and are standing side by side. The two smaller ones are closer together in another area. Each of the immense structures is a 3-sided pyramid. Another structure seen nearby in the photograph is a perfectly rectangular 4-sided pyramid, similar to the pyramids of Egypt and Mexico.

All theories that some natural process could have formed these colossal structures have been ruled out by an expert science writer, David Chandler, author of *Life On Mars*. But the released photograph is not convincing to everyone, because it has a grainy quality to it, and therefore lacks real clarity. However, it has led to quiet speculation that there was a civilization on Mars at one time, if not today, according to those who believe NASA's public statements.

Before all the Mariner 9 reports could be analyzed, plans were underway for the most ambitious exploration project of all. The project was Viking, a space mission using two orbiters and two landers that would rendezvous and search for life on Mars in the summer of 1976. As the U.S. probes were heading out on their 11-month, 220 million mile trip to the planet, the team of Viking scientists declared:

> "If we find life on Mars, we automatically will have invented a brand new science. It will completely convert the science of biology to something else. We will even have to rethink many philosophical positions that man held for many years. The impact of the discovery of life is immense, it is immediate, and it is not debatable."

Those were meaningful words, but there was one big ingredient missing. That team of about 60 Viking scientists were searching for life *according to their perceptions*. And they could only perceive a remote possibility for life on Mars, limited to microorganisms in the soil. In fact, the head biologist of the project was already on record as saying, that the probability of ever finding any kind of life on Mars was a flat zero.[1] What kind of objectivity or attitude is that, for the most important space mission undertaken to date? The answer: it is very representative of the type of scientific thinking by the orthodox community. We have to remember that the results of any research will depend on the caliber and attitude of scientists hired to work in tax-supported space projects. Their perceptions, opinions, and prejudices will weigh heavily on the answers that are determined. Scientific study is seldom value-free.

The Viking 1 spacecraft reached Mars in June 1976, and spent a month orbiting the planet in order to photograph possible landing sites in great detail. Those photographs would be very interesting to see, because the picture that was reportedly used to select the Chryse region was photographed from a distance of more than 1000 miles, and there is a lack of any detail to justify it as a safe landing site. In fact, all the Viking Orbiter pictures that have been reproduced in NASA publications, and in various books and magazines, are but a slight improvement over the Mariner 9 pictures. There is that certain lack of definition, except for the all-too-familiar geological sites that are the known desolate areas. And they are all the lifeless gray type. There were a few "color" pictures that were released, but they are not true color pictures. They were made by superimposing three separate black-and-white images taken through color filters, which created an exaggerated effect. A person looking at any of the "color" pictures would not have any idea what he is looking at, until he reads the corresponding NASA description.

Couldn't NASA have taken real color pictures with the Viking Orbiter? They could. And they did! But they never admitted it, and only released the computer processed gray pictures from high orbits. Pictures taken of Earth by an orbiting satellite at the same altitude and resolution would not show any signs of intelligent life here, nor would gray pictures allow us to determine that there is abundant vegetation growth on Earth.

Before we examine the positive findings, and the illuminating contradictions, it is important to assess how the information from the Viking space-probes was controlled. There are definite similarities to the methods employed on previous missions to Mars and Venus. The pictures and various meteorological readings taken by the orbiters were channeled into the crypto-communication center at Jet Propulsion Laboratory first, where they could be sufficiently modified before being relayed to the main consoles and printout displays at the control center. It may be argued and disbelieved by the team of project scientists, and by just about everyone else, but the fact is, that these scientists do not receive the direct, first-hand signals from the space probes. Political and economic realities dictate otherwise. The scientists are not in any type of position where they would be allowed to present dramatic, undeniable proof of intelligent life or habitable conditions in our solar system. They can be allowed to speculate about microbiological activity because that has no real connection to UFOs. And it is the visiting UFOs that have been the intense focus for suppression by various government agencies since the 1940's.

Neither was the decision where to land the Viking

landing package made by the team of scientists either, because they didn't have the really detailed pictures. It may have appeared to them that they were responsible for the final decision, but in actuality it had to be a form of suggestion by those who knew where a definite desert area would be encountered. The northern hemisphere was in its summer season when the Viking spacecraft reached Mars, and more than half of it had fertile areas of vegetation growth.

From the start, the Viking information was controlled in extreme secrecy. The photographs by the orbiters that were high resolution and color detailed were for top secret examination. The colorless gray photos with low resolution (taken from the high orbits) were screened and sent to the display monitors, and eventually to the general public. People wouldn't clamor for too many, because they were boring to look at. The various meteorological measurements were programmed to provide ambiguous readings of the upper atmosphere of Mars, that could be interpreted into any number of theoretical models for the Martian environment. The July 1977 *Scientific American* states that not a single reading of the Martian atmosphere was taken below 120 kilometers. Now on Earth, 99.9% of our atmosphere is below that height, and scientists are not really sure what the molecular make-up is at that altitude.

Why is everything about the Martian environment taught as fact today, when the real record shows that all so-called evidence is pure speculation? The following is quoted from Science News magazine (7/18/81): "The Viking orbiters, though equipped with water detectors and thermal mapping devices, *provided so little atmospheric data* that researchers are still trying to unearth new findings from data provided by an ultraviolet spectrometer aboard the Mariner 9 spacecraft a decade ago (1971)" - (italics - author). And to further document my case that the conclusions about Mars following the Viking mission were nothing more than a restatement of long-held theories, the same Science News article states that a future mission to Mars should carry various spectrometers to measure the composition of the atmosphere and ionosphere, along with a magnetometer to report on the planet's magnetic field, since *"none of these measurements were made from the Viking orbiters"* - (italics - author).

NASA censors controlled the photographic results of the mission. Space findings regarding the atmospheric conditions were essentially nil. The only real operation left in the hands of the Viking team was the soil analysis experiments by the lander. They were allowed to try and interpret the tests of the little soil samples. Whatever the results or conclusions, they were likely to be debated for years (although it was almost a foregone conclusion that such conservative minds would never interpret any results to be definite positive indicators). Microscopic life would be OK to admit, unless the scientists started to get a little too emphatic about it.

The Viking 1 lander was released from the main orbiter, and went down to a landing on the Chryse Plain on July 20, 1976. A parachute was used to brake the 1200 pound lander as it plunged to the surface. We can understand a parachute working in the Earth's atmosphere of several hundred millibars pressure. But since NASA stated that the surface pressure on Mars is only 7 millibars, and less than a millibar a few miles up, what inflated the parachute and caused any kind of drag to slow down the descending lander? The answer is simple: the same dense atmosphere that was photographed during the telescopic studies, and the same one that the NASA censors deny is there.

We were given indirect evidence of a notable atmosphere, with the first color photograph that was transmitted back from the surface on July 21, 1976. Not many people know that it showed a beautiful blue sky. The San Diego Union newspaper printed the photograph in full color on the front page of the July 22 edition, with an accompanying article titled "Planet Boasts Blue Sky." The picture was more than aesthetic. It looked just like the sky on earth, and strongly hinted that the Martian atmospheric constituency diffused sunlight the same as our earthly sky.

The picture was retracted the very next day by NASA as a false image, and every picture released from then on showed a pink sky and red-orange soil. The space agency claimed that the American flag decal on the side of the Viking lander provided a more proper color code for computer processing, and that the new pictures were more correct. But in fact, it would be very easy to keep the red and blue flag-emblem intact, and assign intense color shading to the rest of the transmitted picture with computer imaging. Except for the first, all the color pictures reproduced from the landing site of Viking 1 (and later, Viking 2) look very unreal. Only the original looks like a natural picture with proper color contrast. See Plate 10.

One might ask why NASA ever released the blue sky picture in the first place. A probable reason is that even before Viking, some scientists had predicted that the Martian sky would be blue regardless of the density of the atmosphere. So when it showed up on the first color photo transmitted back to Earth, NASA censors considered it no big deal, in all probability. But then the reality hit. It looked so stunningly like a picture taken anywhere on Earth, that a few scientists immediately suggested that our old theories of a wispy atmosphere on Mars might be quite wrong. This impromptu statement was picked up by the press. The censors looked at the picture again, and quickly decided on computerizing all further pictures to show an eerie pink sky and unearthly red soil. That would definitely stop the speculations. And they debunked the blue sky picture as a false image. Because it was released, it can be ordered from NASA's photographic contractor. I ordered a print, but it is not as good as the picture from the San Diego newspaper!

Those first few days of reports in the press were interesting. Many articles quoted official statements suggesting possible evidence for life on Mars. Mission Control said that there was ground fog at the landing site every morning. The Viking orbiter provided surprising evidence that Mars was much wetter than scientists had previously thought. The space probe also revealed for the first time that nitrogen was present in the Martian atmosphere - an element believed to be necessary for all life processes. No remote sensing devices had ever detected the nitrogen before.

Viking also confirmed the presence of phosphorous, argon, carbon dioxide, and water. If one considers that oxygen is needed to form water, then all the constituents for life were detected. The northern polar cap was determined to be frozen water, a half-mile thick.[2] Pictures taken in the northern latitudes showed thick fluffy clouds as large as 20 miles long (Plate 12). These clouds were a few miles from the surface and casting distinct shadows on the ground. The atmosphere must be much denser than reported to support these substantial clouds. Later photographs revealed morning mists, and ground fog lining crater basins and valleys. Other regions were covered with frost and snow.

Surprisingly, all this evidence for water in the atmosphere and on the ground did not get much mention in the scientific journals. Most of the public is unaware that water on Mars is very abundant. Students are not taught that in our schools either. And science writers have almost exclusively focused on the familiar pictures of the desert canyons and dry riverbeds, and ask where is the water now that carved these formations. They might as well be asking where is the water that carved the Grand Canyon in Arizona. The answer is, that the water is somewhere else on Earth because the climate shifted eons ago. And the water on Mars is now in different regions also. It's that simple.

But Mars was not shown to be positively habitable by the Viking mission, because NASA released everything in bits and pieces, along with some puzzle pieces that wouldn't fit. Their false data in regard to the reported sub-zero temperatures and rarified atmosphere made an impossible jigsaw puzzle. The public lost interest, and scientists eventually retreated back to the old theories. But before that happened there was one last question to be answered. Was there some form of life in the soil?

The nineteenth century philosopher Johann Goethe once declared, "Experiments are not designed to prove the truth, nor is it their intention. The only point professors prove is their own opinion. They conceal all experiments that would reveal the truth and show their theories untenable." We have seen how the orthodox scientists ignored the early telescopic observations by Lowell and Slipher, which showed their theories untenable. With Goethe's statement in mind, let us discuss the experimental results of the soil tests. It was mentioned earlier in this chapter, that the NASA censors gave the conservative Viking team free reign to interpret the results, because the outcome was a safe bet.

The public was given the impression that the soil experiments disproved any possibility of life. This was not the case at all. Except for one ambiguous result, the indications were very positive. Each of the three biological tests gave positive results, and only an unplanned organic chemistry test (which was never intended to be used as a life detection experiment) lacked the sensitivity to give supporting evidence. The extremely cautious and conservative Viking team stated that biological processes may be taking place in the Martian soil, but that they could not rule out the possibility that unknown chemical reactions were providing the positive responses. Years of laboratory experiments with chemicals failed to duplicate the recorded results of the soil tests by the Viking landers. But there was an unwillingness on the part of the space agency to state that they found life on Mars.

Later, NASA admitted that the planned experiments for Viking could not have provided absolute certainty in either proving or disproving the case for life, and that the question was still open. But by that time, the negative impression had been so firmly implanted in the public consciousness (credit to the censors for very effective psychological planning), NASA's admission went unnoticed. The world believes that NASA "proved" life does not, and cannot, exist on Mars. That is not only a false belief - it is a complete contradiction to the truth.

In my opinion, the soil experiments proved more about life on Earth, than they did about Mars. I say that, because it is very apparent that man's egocentric outlook will not allow him to even admit microbe life elsewhere. I guess if he could, it would be a big step forward for our civilization.

But I and many others do not care to linger behind until the rest of mankind can finally accept life in the soil. Microscopic life isn't the interesting question anyway. We want to see the proof of a Martian civilization and the proof of an Earth-like environment on Mars. We have heard that the canals were positively photographed as early as 1965 by the Mariner 4 probe. We have heard the accounts of human visitors from Mars alighting from UFOs. It was well documented in the UFO journals and books that at every 26-month opposition of Mars (when Mars was closest to Earth), UFO sightings substantially increased. What evidence from the Viking space probes escaped the NASA censors, showing the planet to be habitable?

Mars has some enormous volcanos, the largest of which is Olympus Mons, a volcano that towers high on the Tharsis Plains. Estimates of its elevation range from 15 km to 27 km, and it has been photographed extensively since Mariner 9. Curiously enough, it is the only feature on Mars for which a true color photograph has been released. In March 1980, the space agency published a photographic text entitled *Images of Mars - The Viking Extended Mission*, NASA SP-444. This color photograph of Olympus Mons is on the front cover of the publication, yet there is no mention of this detailed picture inside the text.

This remarkable photograph is reproduced on Plate 11. The detail is clear and sharp. Extensive cloud cover can be seen surrounding the high summit that shows natural earth colors, and there is a subtle hint of foliage. The thick clouds at such a high elevation are the knockout though. They prove that the Martian atmosphere must have a density and pressure at the surface much higher than we have been told. It is probably on the order of 100 times as dense. This estimate would make it 700 to 800 mb on Mars, compared to 1000 mb at sea level on Earth.

When Viking 1 had first begun orbiting Mars in June

1976, a NASA spokesman told the press that space probe readings found that the atmospheric pressure was sufficient to permit the existence of liquid water on the surface, something that earlier studies of Mars had not believed possible. The quoted statement in the UPI report was made by Dr. Hal Masursky, a geologist on the Viking project, and head of the landing site team. But the actual, true pressure was never given.[3]

Back in the early 1960's, a famous Russian scientist carried out a long study of Mars at the Crimean Observatory, which left no doubt that the red color of Mars seen from Earth-based observation is not the color of its surface. The astrophysicist, Dr. N. Kozyrev, published his sensational report in April 1962, based on years of spectroscopic observations which proved that the red appearance was the result of the sun's interaction with an upper layer of a dense Martian atmosphere. Further measurements convinced the scientist that the density of the Martian atmosphere was very near to the density of the Earth's atmosphere.[4]

This study could not be confirmed until space probes could travel to Mars and photograph the planet. By now, everyone has seen the standard hemisphere photograph of the "red planet," taken by Viking 1 in 1976 and reproduced on Plate 13. That picture has been published in numerous magazine articles and science journals, and of course, in all the school textbooks. In actuality, that is not a true picture of the planet. It is a black and white image taken through a red filter by the Viking Orbiter camera, as the space probe neared the completion of its journey to Mars.

The brilliant Russian scientist was entirely correct in his studies. With this book, for the first time the truth can be shown. The Viking probe did carry color television cameras, and from a distance of 336,000 miles, filmed the planet as it really is. That picture is reproduced on Plate 14.

Mars is finally unveiled! The supporting evidence in this book should finally vindicate Percival Lowell, Dr. Slipher, Cedric Allingham, George Adamski and others, who courageously told the world that Mars was inhabited with an intelligent civilization. The false gray, computer-processed, red-orange surface and pink sky photographs can be thrown away, or filed away as irrelevant. The latter were specifically processed to supplement, and boost, the rigid theories of orthodox science.

Since the Viking mission was set up to take true color pictures, as from the interplanetary distance shown in Plate 14, then why were all the orbital photographs released to us in gray? Or taken through those color filters, which gave a very exaggerated effect? The reasons should be clear. True color photography could easily reveal that Mars is Earth-like and inhabited, as the canals and oases would be defined in the orbital pictures.

What then are the temperatures, gravity, and atmospheric conditions on Mars? In reality, we would find their values very close to earthly conditions. The Martian temperatures are moderate, and subject to latitude and seasonal changes, just as on Earth. The gravity and atmospheric density is approximately 80 to 85% of the Earth's, with the pressure dropping off gradually in the higher elevations. So slight is the air difference, that our breathing adaptability would adjust in a very short time.

In the Knickerbocker News (Albany, N.Y.) of December 1981, is a front page article headlined: Soviets recharging efforts for rocket landing on Mars. We shouldn't be surprised. The last line of the article stated that the U.S. Pentagon refused to comment. We shouldn't be surprised about that either. It was confirmed just recently, that the Soviets are planning a manned mission to Mars in 1992. It is unlikely that the arrival of the "earthly UFO" will be kept a secret from the Martian population.

My own views of the government space agency were confirmed recently, when by chance I happened to read an interesting book titled The Making of An Ex-Astronaut. The author, Brian O'Leary, tells how he successfully became an astronaut during the 1960's, and then why he resigned after realizing his personal convictions came into conflict with the true nature of the space agency. He charges that NASA has the same character, or illness, as the Pentagon; that it is self-serving, inflexible, and controlled by vested interests. Behind all the public relations gestures of exploring the unknown, NASA's real goal of putting man into space and on the Moon had a decidedly militaristic dimension to it. And in actuality, NASA's budget is directly controlled by the Pentagon, and it has always been a tiny fraction of the annual military budget of the country.

Time-Life has always been considered the informational medium of the Establishment. In his book, O'Leary states that the press conferences following space flights were surveyed under the watchful eye of the Time-Life censors. In other words, they hold strict control over the presentation of space information to the public. The astronauts cannot interject any unorthodox perspectives or worthy revelations, but simply rephrase the feelings of adventure, God, and country. This Time-Life contract with the space agency is a very sensitive issue. And throughout the complete space program, including the unmanned probes to our neighboring planets, the public became informed of the official statements and the orthodox perspective almost exclusively, since the majority of people read the popular magazines of the establishment, if they read anything about space, - Time magazine and Life magazine.

The former astronaut also reveals that the press services are the only source for space photographs for the scientific community for several months following a mission. This is very significant, because it explains how the government uses the media in establishing the basic presentations regarding space. Let us look at how the system works. As an example, we'll consider a Mariner probe to Mars.

Within a few days of the probe reaching Mars, the National Security Agency reviews the preliminary data and any initial pictures that were received from the probe. After careful screening by the authorities, the safe and inconsequential data is left in the hands of NASA officials. The space agency then releases a dozen or so space photographs from the mission to the media at a press conference, along with some preliminary data from "readings" by the space probe. The information goes out over the press wires, and articles are then written in daily newspapers, and usually brief spots on the evening TV news hail this "latest, historic" space mission conducted by NASA.

Any space mission photograph that is released would not reveal anything but what might be expected, and not being disturbed by what he sees, the science writer for a newspaper or magazine dutifully pens an article rehashing the common orthodox theories on Mars. With the latest photograph and some "official data", it all seems so authoritative. Within a week or two, the public gets a neat review of the recent space mission in *Time* or *Life* magazine. Soon, all is forgotten.

But the scientific community has just begun its procedural routine. Now remember, O'Leary states that the press services are the only source for space photographs for the scientific community for several months following a space mission. With this inconsequential data that has been publicly released, the orthodoxers then argue their superficial differences and trivia among themselves, which leads to the voluminous theorizing in the scientific journals. Sometimes this tortuous theorizing gets reduced for public consumption by science writers in popular home magazines. By then, the theories and dogmatic thinking among scientists have become solidified.

NASA and the government have cleverly distanced themselves from educating the public, by allowing the media and the scientific community to establish (and indoctrinate) the common belief of a lifeless solar system. Of course, the National Security Agency and NASA carefully screen data from continual developments during a space probe mission, but any incidental or minor leaks that might filter down later from the space agency would not make a dent or ripple in the established pattern of thinking, which has by then solidified in the public consciousness and the scientific community.

To publish the truth about space, one is up against almost insurmountable odds. Even this book alone, is competing against thousands of books, journals, magazines, and reports, that differ on almost every point discussed. Simply because their authors have never understood the relationship of space science to the UFO evidence, or they did not search for the real discrepancies in space science findings coming through official channels.

The most significant revelation in *The Making of An Ex-Astronaut* is Brian O'Leary's brief discussion of a *manned* space program that few people know about. We are all aware of Russia's and the United State's public space ventures, but there is a third manned space program. It is with the U.S. Air Force. O'Leary states that it is highly secret, and equally ambitious as the other two. Even as an astronaut, he learned little about it, because it operates under the protection of secrecy accorded to the military. He goes on to say that the Air Force space program has all the capabilities of NASA's projects, and that it has its own military astronauts. Although O'Leary doesn't mention it, it is quite possible that more space probes have gone to Mars than we have been told about. Air Force astronauts could have been rocketed to the Moon in complete secrecy. It's only a speculation, but if they did, it is highly probable that they landed on the back side, which would be far more interesting than the relatively desolate near side that the six known Apollo flights set down on.

The following is a newsclipping from the Contra Costa Times, Walnut Creek, CA., April 15, 1984.

SECRET PAYLOAD GOES INTO ORBIT
Cape Canaveral, Fla. (AP) -

An Air Force Titan 34D rocket launched a secret payload into space at 11:52 a.m. EST Saturday from Cape Canaveral Air Force Station, a spokesman said.

No advance warning was given for the launch, which was announced half an hour after liftoff, nor was there any comment on the nature of the payload.

"It's a classified launch. It's a classified payload," said Air Force spokesman Dick

Castelucci.

The Titan 34D rocket is more powerful than the Titan 3C, which was previously used for secret payloads by the Air Force.

So goes the secret space program. They were using a rocket as powerful as the Saturn V which launched men to the Moon. What was the classified payload? Was it a manned capsule? A large probe destined for Mars? Since the mission was classified, the probable reason for the late confirmation was that the liftoff was too spectacular to go unnoticed, and Cape Canaveral got phone calls from the press.

Who's controlling this secret space program? And for what purpose? The funding is conveniently hidden under our huge defense budget, and nothing is publicly known because everything is classified. A lot can be accomplished in top secret with an Air Force space program that can be super-funded under the Defense Budget, and accountable to no one except the cryptocracy that controls it. Planetary studies in complete uncensored detail may have been accomplished years before NASA's publicized ventures. The following suggests that this is a reasonable assertion.

In 1969, the Air Force published a text on space sciences, that was restricted for academy-use-only at the Colorado Springs Air Force Training Academy. Included in the text was a fourteen-page chapter written by Major Donald G. Carpenter on the subject of UFOs. In a carefully worded discussion, it was stated that UFOs have been visiting Earth for thousands of years, and that "it implies the existence of intelligent life on a majority of planets in our solar system, or a surprisingly strong interest in Earth by members of other solar systems." Cadets were advised to keep an open mind on the subject of UFOs.

The "other solar systems" part can be discounted for the following reasons. When representing an official stand on a sensitive matter, there is always a tendency to give subjective and double-edged answers, so that one answer can never be pinned down as absolute fact. "This, but maybe that" comes across as unconfirmable speculation, and leaves a confusion factor to the suggestion that is being made. However, that is the intent, as no official source is going to present a committed statement, especially on the subject of extraterrestrial space vehicles, when the government is officially presenting a lifeless picture of our solar system.

But the following discussion explains the situation fully. Immediately after the development of atomic weapons on Earth, we were visited by spacecraft from our neighboring planets. Although a few spaceships crashed after encountering unnatural conditions in our atmosphere, there were actually more crashes caused by an aggressive act on our part. For several years, the military had official directives which allowed them to scramble jets in order to try and shoot down UFOs sighted near their bases. It was not until 1954 that President Eisenhower revoked those standing orders, because it was officially admitted that the UFOs had never demonstrated anything of a hostile nature towards us.

However, by that time a few of their ships had been destroyed and their crewmen killed. For this reason, Adamski learned, the interplanetary visitors of our own solar system do not permit passenger craft from other solar systems to approach Earth. Other systems should not have to encounter the arrogance and hostility of our wayward planet. Earth is the only planet in this solar system where war exists, along with possessiveness and greed, and the selfish, personal way of life. What could advanced space civilizations gain or learn from coming into contact with our rebellious nature?

Not until we learn to temper our aggressiveness and arrogance, and willingly become part of the all-inclusive life here in our own solar system, will the UFOs that we see be from another system.

Modesty becomes man well, for
his knowledge is truly small.

V.A. Firsoff

Chapter 6
Unveiling the Real Moon

There is life on the Moon.

This assertion quite naturally seems to be contrary to current scientific opinion and public knowledge about our Moon, and therefore the evidence will be thoroughly developed and presented to the reader. The Moon is not airless, waterless, or lifeless, and there is a considerable body of evidence to prove it. And of equal importance, the UFO situation is closely connected to our nearest celestial body.

Let's first state some realities about the Moon, and then take a careful review of the solid data.

1. The Moon has a substantial atmosphere - 6 pounds per square inch in its lowest elevations.

2. The Moon has a much higher gravity than has been theorized - a value greater than 50% of Earth's.

3. The Moon has water and known vegetation.

4. There are large variations in environment, between the side that always faces the Earth, and the far side that only can be seen from lunar orbit.

5. The Moon is occupied by space people. There are artificial bases on the front side, and more natural bases on the far side. The evidence has been photographed and verified.

To learn the truth about something, a person must not drag along the old perceptions and usual misconceptions. He must temporarily discard them. We do not expect a student to enroll in a college class, only to tell the professor what he thinks he already knows or has believed all along. That person would not be a good student. Nor would one be a good student if he only accepted an authority as having all-inclusive knowledge. He must attempt to learn the new information, and then he will be able to weigh it against the limitations of his previous knowledge. From there he will know the way to go beyond what has been commonly accepted as fact.

Few people know anything about the Moon other than what was shown or described regarding the manned lunar missions of 1969-72. Those landing sites were relatively close to the Moon's equator, and were found to be desolate and barren as expected, -or rather, as predetermined by the earlier (1966-67) unmanned lunar orbiters. For these reasons, we cannot fault people for being conditioned to expect a rather uninteresting companion world, our Moon. However, the evidence in this book will prove that the Moon is indeed a very interesting world.

The astronauts only covered a few miles by walking, or while riding in the lunar rovers, yet there is 14 million square miles on the Moon's surface. And the orbiting Apollo spacecraft only photographed 20% of the surface in detail. The missions had inherent limitations, regardless of both the publicized and unpublicized findings. But nothing was stated by NASA publicly, or released to the scientific community, that would change the long-accepted theories and orthodox ideas about the Moon. A basic falseness has pervaded every official presentation, by statements that the Moon is airless, and that no life exists there. However, a few things did eventually leak out, as will be shown later.

As in the case with Mars, we are indebted to the telescopic record of astronomers. More than a hundred years of observation proved that there are cyclic changes, atmospheric phenomena, and intelligently-directed activity on the Moon's surface. Mists, obscurations, blinking and glowing lights, low-flying lunar objects, vegetation color changes in some craters, dark spots and spheres, moving shadows, and the sudden appearance of inexplicable domes, were all recorded from careful telescopic studies. One can find the detailed evidence in a number of scientific journals and books. Some of the recorded data is open to debate, but most of it is not.

Even conservative science has recognized that strange and inexplicable lights have been seen on the Moon, and scientists have categorized them as transient lunar phenomena (TLP). In an article that discusses a few of these curious reports, the February 1969 National Geographic states:

> "One could disregard such reports were it not that they number more than 800, many of them from respected astronomers. The sightings have been concentrated in a few locations, notably the craters Aristarchus and Alphonsus. They take the form of temporary bright spots, red glows, red and blue bands, veils, violet tinges, and other peculiarities known generally as transient phenomena."

> (Authors note: This 800 figure is extremely conservative, as there have been many thousands of reports. The Royal Astronomical Society of Great Britain recorded at least 1600 observations of strange light formations in just a 2-year study! Many were glows, and many were glittering points of light.)

In 1953, Dr. H. P. Wilkins, a respected astronomer and noted authority on the Moon, wrote that strange domes on the lunar surface had recently been discovered, and he added that their number had been increasing rapidly. Similar reports were made by many expert observers.[1] Wilkins could not explain their sudden appearance. Neither could other astronomers, for the newly discovered domes were near the limits of telescopic resolution, and the blurred features prevented positive conclusions. However, something was definitely responsible for the appearance of more than 200 strange domes.

When this independent information came out in the

early 1950's, the government took notice - to say the least! To be able to see the features with sufficient detail, and therefore identify what was taking place on the Moon, the giant telescopes would have to be used. Accordingly, the Pentagon had top-secret studies done by a few large observatories, including Palomar.

While these studies were being undertaken, a startling discovery was made by the Pulitzer Prize science writer, John J. O'Neill. On the night of July 29, 1953, while observing the Mare Crisium area, O'Neill was amazed at what he saw in the northern region. Spanning two prominent ridges was a straight 12 mile-long bridge. Not only did it cast a shadow, but sunlight could be seen streaming in beneath it. Shortly after he announced his discovery, two top British astronomers, Dr. H. P. Wilkins and Patrick Moore, confirmed the existence of the bridge. In an interview on BBC radio the following December, Dr. Wilkins explained that there was no mistake in these observations - this structure was there now, absolutely regular and straight, and it looked like an engineering job. [2]

Back in the United States, the Pentagon study to investigate the new domes continued. There was an apparent correlation between the luminous events and these dome appearances within various craters. Top-secret discussions allowed the possibility that some sort of building boom was going on, right there on the near side of the Moon facing the Earth. Not by a moon race, but by the visitors on interplanetary UFOs. O'Neill's mysterious bridge was also seen by astronomers working at Mount Palomar, and a spectrographic analysis proved that it was a metallic structure.[3] (Since I cannot find any recent reports that this bridge is still there, I suspect that it was a very large mothership temporarily grounded. If repairs or other operations need to be carried out, a ship will land by supporting itself across two mountain ridges. However, in relation to this mystery, there are smaller permanent bridges that later appeared in other regions, and remain there).

Careful observations over several months during these

top-secret studies confirmed the existence of alien operations on the Moon, and the new evidence dramatically coincided with the constant reports of UFO activity in our skies. The intelligence agencies were responsible for keeping the UFO situation classified, and discredited in the eyes of the public. The National Security Agency could care less about the insistence of organized astronomy which always maintains that nothing changes on the surface of the Moon. Something was causing observable changes up there, but detection was difficult, and only capable at the world's largest observatories. The changes were not due to any natural or geological causes.

In fact, the surface changes that were observed included dome-type hangars, bridge-like structures, and mining excavation along a few crater walls. It was no doubt recognized that strange lights, previously unexplainable as TLP, went hand in hand with these signs of intelligent activity. A handful of men at the Pentagon had its answer on the Moon. They knew that it would be some years before a space shot could be sent to the Moon and send back photographs. There would be plenty of time to organize and perfect the methods required to continue the scientific cover-up and public deception.

It has to be considered a foregone conclusion, that the government (i.e. the Pentagon and its agencies) decided from that time on, that any lunar studies conducted at the giant-telescope observatories were to be organized, and restricted, by national security guidelines. There was no need to worry about the regular astronomical community. They seldom bothered with the Moon, choosing to ignore it in favor of star and galaxy studies. This trend had been the norm since about 1940, when it had been generally accepted that everything that could be determined about the Moon through a telescope had been achieved. Even if they were to inexplicably reverse their abandonment of the Moon, the telescopes at their disposal would not give sufficient resolution to positively reveal these unusual changes. And without a documentable, photographic, proof-positive record, any comment or speculation to the effect that something changed on the Moon would be most debatable, and subject to the weight of orthodoxy prevailing against it.

Since 1953, the National Security Agency had been behind the official censorship of information concerning UFOs, and now it was equally necessary for them to clamp down security regarding any proof of alien operations on the Moon. By 1954, the guidelines and restrictions were set, regarding any photographic studies or announcements by the big observatories concerning the Moon. Later that year, the government moved in the direction of Mars also, initially securing a restriction, and then a blackout of public reports from the Mars Patrol Committee, as noted in the previous chapter. Planetary studies of the Moon, Mars, and Venus, *that had the capability of disproving the uninhabitable theories*, were now a matter of national security.

How can the government have such power? The big observatories do not derive their own source of income. They are not a business. The enormous costs of running their operations are financed by grants and government funding. Whenever an institution is being monetarily supported by the government, (and without the funding would fall under), it is subject to the authority of that power. That is the way our system functions.

For example, take the Palomar Observatory, home of the world's largest telescope. The building of the observatory was funded by three Rockefeller organizations. Later developments and operations were funded by the National Science Foundation and the National Aeronautics and Space Administration (NASA). For many of its early space projects, NASA contracted with the observatory, and engaged the staff to assist in both project planning and post-mission studies. The projects were a combined effort, and obviously there would never be observatory announcements that were in opposition to the publicized achievements of NASA. In between the planetary studies, the staff at the observatories naturally resumed their own role of studying the stars and distant galaxies.

Telescopic studies and speculation of the Moon and Mars became outdated and meaningless in the mid-1960's, for NASA's Ranger 7 returned the first close-up pictures of the Moon in 1964, and Mariner 4 photographed at least a smattering of the Martian surface in 1965. Within two short years, space mission photography surpassed the best views provided by earthbound telescopes, and all planetary descriptions became solely the domain of NASA. The top-secret studies of the Moon by the giant telescopes in the 1950's were now furthered by the top-secret space findings of NASA in the 1960's.

Only the "acceptable" pictures and data were released - a minute portion of the reality. Orthodoxy was left intact. Nothing was released that would undermine the old theories. Scientists were given exactly what they fervently anticipated - photographs of rocks and craters, and a bleak, airless, waterless, desolate picture of the Moon. The government knew that UFOs were on the Moon, but like the UFO activity in the skies around Earth, the truth was fully contained, while officially denied or discredited, as a matter of directive by the National Security Agency.

Just what are the domes that radically appeared to those early observers, including the late Dr. H.P. Wilkins, author of *Our Moon*. Though giving no definite opinion himself, Wilkins noted that most all the domes had a pit at the summit. Most of the reported domes are hangars for the interplanetary ships that travel in our part of the solar system. The "pit" seen at the top is the opening for entrance and exiting.

Something has to be at least a full mile in size on the Moon in order to be detected by a 36-inch telescope, on a night of ideal seeing conditions. Yet an object would have to be many times larger before it could be resolved into something identifiable through a telescope. Even then, our atmosphere would tend to blur the telescopic image. A guideline to remember is: craters of about 4 miles in width are the smallest thing that can be resolved as a surface feature on the Moon. (Luminous events generate their own light, which can even be picked up by modest telescopes, so size is not a relative factor in those observations). In comparison, the Mt. Palomar Observatory has a 200-inch telescope, and this is where the government's secret studies were conducted.

Sometimes, an astronomical report indicated that a small crater had disappeared and in its previous location was a white spot or dome. The new convex surface was sometimes described as elliptical. At a later observation, weeks or months afterwards, the surface feature appeared again as a normal crater. Some of these impermanent domes can be explained as large spaceships temporarily occupying the site.

It would have been difficult to deduce what the intelligence agencies learned from their secret lunar studies, without having known some direct statements by the space visitors regarding their own lunar operations. It can be admitted that the discussion in the previous pages leaned more on logical reasoning than documentation, since the results of the secret studies have not (of course) been published, and also, the astronomical record (of strange lunar lights and unexplainable domes) is too weak by itself to document the foregoing conclusions. However, the confirmation does come from the space visitors themselves, as related in George Adamski's second book, *Inside the Spaceships*. What better way to learn about the Moon situation than direct input from the parties involved? Published in 1955, Adamski's book is the clearest and most complete source of information about UFOs and our interplanetary space visitors.

A contact in August of 1954 presented Adamski with the opportunity of going on board a Venusian carrier ship. During part of the excursion, the spaceship made a close approach to the Moon. While in the control room, Adamski was shown a detailed sectional view of the Moon from close up. An advanced form of telescopic image was reflected onto the large viewing screen, and the mysterious domes on the lunar front side could be seen.

His space friend informed him: "You are now looking at

the familiar side of your Moon, but we are not landing on it. The image is being reflected on the screen from one of the telescopes which was not in operation the first time you were with us. Look closely as we approach the surface and you will note considerable activity. In the numerous large craters which you see from Earth, you will notice very large hangars - which you do not see! Notice, too, that the terrain here is very similar to your deserts. We have built these hangars on such a scale in order that much larger ships than this one can enter easily. Also within these hangars are living quarters for a number of workers and their families, provided with every comfort. Water in abundance is piped in from the mountains, just as you have done on your Earth for the purpose of bringing fertility to your desert areas."

There lies a touch of irony in the following conclusion. At the same time that our government was attempting to define signs of activity on the Moon, our world was under observation from lunar outposts. From these artificial bases, the interplanetary visitors were prepared to monitor our progress into the nuclear age. From their place of observance, *our* signs of activity on Earth must have seemed rather ominous. For we were busily exploding great numbers of atomic bombs in our atmosphere, to test their destructive power.

It's unreasonable to assume that all such activity on the Moon could be conducted in the absence of an atmosphere. It would be impossible to build bridges and primary installations, and impractical to do so, if the people could not comfortably remain outside of their ships. Why build anything, if you are confined to a spaceship due to lack of air outside? What purpose would it serve?

Is there air on the Moon? This question needs a full examination. And on this issue is where the battlelines are drawn. The battle has always been between: selenography - the professional study of the Moon, and astronomy - the study and location of heavenly bodies, primarily stars.

Even before the space age, when the Moon was being observed by men who devoted their lifetimes to the study of it, there was every indication that the Moon has an atmosphere. Yet these careful and precise observations by very prominent selenographers could not make a dent in the rock-hard theories of the orthodox astronomers who had seldom devoted a single month of their lives to lunar observations. It was the late Harvard professor, W. H. Pickering, who wrote:

"The view that the Moon is a dead unchanging world, although based on the most inadequate negative evidence, is so widespread and so firmly rooted in the minds not only of the general public, but of the astronomical world as well, that the united and practically unanimous opinion of all the greatest selenographers has hitherto been able to make but little impression upon it...

"The arguments on the two sides of the case are extremely simple. The astronomers who are not selenographers declare that there is no atmosphere or water upon the Moon, and that, therefore, changes are impossible. The selenographers' reply is simply that they have seen the changes take place."

Comparing the periodic alterations on the lunar surface to telescopically observed changes on Mars, Pickering added:

"The only plausible explanations of the similar changes upon the the Moon is that these changes are due to the same causes. If so, they involve the presence of air and water."[4]

Books were written right up to the time of the space age, expertly documenting the observed natural changes that could only be attributed to the presence of sufficient air and water on the Moon. Yet as Pickering and others noted, nothing it seemed, could shake the entrenched dogma of astronomy. With the coming of the space age though, NASA was able to commandeer the domain of lunar mysteries. And the bureaucratic agency fully understood the psychology of the situation - that the world's greatest selenographers had not previously been able to make a dent in orthodox science, which stated that the world of the Moon is dead and changeless. That situation would never change unless there was undeniable confirmation to the contrary, by space probe findings announced officially through NASA.

The airless and waterless Moon was a religion of the orthodoxers, and if NASA left the religion intact, the government had a made-to-order scientific body that would forever teach, and publicly propound, the belief of a lifeless Moon. The formula was simple: give them only what they expected and wanted to hear. The real findings and properties of the Moon would be concealed, and known only to the cryptocracy in control. Were not the officials able to contain the UFO situation? This would be no different. Economic, military, and political institutions do not publish any truth that would serve to undermine their powerful positions.

The Moon was mainly portrayed throughout the space program as simply a target to send mechanical contraptions to. With our artificial methods of overcoming gravity, and the inherent dangers of rocketry, it was no small achievement by any means. Neither was it cheap. But we were not truly informed about the Moon, because it would have irrevocably changed the course of affairs on the Earth.

It has been mentioned before in this book, but it bears repeating, that NASA's prime mission in the 1960's was to get man into space. But the government considered it imperative not to reveal the truth about space beyond our Earth. The world mentality was not ready for the full reality of space: religions were not ready, institutions based on false knowledge were not ready, political-military ideologies were not ready, the international system of false economics was not ready, many branches of organized science were not ready. One word from the space agency giving a positive indicator of life on the Moon, - indigenous or foreign, moss or space traveler, - would have been all it would take to undermine many powerful institutions. Self-appointed scientific authorities would be exposed for their lack of knowledge, then discredited and disqualified. There would be a student rebellion all over the world. The space agency is controlled by the government, which in turn is controlled by vested interests, and NASA had to follow orders. The truth about space made public, would shake the very foundations of misplaced power.

The answers needed to establish the true lunar environment will require a thorough examination of the selenology record prior to the space age. The reader will see that there is no way NASA could have missed confirmation of the life activity on the Moon with their manned space missions. The early work by expert selenographers will also be supported by up-to-date, documented space science from the lunar missions. The present work will finally prove that there is a true living environment on the Moon.

Two exceedingly competent astronomers published definitive documents on the Moon just prior to the space age. Both men were fully knowledgeable of the telescopic studies and scientific records of the previous 150 years, and in combination with personal observations they were able to prove conclusively, the existence of atmosphere and periodic changes on the Moon. The atmospheric density could not be determined, and was still open to conjecture, but the observable effects of an atmosphere were unmistakable. And these men were top scientists who were completely familiar with the lunar studies of other experts. The first to publish was M.K. Jessup.

Prior to building an observatory in South Africa housing the largest refracting telescope in the southern hemisphere, Jessup had taught astronomy and mathematics at the University of Michigan while completing his doctorate thesis in Astrophysics. His breakthrough on the Moon, entitled *The Expanding Case for the UFO*, was published in 1957.

The second man was V.A. Firsoff, acknowledged to be the top scientist and authority on the Moon. His timely study was published in 1959, and it documented nearly all the lunar information then known by scientific study. Entitled *Strange World of the Moon*, the book presented uncontradictable evidence of a lunar atmosphere, and the highly probable existence of regional water and vegetation. Ten years later, Firsoff conclusively proved this information and more in a second book, through a detailed analysis of information and pictures returned by the unmanned space probes. But we will discuss this 1969 book a little later.

Both Jessup's *The Expanding Case for the UFO* and Firsoff's *Strange World of the Moon* are difficult to find. The latter is even difficult to read, unless you have an exceptional interest in geology, astronomy, and technical science. But a study of these two books would readily prove, that years later, NASA cleverly concealed the truth about the Moon's environment. In the final analysis, NASA only proved one thing for mankind - that it was technologically possible for a spaceship to get to the Moon and back. A technological success for man, but a formidable cover-up for mankind.

Formidable means difficult to surmount. Today it is unlikely that even one person in a thousand believes that there could be life on the Moon. Yet it is there. It has always been there. The government knew it back in the 1950's, with the secret observatory studies. Also,there is an atmosphere which moderates the climate and temperature in certain regions, and one of sufficient density to support vegetation. It is time to re-examine the early evidence of selenography.

The Moon has its own unique time cycle. In 29.5 of our days, it has essentially gone through a full season. Any longitudinal area will have had about 14 continuous days of sunlight (timed by our clocks) as the sun rises and sets, followed by another 14 days of night darkness. Since the Moon's axis is nearly perpendicular to the plane of the ecliptic, there are no different seasons, (no winter or summer), only a monthly cycle.

The late Harvard professor W. H. Pickering photographed the effects of an atmosphere during lunar occultations of Jupiter and Saturn. An occultation refers to the temporary disappearance of a celestial body as it passes behind a closer planet or moon. Separately, when the planets were at the line of contact with the limb of the Moon and partly covered, Pickering's negatives showed a clear, unmistakable dark band crossing the disks of Jupiter and Saturn that measured 3 seconds of arc wide. In other words, the Moon's atmosphere extends 3 miles above its surface with sufficient density to provide a photographic effect. This observation was also made by the expert selenographers, Barnard and Douglas.

The Moon is a much smaller celestial body than Venus; its volume is less than 3% of the size of our sister planet. Therefore the total volume of atmosphere would be very reduced for the Moon. However, the actual density near the surface could be comparatively high. Beyond an altitude of 3 miles the atmospheric density around the Moon appears to diminish rapidly, whereas on Venus the atmospheric range is known to be many times more extensive. The air density 4 miles above the Moon's surface might be equivalent to the air density 40 miles above the Venusian surface. Our present-day theories are inadequate to explain the phenomena. The case for each and every celestial body is dependent on its mass, volume, and *actual surface gravity*. Since it will be shown that the Moon's gravity is 3 to 4 times higher than what has been commonly accepted, there is no simple model or formula to predict each case. And until gravity is absolutely understood, along with its precise relationship to a planet's size and mass, it will not be possible to explain one atmospheric situation in terms of another. To put it plainly, even if the surface air density is known, it cannot be predicted what the atmospheric range and corresponding altitude density would be, until the intricate relationship of gravity to that celestial body is known.

Why is this important? Astronomers have always insisted that the question of lunar atmosphere can be answered by the way in which stars are "occulted" by the Moon. Since stars passing behind the rim of the Moon appear to snap out instantaneously, astronomers readily conclude that there must not be an atmosphere there. If there was a gaseous layer, they say that the effect should be as obvious as the case of a star occultation by Venus, where the extensive atmosphere makes the star appear to flicker and fade briefly before disappearing behind the rim of the planet. But Venus' atmosphere is much denser, and the planet's size too massive, to compare the effects.

William Brian, a recent Moon researcher, suggests that a lunar atmosphere would be very clean, due to the lack of high winds and other weather conditions. Since the lunar atmosphere would not generally be carrying dust and water vapor by surface winds, he points out that light diffusion and scattering effects would be minimal. Therefore the occultation of stars would not be as pronounced, even if the Moon possessed a dense atmosphere.[5]

Firsoff writes in his book that he observed the occultation of two stars in March 1957 while using a 6.5-inch reflector. Neither star 'snapped out' at contact with the rim of the Moon, but dimmed rapidly, then flickered brilliantly, before dimming again and finally disappearing. At the time of observation the Moon was a narrow crescent 2.5 days after the New Moon, and Firsoff stated that the effect could not be seen at a fuller phase, probably due to the background glare of the moonlit sky. Since we are dealing with different conditions for the Moon, the observational results do not come as easily as observing the Venusian atmosphere effects. This instance seemed to be an excellent combination of timing, seeing conditions, and most importantly - professional objectivity.

Indeed, Firsoff wrote that the observation was a clear and unmistakable confirmation of a lunar atmosphere - that there is a gaseous layer, low over the surface of the Moon. To this statement can be added the evidence provided from a study by the American Association of Lunar and Planetary Observers. This group of independent astronomers catalogued dozens of observations of faint meteors flashing near the Moon's surface. An atmosphere around the Moon provided sufficient friction for these meteors to become incandescent to earthbound observers.

Firsoff also recorded that he observed an auroral streamer near the southern pole of the Moon in May 1955. His telescopic view showed a dancing and sparkling glow, from which a faint beam of light suddenly detached and shot up vertically into the lunar sky. As it ascended the beam became more intense, while fading out at the base, and finally disappearing. The length of the beam was estimated to be nearly 100 miles, and the auroral display reminded him of the colorful northern lights he had seen in Scotland, an effect that certainly requires an atmosphere.

The lunar atmosphere could be tenuous and still account for these various observations mentioned, as Firsoff pointed out. He took a cautious approach at the time, which was probably reasonable, due to the accepted gravitational theories of the day. However, other discoveries suggested that basic assumptions about the Moon could be fundamentally wrong, and that the strange lunar world might have many surprises in store for us.

On July 22, 1954, Firsoff telescopically viewed the sunset on the Moon's Apennines, a prominent mountain range bordering the Mare Imbrium. Using different filters for comparison, he proved to himself that sunset on the Moon was really red, an effect that other astronomers had also observed. This was amazing to Firsoff, (he even called it thrilling), for the reddening clearly indicated the presence of a gaseous layer over the Moon containing water and carbon dioxide molecules.

For the sun's light to become reddened, it has to pass through a layer of gas of sufficient density. Noting that this is quite conspicuous at sunrise and sunset on Earth, Firsoff explained that the Moon's atmosphere shows the same positive reaction to sunlight at the end of its day. This meant that the lunar air was dense enough to hold water and CO_2 molecules.

Immediately following sunset, is twilight. There is a small time interval before dark which we call twilight, when our atmosphere is illuminated by the sun which has dropped below the horizon. Without an atmosphere, there would be no period of twilight. As soon as the sun dipped below the horizon, it would be totally dark (nighttime).

Is there twilight at the Moon's terminator, the boundary

between the dark and sunlit hemispheres? When the viewing conditions are favorable, it can sometimes be seen. When the Moon's phase is a narrow crescent, competent astronomers have reported a twilight extension of about 10 degrees beyond each horn. Firsoff also recorded seeing a thin line of light along the entire terminator, rimming the old Moon opposite the crescent.

The twilight arc can only be seen infrequently, because earthshine reflecting onto the Moon overpowers the faint illumination, and the brilliancy of our own sky diffuses the moonlight under question. It must be agreed that it is difficult to confirm from Earth, the subtle twilight effect on the Moon. Yet the twilight "principle" has been frequently observed on the sunlit hemisphere, when penumbra are seen surrounding a dark lunar shadow. The soft shadow that makes up the penumbra could not be possible in the absence of an atmosphere. In fact, the atmosphere would have to be much denser than the old theories allowed.

Why couldn't organized astronomy verify any of the effects of an atmosphere on the Moon? As always, their own conclusions were implicit in their assumptions. They devised experiments to "prove" their obstinate belief in airlessness, and then congratulated each other's work. Firsoff amusingly writes that orthodox lunar researchers used methods which inadvertently succeeded in suppressing the image of the lunar atmosphere, and then concluded that an atmosphere does not exist. Since the Moon was at the borderline limit of telescopic resolution, Firsoff said that the hard-bound theorists should refrain from laying down the law, and pay more attention to the objective record of observations.

Both Jessup and Firsoff cited many cases from the astronomical records where mists, clouds, and fog had been observed in lunar craters. Plato, which lies at 50°N latitude, has been seen obscured by fog at lunar sunrise, or by thin clouds which later dispersed. Mists have been seen in the craters Timocharis and Tycho, while a dense fog was recorded billowing over the walls of the crater Schickard.[6]

Sometimes the clouds or vapors cast moving shadows on the crater floors.

Mists and clouds have also hovered over craters Copernicus, Picard, Eratosthenes, Littrow, Thales, and Gassendi. The same observations have been reported for Mare Serenitatis and Sinus Iridum on several occasions,and Jessup cites a case when fog practically filled Mare Nectaris and extended all the way to the middle of Fracastorius Crater. Firsoff relates many instances in detail, and notes that a complete register of these observations would make a substantial catalogue.

There have been many puzzling features and startling changes observed in the crater Plato by expert scientists. Even if we were to disregard countless other areas on the Moon that have repeatedly shown signs of activity, Jessup states that observations of Plato alone, would prove that there is life and UFOs operating on the Moon. The selenolographers Barker, Pickering, and Wilkins, staked their astronomical reputations on the observed evidence of vegetation in this prominent crater.

Varying fogs and clouds have frequently been seen spreading across Plato from the east after lunar sunrise. At times within this crater, variable bright spots and self-luminous objects appeared to move about. Lights have been seen to form geometric patterns, as circles, squares, and triangles. As far back as 1887, observers in the U.S., Great Britain, and France watched as a large number of luminous lights moved from surrounding lunar craters towards Plato, descended the walls and formed a huge triangle of light on the crater floor. Various unexplainable events were logged every decade for this mysterious crater, and in September 1953, a British astronomer reported a brilliant orange-yellow light, as bright as a first magnitude star, occupying this enigmatic lunar site.[7] Again in 1966, there were reddish glowing spots shining out from Plato, that fluctuated like intermittent blinking lights.

Aristarchus has also been a site for mysterious light patterns and glows. Patrick Moore states that these events, officially catalogued as TLP or Transient Lunar Phenomena, are common in this fascinating crater. Firsoff has suggested that some type of electrical discharge is one possibility for the lights seen in this region, because of their long duration when they appear. In March 1950, Dr. H. P. Wilkins observed a brilliant, oval-shaped glow near the crater floor. Dr. James Bartlett, a professional astronomer, reported an almost identical light at the same spot three months later.[8] And Dr. Wilkins traced dusky bands or streaks along the inner sloping wall that developed during the lunar day, suggesting that it was clumps of vegetation.[9]

Before we take up the question of vegetation, let's analyze the evidence to this point. Fogs, mists, and cloud-like obscurations have been observed in numerous craters and lowland areas of the Moon, generally moving from east to west. Even if some of the obscurations reported were dust clouds, something had to support whatever was floating over the surface. Therefore the Moon has a gaseous atmosphere, capable of supporting vapors and dust particles. This was also inferred by the meteor flashes, star and planet occultations, and subtle twilight effects. Mr. Jessup believed that many of the mysterious lights and glows, recorded over the past century by competent observers, were electromagnetic phenomena of UFOs, and that the luminosity was due to the ionization of the local air on the Moon by the forcefield of the spaceships.

Mr. Firsoff prudently avoided any mention of UFOs, but cleverly threw in a statement that some of the anomalies on the Moon were once thought to be the industrial activities of the Selenites (Moon inhabitants). Firsoff was straight science all the way, using observational data and scientific reasoning, but made one casual comment to the effect, that it was difficult to contemplate certain lunar mysteries unless we were to assume they represented the efforts of Martian colonists on the Moon. Perhaps he was seriously suggesting that, to the reader's subconscience.

If an atmosphere of sufficient density exists on the Moon to produce the effects which have been discussed, it adds a very important dimension to the lunar surface conditions. The temperature difference between night and day would not be as extreme as our scientists have stated in the past. There would be constant mixing by air movement, not only along the terminator, but also according to temperature gradients of the local landscape, and the changing incident angle of sunlight relative to latitude. On the lunar nightside, the atmosphere would act as a thermal blanket. The overall conditions would be much more moderate than previously thought.

Both Firsoff and Jessup explained the problem of seeing the Moon's true colors from the Earth. In fact, the Moon is quite colorful, but it has to be seen by indirect methods, using a fair-sized telescope, polarimetry, and dichromatic and monochromatic filters. Otherwise, the actual lunar colors are obscured, or negated, by at least 5 miles of sea-level density Earth air. Firsoff points out for comparison, that using a telescope to view Earth mountains 7 to 10 miles distant produces the same effect. The interference of our own atmosphere causes distant mountains to show very little color, even when the sides are known to have the variances of brown timber, evergreen, bare rock, and snow.

But with professional methods, the colors and hues of the Moon's surface are quite visible. Firsoff made several hundred observations over a period of three years, and found considerable agreement with the results of other painstaking researchers. There are various shades of brown, from rusty-brown to chocolate tones, inside lunar craters. There are broad areas of greenish tint, and a noticeable cycle of green variation in some of the craters. This two-week (Earth-time) cycle begins with grey-olive green in the lunar morning, later becoming a bright green, followed by a khaki shade, and finally a yellowish tone in the lunar evening. The Sea of Tranquility is very green, Mare Vaporum a bottle green, and Oceanus Procellarum a soft yellowish-green. Blues, violet, and red have also been recorded. Firsoff mentioned a letter from a scientist friend, who suggested that a purple color occasionally seen in some craters resembled the color of heather in bloom. From the results of his own observations, Firsoff stated that frost appeared to rim various craters before daylight, and that the lunar Appenine Mountains seemingly had snow on its highest peaks.

Summarizing the data of experts, Firsoff postulated that the regular alterations of color in certain areas on the Moon could possibly be due to biological activity. He stated that seasonal changes are definitely there: that areas darken and expand, only to become paler and contract, or disappear entirely, and then colors reappear. The changes of color and hue are definitely not the result of shading, or light abstractions, according to the sun's position in the lunar sky. Something changes on the surface in a cyclic fashion, within local climates and a lower atmosphere that "perpetually balances between precipitation and evaporation," according to Firsoff. He confidently asserted that life may have secured a foothold.

Noting that astronomers had long scoffed at the idea of life there, he explained that vegetation seems to be the reasonable answer for the cyclic radial bands overrunning crater walls, the dark markings in Eratosthenes and Plato, and some of the conspicuously green areas. The evidence for a lunar atmosphere suggested also, that ultra-violet radiations from the sun would be effectively blocked, negating the often-used argument that uninhibited UV rays would be too deadly for life to exist on the Moon. (It was later proven that the destructive radiations of the Sun do not reach the lunar surface, by the U.S. Surveyor III, a lander probe).[10]

His book is a monumental scientific treatise, skillfully documenting the telescopic work of experts and authorities on the Moon. His evidence cannot be easily refuted. The top scientific selenographer of the world stated at the conclusion: "There does not seen to be any sufficient reason why plants, even of a highly organized type, should be unable to exist on the Moon." Even animal life could not be ruled out completely, he added.

M. K. Jessup, writing two years earlier, also presented a competent review of the astronomical reports. The telescopic record showed that many surface effects on the Moon were clearly visible. He stated that the darkening within many craters, including the prominent Eratosthenes, could be seen spreading for miles over the floor, and even up and over the crater walls. And they were not shadows, because the sun was at such a high altitude to make shadows impossible. In the lunar afternoon, the dark patches often moved in directions opposite to those of the lengthening shadows prescribed by the position of the sun. Jessup emphasized that the changes in color were consistent with a short-cycle growth and decay of vegetation.

He cited many books and articles by men who staked their astronomical reputations on the fact that vegetation grows in many areas of the Moon. The crater Plato was a certainty. But our textbooks never changed. And therein lies the problem. Telescopic evidence no longer gets a hearing, because NASA "evidence" has preempted any earthbound studies. But the truth still exists in the telescopic records of the selenographers.

Jessup was more interested in the physical changes, obscurations, and lights that had been observed for more than a century by lunar experts. For these were indicative of UFOs and UFO activity. Some of the apparent changes along the interior walls of craters and ridges seemed to indicate surface mining. Parallel ramparts and geometric walls suggested mammoth construction at work from time to time. Glowing and flickering points of light indicated intelligence operating on the Moon. There have been many recorded observations of lights moving across large distances on the Moon, sometimes singly, while at other times traversing in groups. One report noted that it took one hour and a half for a procession of about fifty lighted objects to cross the Moon.

Jessup also felt that some obscurations, described as local clouds or haze, were due to the presence of one or more UFOs temporarily occupying a site. There have been many reports of transitory clouds obscuring sizeable areas on the floor of Plato. The descriptions provide evidence that some of these clouds are self-luminous and give off a glowing light. The reports are of various colors, such as white, red, orange, reddish-purple, and blue.

There are also more permanent spots of light, and straight lines on the floors of some medium-size craters. Many of these lines were observed to be in pairs, sometimes parallel and sometimes intersecting. The glowing spots seemed to connect the lines at regular intervals, and Jessup said that this lunar mystery was a sign of intelligently controlled activity on the Moon.

Controlled activity can be translated into more specific terminology - artificial bases of the space travelers. Gassendi Crater is a prime candidate, for it has a peculiar geometric pattern of lines on its floor, and numerous TLP have been seen here over the years. But Plato is, according to Jessup, the essence of life, intelligence, and UFOs on the Moon. Varying lights have been seen to move about, and fixed bright spots were found to be in a patterned relationship to several intersecting lines. This is the place also, that clouds and obscurations were observed by astronomers, and where irregular surface darkening, unrelated to the position of the sun, indicated vegetation growth. This would appear to be an ideal location for the space people to park their ships and conduct outpost operations. There are undoubtedly dozens of these bases, located all over the visible side of the Moon, directly related to the dome mystery discussed earlier in this chapter.

Before the modern era of UFO sightings, the unpredictable lights on the Moon puzzled, startled, and amazed the earlier observers. Hundreds of these transient events were recorded by lunar observers over a full century. As early as 1869, there was a coordinated effort by observatories around the world to investigate the mysterious activity. What prompted this special study were a number of reports of strange lights in the Mare Crisium. Observed night after night, a series of blinking lights would usually form straight lines, or geometric patterns of circles and triangles.

For two years these events continued, and the Royal Astronomical Society of Great Britain charted over 1600 observations of the strange lights, which had been made by astronomers and various observatories around the world. Detailed graphs showed that there were specific patterns to the lights, which often pulsated in their intensity. The remarkable lunar display suddenly stopped in April 1871, and the findings of the Royal Society were published shortly afterwards in their annual Journal (1873). The conclusion from their two-year study read- that the lunar lights were "intelligent attempts by an unknown race on the moon to signal Earth."

There is an amazing footnote to this. The lights were seen concentrated in the Mare Crisium, the same place where the giant "bridge" was later discovered by John J. O'Neill and Dr H. P. Wilkins.

Closer to our own era, strange lunar events started to be associated with UFOs and space visitors, since there was so much UFO activity in our own skies. While routinely studying the Moon, some individual astronomers just happened to be looking at the right place at the right time, to witness actual space-flight over the lunar surface. On October 12, 1954, an astronomer using the Edinburgh Observatory telescope watched a dark sphere travel in a straight line from the crater Tycho to the crater Aristarchus. The distance covered took a period of twenty minutes, and this roughly calculated to a speed of nearly 6,000 miles per hour.[11] In September of the same year, an object was sighted by two men using a six-inch telescope. Again, it was reported to be a dark spherical object, and over a period of forty minutes they watched it leave the northern area of Mare Humboldtianum and move upward into space.

There have been many reports of black bodies crossing the surface of the Moon, and there is significance in this description. For when similar objects are observed moving around close to the surface, or are found to be occupying craters, the visible effect is normally bright luminosity, or glowing lights. What glows? A spaceship does not glow of itself. The luminescence is the direct effect of a ship's energy force-field ionizing the air around it. This is another indication that there is a lunar atmosphere; otherwise, the objects on or near the surface would be seen as dark objects, the same as their counterparts flying above the lunar atmosphere.

This chapter has introduced and summarized, the state of knowledge about the Moon at the beginning of the space age. Telescopic documentation had brought us to the very threshold of discovering life beyond our planet. Were we, as a civilization, ready to cross that line and know the truth? Would we be willing to leave the ignorance of the past behind? Would our authorities allow us the privilege of knowing the truth about the Moon, and chart a new direction in human understanding? We were at a cosmic crossroad. Proceed to the way of new knowledge and light, or keep on the old path of doubt and darkness, isolated from the rest of the solar system.

V. A. Firsoff presented the scientific and telescopic evidence for the lunar atmosphere, climate, and cyclic vegetation. Jessup presented the conclusive documentation for UFO activity on the Moon. Both men were expert astronomers, and authorities on the history of telescopic observation of the Moon. Their books stated many of the true facts about our neighbor in space. An inhabited environment was about to be discovered.

Is it possible that NASA did not see any of this when they sent probes and men to the Moon? One can be certain that they saw everything. What would NASA have us believe? That 150 years of telescopic evidence suddenly disappeared from the face of the Moon? Of course, it had not, but who was ultimately pulling the strings behind this consummate deception?

Chapter 7
Apollo Goes to the Moon

We have seen a technical picture of the Moon from the telescopic records. At about the same time that evidence was first presented in the 1950's, George Adamski gave a close-up view of the same picture, a privilege provided through his space contacts after his meeting the scoutcraft visitor in 1952 (*Flying Saucers Have Landed*). As Adamski explained it later, "I was offered a ride, to which I gladly accepted, and this enabled me to get a view of outer space. I had the privilege of learning what I could." He fully recounted his experiences with the publication of *Inside the Spaceships*. In fact, his book was published a few years *before* the scientific researches of Firsoff and Jessup went into print. His descriptions of the Moon provide a remarkable comparison to the telescopic evidence.

The scoutcraft left the Earth for a short trip to the outer regions of our atmosphere, to dock and enter a large mothership hovering in outer space. At one point, Adamski was given a brief tour of the laboratory of the mothership, which by then had positioned itself much further out in space.

While in the laboratory, Adamski was shown the familiar side of the Moon by instruments capable of transmitting close-up pictures. The Moon proved to have an atmosphere, although naturally not as dense as the Earth's, for it is a far smaller body. The pilot in the laboratory ship explained, that what our own scientists have observed as mild movement of air within craters, are in actuality, shadows of thin clouds. He indicated that heavier clouds regularly formed over a temperate zone on the far side of the Moon, beyond the rim. The space visitor emphasized that the Moon is not a dead, useless planet, but in fact is quite capable of supporting life, because any body of that size must have an atmosphere to offset internal pressures, else it would vanish from space through disintegration.

While still forty thousand miles from the Moon, Adamski was able to view the landscape by an advanced type of telescopic image. On the near side of the Moon which is always seen from Earth, the surface did not differ much from our own western deserts. Many of the craters proved to be large valleys, and deep ruts could be seen crossing their surface, indicating a heavy run-off of water in the distant past. Surrounding these valleys were rugged mountains, and on the flanks were definite traces of ancient water lines. Adamski was informed that much water still exists within the mountains.

The tenuous clouds that formed, only to disappear and give up their moisture, sustained a small growth of vegetation that Adamski saw in some of the valleys. While observing a close-up view of the rugged habitat, he noticed a small animal suddenly run across the area under view. In combination with the atmospheric information and scenes of vegetation, this was not too startling to see.

At a lecture in New Zealand in 1959, Adamski commented further about the Moon's front side. We would find dwelling places in several crater areas, for there were bases constructed by the interplanetary space travelers. Naturally, there would have to be a number of people at those sites in order to take care of those bases. No different than our operations at isolated areas on Earth, on the Moon people are needed to maintain ship operations and power stations, be it hot climate or cold desolation. Just like we station people at our own Antarctic bases, people have to be at these outposts on the Moon. This explained many of the strange lights that blazed out from crater floors, noted by astronomers over two centuries.

How is it that our six announced Moon landings showed an opposite picture? All one has to do to answer this question is check a topographical map of the Moon to see where we landed. NASA did not plan to go anywhere near the alien bases. NASA stayed at least a hundred miles from the life-supporting craters and valleys, and set down in the desolate regions: the flat expanse of the maria (Apollo 11 and 12), barren plains (Apollo 14), an ancient lava bed (Apollo 15), the Descartes highlands (Apollo 16), and the rolling hills of Taurus-Littrow (Apollo 17). NASA knew that these were uninspiring, inconsequential places. NASA did not go to the Moon looking for life. The inside planners knew it was there. They guarded against any chance of proving it, and shocking the world out of its conditioned ways of thinking.

Yet extreme precautions had to be taken, for the alien inhabitants might show up at the chosen badlands of the Moon to monitor our first excursions there. NASA could easily confine the activities of our astronauts to certain landscapes, but obviously would have no control over any rendezvous activity by extraterrestrial spacecraft. But when it came to what the public would see, nothing was left to chance. Any accidental discovery or evidence that might be encountered by our astronauts, showing a living environment or UFOs on the Moon, would only be known by those in charge, through separate and secret communication channels. Live pictures from the Moon were on an 8-second time delay to allow censoring if needed. This was not a voyage of discovery. Everything that the public was to see had been planned. The public would be shown a totally bleak and desolate landscape. Naturally, after sticking a flag in the ground, the astronauts would be shown bouncing around in an apparent low-gravity, and airless environment. The cryptocracy's overriding script of the space missions is to keep life as we know it confined to the Earth.

Let's further answer the question of how NASA knew where to land men on the Moon and avoid any dramatic confrontation with things that are not supposed to be there. They and their predecessors had been behind all the secret Moon studies conducted at the large observatories. Later, when unmanned space probes were sent to the Moon, five

Lunar Orbiters successfully photographed virtually all of the Moon's surface. High-resolution photographs were taken from a 25-mile altitude, and from possibly much lower orbits. Every region on the Moon was known in sufficient detail. The public and orthodox scientists were put to sleep with a small number of low resolution pictures that showed nothing but the expected.

At the same time, NASA was compiling studies of past reports of extraterrestrial activity on the Moon. One of the documents was called the *Chronological Catalogue of Reported Lunar Events*, which listed the locations of mysterious lights and clouds observed by astronomers for more than a century. NASA was also doing its own observing, in a special study called Operation Moon Blink, possibly to re-confirm certain areas with modern-day sophistication. For a long time now, the government and Air Force knew why UFOs were here and where they were from. NASA certainly knew that they were not going to be sending our astronauts to a dead, burnt out planet. But they were fully prepared to present that picture to the watching public.

Everything was at stake. The higher ups knew the full consequences if anything about the real nature of the Moon was released. Thousands of so-called authorities would be discredited in one stroke. It would not matter if it were astronomy or political sophistry - all orthodox thinking and fraudulent preaching would be tagged as nonsense. Much in our educational system would be exposed as fiction. If the real truth from space were released to the public, the masses would suddenly know as much, if not more, than the so-called authorities in the field of space knowledge. Just the thought of that would be quite horrifying for those in their established positions of certified authority.

The censors had been in the business for twenty years prior to the manned lunar missions. They knew where to set those landers down, for there *are* vast areas of bleak desert and barren plateaus. And the pictures that they would present of the Moon were destined to keep the lifeless theories intact. Any incidental evidence to the contrary, or unplanned development (such as an extraterrestrial vehicle arriving to watch our activity), would be censored, obviously. There would be one picture, and one picture only, that would be instilled in the minds of the public. That being, - a bleak, desolate, airless, lifeless orb, that people would just as soon forget about. And they did, after only a few lunar missions. The public decided that it was a pointless waste of money to go to such an uninhabitable, rocky wasteland. What was the point of duplicating the feat over and over?

The answer to that particular question was that there were a lot of economic reasons for the aerospace industries to keep the moon missions going. And it was important to get man into space. With that I agree, for how else can mankind begin to learn. Eventually though, interest waned from all quarters, the federal budget cut off funds, and nothing could justify the expense of sending any more rockets to the Moon.

All of our lunar mission astronauts were well-trained, and capable men for the task. All but one were military pilots, and the Apollo program was a government project, of course. Whether any number of astronauts saw UFOs or related evidence at some point in the missions, those facts would only be known to the authorities in control. The astronauts could not make any statement along those lines to the public or to the press, or else they would be breaching national security. When questioned during post-mission interviews, some have answered with vague, noncommittal opinions. But no definitive statements regarding their sightings in space have been given by the astronauts, in keeping with NASA's strict policy of silence concerning UFOs.

There have been several magazines and books that have published transcripts of supposed lunar-mission conversations between the astronauts and mission control, when bogeys (unidentified objects) were sighted, sometimes trailing their spacecraft for hours. While I am quite certain that the space missions were kept under regular surveillance by our space visitors, and that extraterrestrial bases were seen on the Moon by the astronauts in lunar orbit, I doubt that any of these alleged transcripts are true accounts. Most are quoted as unconfirmed reports; the rest are ambiguous, and much is simply read into the partially deleted accounts. NASA knew that the space visitors were up there, so rigid procedures were established beforehand in order to keep the expected sightings secret and classified. Coded signals, in conjunction with a crypto-communication channel, were used to send information to the high security room at the Space Center, thereby keeping the reports on alien activity secret from the millions of television viewers watching the flight, and just as importantly, secret from the main body of NASA personnel at Mission Control.

Anonymous sources from NASA have stated that the early reports of UFOs and alien bases on the Moon were suppressed, so as not to cause public panic. There is little doubt also, that the astronauts were fully briefed and instructed prior to going to the Moon, so they would not be alarmed at what they saw there. But because of national security, they cannot discuss it.

A senior NASA engineer confirmed that every space mission encountered UFOs. His very interesting book was first published in France in 1975, with the American edition following a few years later. The author, Maurice Chatelain, had been in charge of the design of all communication and television systems for the Apollo program. He relates in his book, that beginning with the Gemini flights, sightings of Unidentified Flying Objects were a routine occurrence, but that these events were never discussed outside NASA.

Confirmation of the truth behind the UFOs stepped up dramatically when Apollo set out for the Moon. In December 1968, astronauts Frank Borman, James Lovell, and William Anders made their historic flight to our companion world, and as their Apollo 8 spacecraft came out from behind the far side on its first lunar orbit, Lovell radioed: "Please be informed that there is a Santa Claus." One might argue that it was just a light-hearted comment with no real meaning, but others have suggested that the hidden meaning behind those words was that alien bases existed on the more habitable far side, surely a fact that had been known by space authorities in both the U.S. and Russia, since unmanned probes had previously photographed the far side in detail. The detailed pictures had always been suppressed, although in 1959, an unnamed scientist in Russia frankly told the press - "The world is going to be very surprised." But with Apollo, here was man's first in-person, visual confrontation with the evidence.

Maurice Chatelain reveals that all the later Apollo space missions were followed - often quite closely - by extraterrestrial spacecraft, but that Mission Control had strict policies in order to conceal this information from the public. Two UFOs followed Apollo 10 around the Moon, and during its homeward trek. While Apollo 10 was in lunar orbit, the UFO base in the Crater Aristarchus put on a dazzling display of blinking lights, brilliant enough to be seen by astronomers in Europe and America. Dozens of reports of the crater lights were made by earth-bound observers. The spacepeople were intently watching our first attempts at interplanetary travel to one of their worlds. They were not going to ignore us, for earthman's misguided and nuclear-weapon mentality was no longer confined to the Earth. They knew that with such wayward thinking, there were potential dangers to their living environment, as we shall see.

With Apollo 11, the Eagle LM landed, and man set foot on the Moon in July, 1969. A spectacular achievement considering our fledgling space technology, and mankind was justifiably proud. Every newspaper and magazine carried a picture of man's footprint on the Moon, and NASA decreed that this was the first imprint on the Moon's dusty surface by a human being.

But NASA knew there were other footprints on the Moon, though not at the chosen Tranquility Base, and not oversized astronaut boots. After Apollo 11 landed, two UFOs hovered near the site, and Edwin Aldrin took several photographs of them before he and Armstrong climbed out of their Lunar Module.[1] That fact is a certainty according to flight communication director Maurice Chatelain. What is also a certainty is that NASA had fully prepared our astronauts on how to deal with the fact that they were traveling to an inhabited world, and to expect harmless surveillance by extraterrestrial spacecraft. They were further instructed as to why man on Earth was not ready for this information. It seems the space program was designed to concentrate on advancing our scientific technology, and to expand man's thinking, step by step - in a controlled manner. It was the perception of the authorities in control, that our civilization was not progressed enough to come face to face with evidence of extraterrestrial life. That evidence could be, *and would be*, completely censored from all lunar mission communications and operations. Appropriately then, man would be seen stumbling around the lunar surface, not stumbling into life on the Moon. According to those in control, that is all that the public would be able to accept.

The problem with keeping mankind in its infant stage by not releasing any truth about space conditions, be it the Moon, Mars, or Venus, is that it allows the cryptocracy to keep this civilization on the road of nuclear insanity. Our authorities would not tell the public of finding an extraterrestrial base on the Moon, any more than they would tell us if they found one in the mountainous highlands of Tibet. And the space visitors do have bases on Earth, in remote areas that are virtually inaccessible by our methods of air and land travel.

Now back to the potential danger for the extraterrestrials by our going to the Moon, as I mentioned previously. With our flight system down pat, Apollo 13 was launched as the fifth rocket to go to the Moon, and third proposed landing. We all remember that this ill-fated trip had to return to the Earth without making a lunar landing, because of a mysterious explosion in one of its oxygen tanks. Mr. Chatelain states that there was a lot of talk and speculation within the space agency about the unsuccessful mission. It seems that Apollo 13 was carrying a secret payload - a nuclear device that was to be detonated on the Moon's surface. The nuclear test would be measured by the seismographic packages left on the surface at the two previous Apollo sites, in order to determine the infrastructure properties of the Moon. A predominant opinion circulating at the space agency was that a UFO trailing Apollo 13 deliberately caused the mysterious explosion of an oxygen tank in the service module, in order to prevent the planned nuclear detonation.

We could not consider an extraterrestrial civilization to be advanced, and then expect them to sit immobile on the Moon blissfully awaiting our arrival, knowing that we might possibly bring barbaric ideas that could threaten living conditions on the Moon. With their advanced technology and instrumentation, they can determine precisely what devices are being carried along into space and exactly what we intend to do. And with the Apollo 13 incident, we can interpret their action as saying: "We'll let you set up your plaques, flags, and probing instruments, but your atomic blasts will remain confined to Earth, not here thank you."

The public displays and hoopla attending our Apollo program can be looked back in retrospect, as profoundly ironic in part. Space officials were "concerned" that our moonwalkers might bring back some unknown pathogenic microorganism from the Moon, and therefore had the Apollo 11 and 12 astronauts in quarantine for several days upon their return, to check for any possible contamination. Yet the same space officials were unconcerned about spreading radioactive contamination around the Moon, to do some infrastructure tests. A big public display of concern over possible bacteria from the Moon, but secret plans to throw around our nuclear garbage. The preposterous schemes of our "experts!"

Apollos 12, 14, 15, and 16 sighted UFOs and man-made structures on the Moon. Many photographs were taken, and some of the unclassified pictures are reproduced in Fred Steckling's recent book, *We Discovered Alien Bases On The Moon*. He obtained them from NASA's Science Data Center. Steckling's well-researched evidence will be referred to later in the book.

There was no public discussion by our astronauts, other

than terse comments like seeing things during the missions which they were unable to explain. The men behind the scenes were responsible for the absolute silence regarding the evidence, because it just was not the "right time." We cannot lay any blame on our astronauts, for they were under national security orders, and could do nothing but comply. They were not serving the public; they were serving our government.

But it appears that seeing the truth firsthand, and then seeing that such an erroneous picture was being given to the public, weighed unbearably on their minds. A glorious future was being denied, because it wasn't the "right time." There was a tendency towards a complete personality change following their Moon experience. Some of the astronauts had bouts with severe depression after their return from space. Others became deeply religious, even what we might call fanatic. I attended a lecture given by one of the Apollo astronauts not long ago. He repeated at least ten times during his talk, that "the only thing worth knowing is that Jesus walked the Earth 2000 years ago. Not that man walked on the Moon."

What was happening back on Earth during the period of the lunar missions? The answer provides part of the reason why it wasn't the "right time" to disclose any of the truth about the Earth's companion world. We went to the Moon for four years, beginning with Apollo 8 in December 1968, and ending with Apollo 17 in December 1972. Those same four years were the peak of the Vietnam War. For an illustrating example, Apollo 17 was returning from the serenity of space to our war-torn Earth, just at the time the heaviest, most destructive bombing since WWII was being ordered by President Nixon against North Vietnam.

For our world of economic forces, it will never be the "right time." Wars, and preparations for war, are but a part of the false economics that necessitate the truth be concealed, and which require the mandate that life does not exist in space. For if it were revealed, everyone would want to know who these people were up there on the Moon. Even part of the answers about the Moon would extinquish much of the untruthfulness in this world instantly. Vested interests would no longer have the world's mindless support of wars, and preparations for war.

The public read a few headlines, watched the televised blur from the Moon a few times, and then the Moon was history. Interest soon plummeted, as one would expect, and when national television tried to briefly cover the live lift-off for the Apollo 13 mission, the network's switchboard was flooded by calls from angered viewers because their sports programming had been interrupted. Also as expected, the scientific community heartily welcomed the space agency's public relations image of the Moon as simply a geologic paradise, and waited to see the rocks.

NASA could have staged a trip to Egypt in the same manner that they went to the Moon. Three-fourths of Egypt is the barren and hot Sahara Desert. Set a lander in the middle of the desert, a couple hundred miles from the pyramids, the fertile Nile, and bustling Cairo, and nothing would be seen. Our astronauts would be obliged to bring back buckets of sand. Egypt would be forgotten as an uninteresting wasteland, if our only information was from a NASA space mission. A land of grandeur and mystery, reduced to nothing by only concentrating on the expanse of sand.

Regarding the Moon, NASA did release some contradictory information, sometimes inadvertently, and sometimes with discretion. Orthodoxers ignorantly ignored the evidence, just as they had ignored the earlier records of telescopic observations. It required much painstaking and meticulous study to dissect the real picture of the Moon from the phony public relations image. Again, we are indebted to the world's leading selenologist, Dr. Val A. Firsoff, who in 1969 published his timely book, *The Old Moon and The New*. NASA's smokescreen might be able to pull the wool over the public's eye, but could not do the same with an expert who had spent years in telescopic observation, and who also knew the full history of telescopic records and scientific evaluations. If NASA's public relations picture of the Moon was even in the least bit accurate, then we may as well junk all our telescopes as being worthless instruments.

Before we review the actual space findings from the lunar probes and landings, I would like to clarify something about my earlier discussion of Firsoff's *Strange World of the Moon*. Some people might read his scientific treatise and then conclude that I preferentially picked evidence from the book which was most favorable towards postulating life on the Moon, while overlooking discussions that seemed to be less supportive of this premise. That is not the case for the following reason. While reviewing his book, I had the benefit of knowing the cumulative evidence of the past 25 years. I was completely familiar with recent, verifiable evidence about our Moon, which in fact confirmed much of his earlier scientific evaluations. Likewise with his second masterful document. His books had a few open questions, simply because the true nature of the Moon's gravity and atmosphere had not yet come to light. Firsoff's analysis was valid in all other respects, and the whole picture becomes remarkably clear with our more recent knowledge regarding the lunar gravity and atmosphere. We are going to discuss these important things shortly.

But for the moment, we must remain patient, because it is important to study things in logical sequence. Most people are impatient and want to know the advanced answers about something, before having a good understanding of the basic. And yet if one were to first give them the full truth, what would happen? The people would not believe it, because it conflicts with their conventional beliefs and impatient thoughts. These habits must be replaced with disciplined learning and thinking, so that they will be better able to evaluate information, and understand what is being given. If I had simply written the final truth about the Moon first, and let it go at that, many would reject it for not conforming to their conditioned beliefs. You will find this true in every field of knowledge, be it philosophy, history, science, religion, politics, etc. For when people with superficial knowledge are confronted with the real truth about something, they cannot properly evaluate it, and being confused they dismiss it. That is how humanity perpetuates its ignorance.

Firsoff got right to the point in his later work. Changes and events on the Moon were constantly being observed by top selenographers, and he charged that astronomers who automatically rejected the telescopic reports only knew the Moon from photographs. From time to time, clouds and obscurations appeared, and then disappeared. TLP's were being observed frequently. Mists, luminous hazes, gases venting from volcanos, vapor clouds, and inexplicable lights were being seen and recorded. A lot of things were actively going on through the eye of a telescope, but NASA's black and white, still photography from a 60 mile-high altitude showed little of it. Only one Lunar Orbiter V photograph showed fog within Crater Aristarchus.

High resolution photography around the Moon indicated that volcanic activity had been the major factor in molding the lunar surface. It appeared that lunar volcanos continued to have eruptions and vent gases, first recorded spectrographically by N. A. Kozyrev in November 1958, while he was studying the area of Alphonsus Crater. Volcanic activity was apparently confirmed there again in 1959, and near Aristarchus in 1963.

But orthodox astronomers resisted fiercely, and insisted that every hole and crater on the Moon, new or old, came about from meteoritic impact. To make this theory completely official, Cornell Aeronautical Laboratory issued a report by designated authorities in August 1964, that deemed everything an impact feature, including Oceanus Procellarum with a diameter of 1500 km! Three years later, when crater chains were photographed on the far side of the Moon by the U.S. Lunar Orbiters, American cartographers refused to chart them correctly when compiling the NASA Farside Chart, because such crater chains were impossible to explain by the meteoritic impact theory! (Crater chains could only develop if volcanism was a major factor in the Moon's history.) Yet the Russian map that was compiled from their own lunar photography, clearly showed the crater chains that exist on the Moon's far side. (For most people it comes as a shock initially, the realization that many so-called authorities only see what they want to see. But it's time the people start waking up!)

What was NASA's role in this debate between selenographers and the regular astronomical community? NASA made it a point to bolster the meteoritic side of the controversy, by instructing the astronauts to describe the Moon with the same exact attitude. When the Apollo 8 crew came out from behind the Moon on its first orbit, Mission Control radioed up: "Apollo 8, Houston. What does the ole Moon look like from 60 miles? Over."

Captain James Lovell replied that the Moon looked like gray plaster of Paris with quite a few craters, most of them looking like they were hit by meteorites or projectiles of some sort. Those were the first words describing the Moon, carried on live television around the world. Then, Colonel Frank Borman transmitted his thoughts from afar: that the Moon was a great expanse of nothing - a primeval, foreboding pumice stone that looked lonely and uninviting. Major Anders read from the Bible, and later added that the Moon looked like a sandpile his kids had played in for some time - all beat up, no definition, just a lot of bumps and holes.

This was the first stage of negating the true nature of the Moon. The astronauts were army officers, and according to Firsoff, could be excused, because 'Orders is orders.' But scientists are obligated to exercise more objectivity.

Why would NASA want to negate the major role of volcanos on the Moon? Because volcanos are directly related to the atmosphere around a planet, and the fumes erupting from a volcano are about three-fourths water vapor. NASA will not confirm even a remote indication of air or water on the Moon. The following is a perfect example of how they explained away more direct evidence.

In early 1971, sensitive instruments which had been left on the Moon at the Apollo 12 and 14 landing sites detected water vapor erupting from cracks in the lunar surface. These cracks had just formed, since seismometers at both areas were registering the tremors of minor moonquakes. On several occasions, the sensitive equipment registered large clouds of gases passing by both sites, which were approximately 100 miles apart. Physicists John Freeman and H. Dent Hills of Rice University issued a report, stating that the instruments had detected a vapor cloud covering 100 square miles on March 7, and that the vapor was 99% water. The men expressed an opinion that there is water beneath the surface of the Moon at those Apollo sites.

Caught off guard, NASA spokesmen discounted the scientists' report, by claiming that the Apollo instruments had probably detected the contents of a urine bag inadvertently left behind by the astronauts, and which somehow ruptured. This most incredible explanation suited the orthodoxers, as NASA knew it would. Another aspect of this incident, apparently was not even questioned. If the Moon was airless, what was supporting such a vapor, which could cover the distance of 100 miles between the two Apollo sites?

NASA never issued any direct statements, but a lot of evidence for the Moon's atmosphere became apparent later, as a result of careful investigation of both lunar photographs and operations. This type of expert analysis confirmed what had been suspected from the telescopic studies and color filter photography of the 1950's - that there was a definite atmosphere on the Moon, and according to Firsoff, one of far greater density and mass than is conventionally admitted. He adds that the biggest obstacle to seeing air on the Moon, often lies in the subconscious mind, - a "superstitious fear, almost a hatred, of the idea of life on other worlds, especially the near ones." This attitude is particularly acute among common-variety scientists, and therefore potential discoveries are held back, because of a psychological problem obstructing proper scientific investigation and evaluation. Timid and superstitious minds cling fiercely to mathematical theories that make life impossible on other planetary bodies.

The belief in the airlessness of the Moon is wedded to the 1925 theory of Sir James Jeans, which stated that since the mean molecular velocity of a gas exceeds a quarter of the velocity of escape from the Moon, any gaseous layer would rapidly dissipate, and it would be impossible for the Moon to retain any given atmosphere. However, Jean's theory is based on the Moon having 1/6 gravity, and there are other invalid assumptions in his theory which Firsoff fully analyzes. The critical analysis is too complex to discuss here, and beyond the scope of this book, but suffice it to say, that Jean's 1925 theory is wrong for many reasons, and the orthodoxers can no longer hide behind it.

Let's briefly recall the earlier discussion concerning telescopic observations of the Moon, where the atmospheric effects were recorded by selenographers, but always questioned or ignored by ordinary astronomy. Why couldn't selenographers show unmistakable evidence of the lunar air, or directly determine its constituency? Earth-based spectrographic analysis would be unable to detect earth-type air and gases on the Moon, since lunar absorptions would be entirely blanketed by the stronger telluric lines from our own atmosphere. Also, argon and nitrogen that might be present could not be seen or measured, since they absorb only in the ultra-violet, which is effectively blocked by our ionosphere. Because of our own atmospheric interference, the only way to determine the makeup and density of the lunar atmosphere would be by spectral observation from space, or from the lunar surface itself. Only NASA has that information, and they did detect a sustantial atmosphere. Its exact composition and density is undoubtedly far different from the official statements, and remains highly classified information.

A detailed look at some of NASA's color photographs provides evidence of the Moon's atmosphere. In their official publication,"Apollo 8 - Man Around the Moon" (EP-66), are three color photographs which confirm the presence of a dense atmosphere. Along the entire visible rim of the Moon, as seen and photographed from space by the Apollo 8 astronauts, there is a substantial brightness of the limb - an effect that can only be attributed to a gaseous layer around the Moon. Mars, Venus, and the Earth all present this same limb brightening due to their atmospheres.

On page 12 of the Apollo-8 booklet is a space photograph of Earth, showing the Earth's own limb brightness. On page 14 of the same booklet is a full picture of the Moon, taken by the astronauts from interplanetary space, and it shows an identical limb brightening along the rim. Firsoff points out that both of the space photographs of the Earth and the Moon were taken on the same film with the same camera, and since we accept that there is an atmospheric blanket around our planet, it would be quite illogical to deny the same such reality behind the same limb brightening in the case of the Moon.

Both the Orbiter probes and Apollo missions photographed the faint haze of light spreading out over the lunar horizon just prior to sunrise, and the soft illumination of lunar twilight after the Sun dipped below the Moon's limb. These effects require an atmosphere. Oblique pictures, such as Plate 17, clearly show soft gray shadows made by an evening sun on the lunar far side. Yet astronomers believing in an airless Moon have always insisted that all lunar shadows are pitch black.

William Brian, author of *Moongate: Suppressed Findings of the U.S. Space Program*, fully discusses the Apollo 14 flag waving, an incident known by many space science researchers. After the Apollo 14 astronauts had set up the small flag pole, and while the on-site television camera was running, a gust of wind kicked up and caused the flag to billow and wave. Brian obtained a copy of this Apollo 14 film and analyzed it closely. He states that the astronauts were not even close to the flag when it started waving, but immediately upon seeing it, both ran to block the camera's view of the flag. One astronaut even put his arm in front of the lens, because nothing so shocking as an atmospheric wind is allowed on the Moon. Anyway, the evidence is not supposed to be seen. NASA didn't bother to comment, and the whole incident was conveniently forgotten. Keep the orthodoxers preaching airlessness is the rule.

The later Apollo missions used a type of starched flag that would stay rigid at all times. More like metalicized cloth, probably imbued with fine metallic webbing, it had a fixed "waving" shape. On these later broadcasts NASA emphasized the need for this ingenious design, so that the stars and stripes could "wave" in an airless world.

Another trick in order to completely instill the idea of an airless Moon was conducted on Apollo 15, the mission immediately following the original flag waving incident. This scheme could easily be called mind control, and apparently NASA has no plans to ever tell the truth about the Moon, because this false display preempted any future possibility of telling the truth. In order to show that there was a vacuum or airless condition on the Moon, an astronaut was instructed to demonstrate Galileo's gravity experiment. It was a rather simple procedure to impress the public. In a vacuum all bodies drop at the same rate, regardless of weight or shape, since there is no air resistance. So at the Apollo 15 site, a hammer and a feather were dropped at the same time, to supposedly show that they fell at the same rate. Since they did hit the ground at the same time, the feather must have contained a metallic slug. The whole demonstration was designed to reinforce a conditioned belief of an airless Moon.

The real evidence was different. Firsoff points out that during the landing of Apollo 12, the dust raised by the retro-rockets took many minutes to settle. If in a vacuum, all the dust should have been down in a matter of seconds.

The early U.S. and Soviet rocket probes slammed into the Moon at thousands of miles per hour, causing huge dust clouds to rise several miles. How could these clouds be raised to such heights without an extensive atmosphere?

Of course, if we were to check any science textbook, we would still find it written that the Moon environment is almost a total vacuum, the most liberal estimates giving it a value of 1/1000 or 1/10,000 the density of the Earth's atmosphere. Those numbers will never change, simply because man and his ego wants to believe that he lives in the only habitable world. Orthodoxers cannot "see" air or water on the Moon, (and NASA will not confirm it), because to admit that it is there, leaves the question of life on the Moon wide open.

Should not a visible daytime sky have shown up in some of the lunar photographs taken by the astronauts on the surface? Yes, but NASA took extreme precautions in dealing with surface photography, so as not to publicly disclose this supporting evidence. Except for the suppression of the lunar sky, there did tend to be a gradual progression of showing colors and realism as the missions continued. Apollo 11, 12, and 14 landing sites were like barren gravel pits, and the photographic score was dull and dreary, like taking black and white pictures inside a faintly lit cave. Whereas Apollo 15, 16, and 17 were in more interesting geological locations, and the on-site photography brightened up a bit. It started to look more natural and realistic. In fact, the picture portfolio for Apollo 17 has some panoramic shots that approached earthly colors, except for the black sky on the horizon.

NASA scheduled each mission so that the landing site would be just near the dawn side of the terminator. This allowed the astronauts to see the surface features in sharp relief, since the sun would be behind them at a low angle of about 7°, and that would make landing the Lunar Module much easier and safer. But as you recall, a lunar day progresses at only 1/14th the rate of an Earth day due to the slow rotation of the Moon, so it was still early dawn for the first three Apollos when they left the Moon. Consequently, their activities were photographed in subdued illumination. However, the latter three missions spent more time on the surface, lasting until the equivalent of mid-morning, and the panoramic scenes brightened up in their colors. A dense lunar atmosphere is suggested in a few photographs from the missions. An appreciable atmosphere would show up as a light sky by mid-morning, and in one Apollo 16 photograph the morning sky is brightly illuminated. William Brian offers possible photographic evidence of light diffusion by the lunar sky, in the book *Moongate*.

Those few photographs are the exception. Virtually every picture released by NASA shows a black sky, as part of their efforts to conceal evidence of the lunar atmosphere. The soft blue or blue-white morning sky on the lunar horizon may have been filtered out originally by the astronauts' cameras. Wratten filters, or their equivalent, were probably used. A Wratten-12 filter will entirely suppress any blue of the sky, and also cut off the violet part of the spectrum. Used in combination with another filter, the whole visible spectrum of the sky could be eliminated. If any original photography brought back by the astronauts turned up unsatisfactory, the sky could be made black during processing. NASA was selling an airless Moon, hence it was mandatory to produce black sky photos.

Given the evidence already presented for the lunar atmosphere, it is reasonable to at least speculate on the changing illumination and color tint of the lunar daytime sky. Early morning on the Moon may be like our own softly illuminated pre-dawn sky, - a dark blue or blue violet. In that case, it may not be any different at a Moon base, than at our inhabited areas above the Arctic circle, where the population lives in periods of six months of days followed by six months of night. The 4000 inhabitants of Spitzbergen, which lies seven hundred miles north of the Arctic Circle, do not see the Sun from the end of October to the middle of February. During this time the sky is neither dark not light, but rather like twilight, and the people accept it as very natural. Perhaps the sky over the Moon is similar.

It is William Brian's contention in *Moongate*, that stars would not be visible from the Moon, unless there is an atmosphere to spread out the starlight. This is precisely the case on Earth. Except for a very few bright stars, most would be too faint and distant to be seen by an unaided eye, without our atmosphere acting like a giant lens and making the stars twinkle.

The Earth's atmosphere performs like a giant lens in making the thousands of distant stars visible. We know this, because the astronauts have stated that they could not see any stars when looking out from their space capsules above the Earth's atmosphere. This was confirmed again recently, when a space shuttle procedure was televised on an ABC news report in February, 1984. William Brian informed the author, that while watching the news coverage of the astronauts performing maneuvers outside the shuttle, one of the astronauts was heard to say, "Just for the record, I don't see any stars out here."

Also for the record, this incident adds further support for Adamski's early space information in *Inside the Spaceships* (1955). On Adamski's first trip into space aboard a Venusian mothership, he mentions that he looked out through a porthole, and "was amazed to see that the background of space is totally dark."

If, according to NASA, there is no atmosphere on the Moon, then the stars should not be visible to a lunar astronaut. However, this was not the case. I attended a lecture given by Apollo 15 astronaut James Irwin, in Walnut Creek, California, on May 6, 1984. While narrating a short film of his Moon trip, Irwin stated that he "could see the stars so clearly, while standing around on the surface of the Moon."

Our own NASA astronauts have stated that stars cannot be seen from their space capsules outside the Earth's atmosphere. So to be seen from the lunar surface, the Moon must have an atmosphere acting as a lens. The early dawn sky still showing its twinkling stars, must have been a beautiful sight to Irwin, in order to make such a memorable impression.

Regarding the lunar surface, we must admit that there are some desolate conditions and at times a harsh climate, on the front side. Therefore, the Moon bases on this side might not be palatial. But what of it? People living above the Arctic Circle are not in a palatial dwelling place either, yet we know that people live there happily, and without real difficulty once they adjust to Nature's conditions. In fact, it suits them just fine. So it's all a matter of reference. Actually, when considering the Moon, and comparing their conditions to conditions in some of our urban cities - smog, overcrowding, traffic, crime - the Moon bases might be considered palatial!

It would be illogical to find an atmosphere without finding water. Firsoff points out that since hydrogen is the most abundant element in the universe, followed by the second most active element oxygen, water (H_2O) must be the commonest of compounds. Saying that we should *expect* to find evidence of water on the Moon, he adds, that *its absence would be even harder to explain* than its presence. Yet orthodoxers view such an idea with shades of horror, for the corollary of water is life.

There is much evidence showing that water existed on this side of the Moon in the past. About twenty-five dried-up riverbeds were confirmed by lunar photography. Schroeter's Valley is more than a mile in width, winds for 150 miles, and is 200 feet deep - a depth that would take centuries to carve. Hadley Rille is more than a 1000 feet deep in places. Apollo 15 and 16 astronauts described seeing ancient waterlines surrounding the bases of the lunar mountains near the landing sites.[2] Countless deep ruts flanking the Lunar Alps indicate a heavy runoff of water previously. There are many small craters, only a few hundred meters in width, that are perfect bowl shape, - so neat and round, "as though they had been turned out on a lathe." Firsoff attributes this description to G. P. Kuiper, and is absolutely convinced that these small craters were formed by phreatic eruptions of water from below the surface.

And indeed there were many full-size lakes in earlier times. The geological evidence was shown clearly in a number of the Orbiter photographs. These included pictures of Riccioli Crater, and areas in the southern hemisphere on the far side. The most distinctive and prominent feature on the backside is crater Tsiolkovsky, often called "The Lake." See Plate 18. This is a unique area and it was photographed extensively during the lunar missions. Firsoff did a thorough analysis of the photographic data, and concluded that the longitudinal striations and grooves on the two aprons along the west side of the crater were made by the movement of ancient ice glaciers. The region near the now-dry Riccioli

Lake also has the distinct markings of former glaciation.

Clearly, the climate has shifted around on the Moon. What the geological forces were, to develop vast areas of desert on the front side, no one knows. They may have coincided with a major magnetic pole shift or a change in the axial tilt, or even a gradual slowing down of the Moon's rotational speed to its present synchronous orbit with respect to the Earth. Actually, the apparent revolution of the Moon around the Earth is an optical illusion. Both planets travel around the Sun together, but continually modify each other's path due to gravitational attraction. Because the Moon is a lighter body, its orbit is more displaced than the Earth's, and therefore it appears to circle us. But in fact, the orbits of both planets are always concave toward the Sun. So while we both revolve around the Sun once in a year's time, the rotational speed of the Moon causes it to keep the same side (hemisphere) facing the Earth.

A lot can be inferred from the photographic evidence of dried-up lakes and riverbeds, a past ice age of glaciers, and the ancient waterlines along crater walls and mountain flanks. Read the following carefully. For surface water to have existed on the Moon, there had to have been an atmosphere of sufficient density and pressure to keep the water in a liquid state. William Brian deduces further that the Moon had to have a high gravity to hold this atmosphere, and that if it had a high gravity at one time, it must still have one. Since it still has a high gravity (proved in *Moongate* using NASA documentation), then it still should have a dense atmosphere.

During an eon of climatic change, geologic processes gradually shifted the water to new locations, and slowly developed a more natural environment in areas on the far side of the Moon. While on the front side, water became primarily harbored beneath the surface in the mountainous regions. Yet enough moisture is present in the lunar atmosphere to form thin clouds and sustain the sparse vegetation on this side. Those effects were treated thoroughly in our earlier discussion of telescopic studies.

The important fact to realize is that whatever water was there in the Moon's past history, is still there in the widely diverse lunar environment of today. Only traces in the desert areas, but significant amounts further into the temperate zones where localized conditions can sustain large bodies of surface water. We would expect to find snow and ice closer to the poles. This is all consistent with our established proof of an atmosphere.

Chapter 8
The Moon Shows a Living Environment

Most people have not had a passing thought about the Moon for more than a decade. They were conditioned to believe that the Moon was a desolate and uninviting place, as a result of the publicity during the manned lunar expeditions. I do not blame the public for its acceptance of the negative image of the Moon, and its subsequent disinterest following the Apollo missions. Nothing else was being publicized to challenge that image, and like everyone else, I never gave a thought to our companion world in space either, until the year 1974. Perhaps the following will give the reader a little insight as to how my previous unthinking-acceptance of NASA's official statements underwent a dramatic reorientation over time, resulting in a different picture of the Moon that was entirely more accurate.

Following my sighting of UFOs in New York, which I described earlier in this book, I read a few books on the subject. They made a good case for the reality of UFOs, but beyond that, the books could only speculate as to what was behind the UFO mystery. It is important to mention also, that I avoided reading any nonsense paperbacks, or any psychic books which attempted to make a perversion of this field. I knew that any evidence on UFOs, and that any accurate information would have to be related to the proper understanding of space sciences in our world. It was then that I discovered George Adamski's *Flying Saucers Have Landed*. This was a remarkably informative book, backed with acceptable evidence.

It was only a week later that I sat down to read his second book, *Inside the Spaceships*. Here were direct answers on the subject of UFOs and interplanetary space. To say that it uplifted my thinking would be quite an understatement. Every discussion in his book carried an impression of truth. Yet being scientifically trained, I felt that I would need to honestly question his statements regarding the Moon. This was 1974, and though I had never paid any real attention to NASA's Apollo program, other than the first landing perhaps, I knew that the space agency had not even remotely suggested life on the Moon. So my position initially was - I wonder...was this possible? I was always an independent thinker, and so it was a natural assumption for me to conclude, "This is going to take a lot of research to fully answer" (concerning life on the Moon). Until there was some completeness to my research, I accepted it as a possibility.

It did not take long to find that NASA's official "evidence" concerning the Moon had been challenged by proficient space researchers. A lot of suppressed information had been uncovered in recent years, which contradicted NASA's official presentation of a "lifeless" environment on the Moon. The discrepancies unearthed by ambitious researchers made some waves in popular science and UFO magazines, and a few authors expanded their research to full-length books. But the revelations could do little publicly, to dent the armor of NASA's simplistic and safe presentation on the Moon.

I perused through a few of these publications, and then decided to collect and file pertinent articles on the Moon, and everything connected to space and the other planets. I reviewed science magazines, NASA publications, National Geographics, current news clippings on space, and even orthodox publications on astronomy. I made notes, and later these provided clues from articles which I had previously filed away as uninteresting. Research is often like putting a puzzle together. Some pieces don't seem to fit together until you see more of the picture later on.

I collected Moon maps, photographic books on the Moon,

and reliable documents. I sifted information from obscure publications which have a very limited circulation. At the same time, I was amassing a reference library of books. I picked up information from correspondence with other space science researchers. A lot of invaluable information from the space program has never been officially publicized.

A lot of people associated with the UFO field have shown a very limited approach. While being very objective and thorough in presenting the real evidence for UFOs, at the same time, they have demonstrated in their writing a superficial awareness or research into space sciences. The overriding themes of their presentations are therefore personal and meaningless speculations.

With my growing library on the Moon taking shape, it was apparent to me that Adamski's early writings were much more than a possibility. They were accurate. In fact, I came to realize something else. While his account was being rejected at the time (1955) by the ordinary scientific community, the intelligence agencies knew that that information was dead serious. Privately, they accepted that information in agreement with their own secret studies, and acted on it. By this I mean to say, the intelligence agencies worked to suppress any corroborative information resulting from earth-based studies.

In his 1955 book, *The Flying Saucer Conspiracy*, Donald Keyhoe mentioned that many private astronomers had turned their telescopes towards the Moon following Wilkins' announcement of the mysterious bridge in 1953. It was inevitable that other anomalies would be observed, and by chance a few reports might find their way into the national press. After Wilkins' and O'Neill's initial disclosure, they were put under pressure to stop talking. The bridge discovery had occurred after the publication of Dr. Wilkins' book, *Our Moon*, in which he had cited the newly observed dome mystery.

It was around this time, Keyhoe learned, that the large observatories were making secret observations of the Moon for the Pentagon. He received confirmation that big-named astronomers were in on it, doing observations at Mt. Palomar and the Naval Observatory, and at other astronomical sites. Saucer bases, and varying types of large scale construction, were confirmed to exist in and around many prominent craters. These were top-secret studies by the Pentagon for the U.S. government. Later, NASA was under the same tight bureaucracy. Does anyone seriously think that the government would relax its control, throw fate to the wind, and allow its subordinate space agency to announce any true findings that they wished to the public?

Those secret studies were done at the giant observatories. The telescope at Mt. Palomar is 200 inches in diameter, the world's largest. Outside of these large observatories, observers had no chance of seeing the building boom or saucer bases. The resolving power of even modest-size telescopes was too limited. And amateur astronomers, with telescopes ranging from 6 to 15 inches in diameter, were virtually using binoculars compared to Mt. Palomar.

Although discernible activity was beyond the range of private equipment, sometimes an effect was large enough to show up as an unexplainable anomaly on the Moon's distant surface. The observances seldom got more than a brief note in astronomical journals, but occasionally a report was picked up by the wire services. It had about as much effect as a UFO sighting report in the newspaper. But the silence group was taking no chances. Although reports made by amateur astronomers were more suggestive than definitive, they could have led to further speculation, and eventually have led to exposure of the secret moon studies, according to Keyhoe. Not realizing that a report would be a concern to a group of censors, private astronomers, in a number of cases, suddenly found themselves contacted by intelligence officers who asked questions and generally confronted them in an intimidating fashion.

But George Adamski's evidence on the Moon was the biggest threat to the censors, because of his well-recognized position in the UFO field. Whereas isolated and little-known astronomical reports of unexplainable lunar phenomena couldn't by themselves provide any real picture of the Moon's environment, Adamski's books were educating the public to information he had gotten first hand from his experiences within the ships. Here was a full picture of the lunar environment. While ordinary astronomy rejected the descriptions as impossible according to long-held theories, the Pentagon silently accepted Adamski's information and *rejected ordinary astronomy*, since the government was sitting on top of full knowledge about UFOs and the secret Moon studies.

A world-wide audience heard the truth about interplanetary visitors and spaceships throughout the 1950's and early 1960's, through the international recognition accorded Adamski. He was treated with much respect by heads of government and influential leaders during the times of his world lecture tours, and in the U.S. he had frequent contact with important men in governmental space industries. Adamski never disclosed confidential information which he often received from scientists, but he realized better than anyone else how much the government had confirmed his own space information early on.

An ongoing coverup was orchestrated by the Silence Group during the space program developments, which insured their plans to fully discredit the reality behind the UFOs. The truth behind the interplanetary UFOs, which had been widely accepted during Adamski's time, was offset and increasingly displaced as time went on, by the false picture of space findings put out by the government. The Silence Group knew that the UFO evidence would become a confusing mystery, and therefore the reality less accepted, after the space agency could develop an "official" lifeless picture of the Moon and planetary environments from minor space probe readings.

The Moon certainly became a fixed picture in the mind of the public, following the six manned missions to the lunar surface from 1969 to 1972. Yet that picture has been challenged by meticulous researchers who found discrepancies and contradictions in NASA's public reports, along with alternate lunar findings, and unpublicized official evidence. Although many books left the coverup penetrated somewhat, they came up short on establishing the true lunar environment. To further break open the coverup, I decided to carefully analyze the telescopic record, which was reviewed in the preceding chapters. With the more recent documentation of unpublicized Apollo findings, it will be possible to discuss the actual climatic environment on the Moon, including the atmospheric density, local temperatures, lunar gravity, and the environmental differences between the near and far sides of the Moon.

Fred Steckling, author of *We Discovered Alien Bases on the Moon*, knew that the telescopic records of selenographers had proved the existence of an atmosphere and water on the Moon. He decided to investigate the available photographic record of Apollo, to find NASA's own confirmation of lunar air and water. Having been a long time pilot, Steckling was exceptionally qualified in examining thousands of aerial photographs from the lunar space missions. He studied these pictures at NASA's Science Data Center in Washington, D.C., and collected many during his patient years of research. Although thousands of Moon photographs were taken, and are technically speaking "available to the public," few, beyond the initial batches of pictures provided for each Apollo mission, have ever been published. Selections from those "initial batches" have been reproduced repeatedly for sporadic magazine articles and general books on the Moon, and this is why the Moon seems so "familiar" to the ordinary person. Perhaps it is now easier to understand how exhaustive the research of Steckling was, in his twelve year investigation of more than 10,000 Apollo and Lunar Orbiter photographs.

In his book Steckling reproduced 125 official NASA photographs, many of which confirmed alien activity on the Moon. Several provided evidence of weather and water on the Moon - clouds and natural lakes in the northern highlands, and what even appear to be artificial reservoirs near craters Plato and Krieger, both long thought to be areas where extraterrestrials have bases.

Although some pictures lack good clarity, and are open to question as Steckling himself admits, many of his pictures are decisively distinct and irrefutable evidence.

Alien activity on the lunar surface, as seen from a 60-mile high orbit, is often difficult to define from NASA's unclassified photos. However, some do seem to show domes, installations, platforms, and other unnatural arrangements in and around crater areas. Sometimes symbols and markings on the surface appear to be associated with these apparent constructions. Many pictures show features indicative of mining operations.

Steckling reproduced a dozen Apollo photographs of UFOs on or near the surface of the Moon, including the remarkable picture of a large cigar-shape craft taken by the Apollo 16 mission, and printed on his bookcover. His research was thorough, and his text well written. By carefully examining the official reports, catalogs, and photographic record, he was able to verify the evidence that extraterrestrials have bases on the Moon. He concluded that our government cut short our Moon exploration program because they found too much up there, or at least all that was necessary for the officials to know. Steckling and others, myself included, believe that after the public Apollo missions, the lunar exploration continued under the complete secrecy of the manned Air Force Space program.

When people think of the Moon, they picture a rocky and dust-covered surface in black and white images. These were the predominate images of the barren Apollo landing sites. Occasionally, some off-shade color pictures were thrown in with the initial batches released to the public, which did little to improve on this overriding perception. Particularly with the early missions, NASA was cultivating a predominate image of the Moon as black and whites, and grays. All the unmanned lunar orbiters photographed in black and white. The Apollo landing sites were near the dawn side of the terminator, and the scenes appear to be in twilight. When the sun is low on the lunar horizon, the ground looks gray in photos. Of course, the lava plains would always look gray.

But in extensive regions of the Moon, the ground appears as brown dirt or natural soil when the sun is overhead. Many color pictures of the backside taken by Apollo show this true color brown, along with different shades of green in and around craters, and covering the highlands. One must search to find these pictures in various books and publications. NASA did release an extensive portfolio confirming the diversity of colors in regional areas of the Moon, which Firsoff and others originally described during their years of telescopic research. For most of its surface, the Moon is a colorful and natural habitat. From the high orbit of Apollo 10, pictures of the panoramic farside are shown in Plates 19 and 20. One can understand why the Apollo 15 crew, upon seeing that our Moon was not barren and gray, exclaimed in their own words: "It is dynamic and beautiful," when rounding the Moon.

Soil brought back from the Apollo landing sites was used in laboratory tests. It was found that some terrestrial plants and vegetables grew "greener and hardier" in lunar soil than in earth soil. When both lunar and earth soils were mixed, an experiment was tried using liverwort seeds. A liverwort plant sprouted from the seeds and grew at four times the ordinary rate. These tests proved that Moon soil is a good source of nutrients and sustains biological activity. A close-up picture of lunar soil at the Apollo 17 site is shown on Plate 16.

This book has discussed evidence for water on the Moon. Steckling's book shows pictures of clouds near crater areas on the lunar surface. As previously noted, early telescopic experts were convinced that they were observing cyclic growth of vegetation in certain crater areas, and staked their astronomical reputations on that conclusion. Of course, they were correct, but if NASA were to publicly confirm it, the complete picture of space would change, and life beyond the Earth would today be on everyone's mind.

There are many complexities in discussing lunar photography. Except for the on-site pictures and films, all

Plate 17. Doppler Crater on the Moon's farside, showing the soft
illumination and shadows of a late lunar evening. (Apollo 17 photo)

Plate 18. Often referred to as "The Lake," crater Tsiolkovsky is a
distinctive feature on the lunar farside that was photographed
extensively during the Apollo missions. (Apollo 13 photo)

Plate 19. The colorful farside of the Moon, as photographed during the Apollo 10 mission.

Plate 20. Another colorful panorama of the Moon's farside, also seen during the Apollo 10 mission.

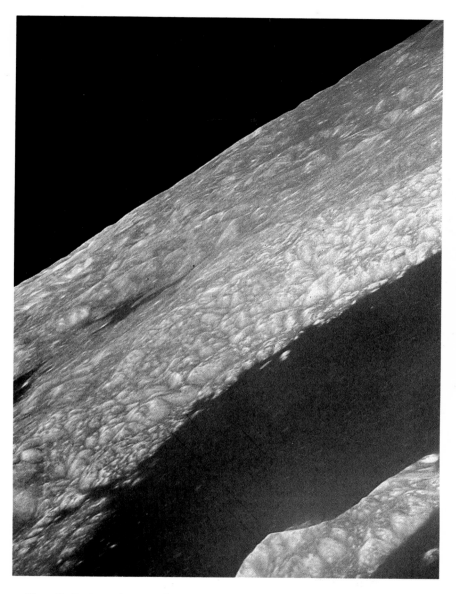

Plate 21. Perhaps the most dramatic portrait of the Moon's farside that has been
publicly released. This Apollo 8 photograph gives a majestic view of the
temperate zone - a regional area on the lunar farside that proves to have a
liveable environment.

Plate 22. Venus (Mariner 10 photo, 1974)

ВЕНЕРА-9   22.10.1975
ПРЕОБРАЗОВАНИЕ 17.01.1976

Plate 23. First picture of the surface of Venus, taken by the Russian
lander Venera 9 (1975).

Plate 24. Single frame from a remarkable 8mm movie film of a Venusian Scoutship that was sighted and filmed by Madeleine Rodeffer at her home in Silver Spring, Maryland, on February 26, 1965. Adamski had been a guest at the Rodeffer home, and he was present the day the film was taken. Madeleine Rodeffer was a close co-worker of Adamski's, and it was during this time that Adamski was lecturing and meeting with government and space officials in the Washington, D.C. area.

Plate 25. An official postal stamp issued in 1977 by Ecuatorial Guinea, honoring Adamski's contributions towards peaceful interplanetary cooperation.

Plate 26. Mercury photo (Mariner 10).

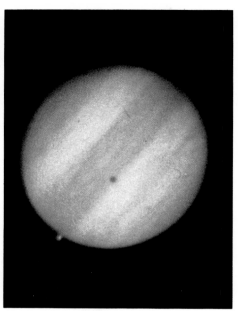

Plate 27. Jupiter (Pioneer 10 photo).

Plate 28. Saturn (Voyager photo).

Plate 29. A NASA drawing showing the known planets of our solar system. In successive orbits from the Sun: Mercury, Venus, Earth (and Moon), Mars, Jupiter, Saturn, Uranus, Neptune, Pluto. Notice the asteroid belt between the orbits of Mars and Jupiter.

Plate 30. The notable UFO books by Scully, Allingham, Cramp, Miller, and Chatelain.

Plate 31. My favorite picture of Albert Einstein, shown here with the Hopi Indians in Arizona.

In this century there have been frequent landing by spacecraft, on the lands of the Native American Indians. Traditionally, their knowledge about the space visitors has been kept secret, and held in sacred reverence by the Indian peoples. I am reminded of the statement by Black Elk, a holy man of the Sioux, referring to the Daybreak Star (Venus) rising in the east... "It shall be a relative to them, and who shall see it, shall see much more, for from there comes wisdom; and those who do not see it shall be dark."

pictures of the Moon were taken from high orbit, about 70 miles up. Astronauts in their Apollo spacecraft photographed about 10% of the lunar far side, and NASA did release some orbital photographs in fair color. A few area photographs show natural browns, prominent greens, and shades of fawn and pink, all in the same picture. But since they were taken with low resolution from high orbit, one cannot positively identify the environmental conditions that produced the color effects in these few examples. The greens in one picture might be related to area vegetation, while greens in another picture wouldn't necessarily mean anything.

Most of the pictures can be said to have exaggerated color schemes and shadings. The source of various color effects are impossible to define, and when viewed from such a high orbit, the Moon appears to have bleak, featureless surroundings. Of course, it was NASA's intent to keep pictures of the Moon ill-defined, particularly those of the far side, beginning with the early black and white photography. Now, the low resolution shots with nebulous colors were just as unsatisfactory. As an explanation, NASA stated that it had difficulty in obtaining accurate surface colors with their orbital photography, due to different film batches and cameras, and various underexposure effects.

However, we are able to compare the lackluster results of the supposedly difficult lunar photography with the superior results of earth photography from early Gemini space flights. Gemini 11, while orbiting 470 miles above Earth, photographed regional areas of our planet in perfect color, and with far greater resolution than NASA's moon pictures. Since Apollo spacecraft were at an orbiting altitude six times closer to the Moon's surface, why was the photographic resolution of lunar pictures not even equal to Gemini pictures? The problems of color may have somewhat believable explanations, but it is obvious that the resolution was kept artificially low for lunar pictures, since camera equipment used on the earlier Gemini flights had proven that better capabilities were available. NASA clearly chose to use camera optics and film which would produce certain desired effects while photographing the Moon.

The little that has been released of the lunar far side is low resolution and nebulous, unless it was a barren crater or inconsequential shot. NASA provided results which instilled the idea that there is not much difference from the Moon's front side. Unlike certain space data, the photographs are not actual fabrications. But since their quality and resolution are so artificially low, the implied, overall picture of the Moon is not genuine.

The release of low resolution Moon photographs with inconsistent colors was all that NASA had to provide. These were readily picked up by the anxious media and disseminated to the public in common magazines, accompanied with write-ups highlighting the undisturbed orthodox theories. Everything seemed to be conveniently confirmed by pictures that wouldn't require a second glance. The scientific community speedily incorporated the pictures into textbooks and other publications, along with their patented orthodox views of the lifeless Moon. The old theories were now published as "scientific truth", and the Moon was history.

NASA simply showed that they went to the Moon, and left public education in the hands of the scientific community, where it had always been. Therefore, the coverup scheme is decidedly simple. The orthodox scientific community does not question NASA's simplistic evidence, any more than they question their own theories, so certainly the public is not going to be questioning anything. While browsing through an occasional magazine article or book, a person will naturally think that he is seeing the latest facts and findings, supported by NASA pictures outlining the text, when in fact he hasn't actually been shown anything new. Just an ongoing and deceptive image, which can be traced all the way back to those deceptive, low-resolution photos from high lunar orbit. The orthodoxers were happy with them, and then beefed up their theories in conservative journals and textbooks. NASA's coverup methods follow a rather routine procedure.

There were contradictory space findings of another

matter that turned up in the scientific literature, and prompted engineer William Brian to investigate the true nature of the Moon's gravity. The results of his careful research was published in 1982, entitled *Moongate: Suppressed Findings of the U.S. Space Program*. His detailed analysis of NASA reports and mathematical data proved that the lunar gravity is much higher than we have been told, and Brian charges that NASA officials continued to publicize the common 1/6 gravity figure in order to perpetuate the airless image of the Moon. The secret gravity findings were learned very early in the lunar exploration program, causing setbacks in plans, and revisions in spacecraft design.

The theory of one-sixth gravity on the Moon has long been based on Newton's Law of Universal Gravitation, which was originally published in 1687. Newton's law holds for bodies *within the gravitational sphere of a single planet*, and it is a proven cornerstone of science, but the extension of this principle to planetary relationships was a modern-day postulate based solely on inductive reasoning. The true gravity on the Moon can only be positively determined by observing the action of falling or orbiting bodies in the Moon's vicinity. When space probes were first launched to the Moon by the United States and Russia, only then was it possible to calculate the surface gravity directly, - by radar tracking each point of the trajectory, and then calculating the actual neutral point distance. This is a point between the Earth and Moon where the force of attraction is equal in both directions. It was mandatory to determine this distance in order to insure safety and success in future missions.

Based on Newton's law, astronomy books and publications had always assigned the neutral point distance to a range between 22,078 and 25,193 miles from the Moon. The difference in the reported figures is due to the elliptical path of the Moon. The lower value is when the Moon is at perigee; the higher value is when at apogee. If the Moon had 1/6 gravity, the neutral point would always lie within that range.

But during the time of the historic Apollo 11 space mission

in 1969, a new neutral point distance was referenced in several sources. The official figure given was 43,495 miles from the Moon, first reported by Time magazine in its July 25th issue, and also in the 1969 book, *History of Rocketry & Space Travel* by Wernher von Braun and Frederick Ordway. Later publications quoted figures from 38,000 to 39,000 miles. Even with the slight inconsistencies in figures, the actual neutral point distance is significantly different from the old astronomy calculations of 22,000 to 25,000 miles.

Since Wernher von Braun was the Director of the Space Flight Center at the time of Apollo 11, he would have been in a position to know the exact figure of 43,495 cited in his book. William Brian states that while the actual neutral point distance didn't show up in public literature until 1969, the space agency must have determined it several years earlier, in order to successfully conduct the Lunar Orbiter and Surveyor probe missions. This means that around 1959 or soon after, NASA knew that the Moon's gravity was much higher than the commonly accepted 1/6 value. But the space agency kept the higher gravity data secret, because it would have seriously undermined the orthodox theories of an airless Moon.

By using the new figures, the Moon's gravity turns out to be 64% of the Earth's surface gravity. Further analysis of Apollo flight times and spacecraft velocities corroborated the high lunar gravity being near 64%. More supportive evidence was added by a thorough examination of the astronauts' performances on the lunar surface. Keep in mind that with the new gravity figure, a 150 lb. man would weigh just about 100 lbs. on the Moon, not 25 lbs. as old theories stated.

According to William Brian, many filmed sequences at the Apollo sites showed that the men and the rover vehicles were definitely operating in high gravity conditions. But these details were not readily apparent on the televised showing, due to a delayed transmission from NASA control center whereby procedural manipulation of the film speed created semi-slow motion effects. For the television viewer, the net result was an exaggerated appearance of jumpy movements and kangaroo steps. Yet it can be clearly seen, that even while running, an astronaut did not step any further, or higher off the ground, than he would have on Earth.

Prior to Apollo, many scientists had predicted that astronauts would be able to perform extraordinary feats in the assumed one-sixth gravity. Whirling leaps and super gymnastic abilities on the Moon were expected. But in fact, the record shows that nothing of the sort occurred. An interesting example is the case of astronaut John Young, who attempted several standing jumps. The event was apparently unplanned, or NASA overlooked something during this filming from the Apollo 16 site. According to common assumptions, John Young should have been able to leap 4 feet in the air if there was one-sixth gravity. But in full view of the camera filming, his vertical jumping distance never exceeded 18 inches, despite several attempts. NASA had the slow-motion effect in operation, but overlooked the vertical height discrepancy.

William Brian devotes a whole chapter to astronaut experiences on the Moon, including their operation of the battery-powered lunar rovers. His competent analysis of the engineering design, and their actual performance on the lunar surface, shows that the vehicles would have been disastrous in a one-sixth gravity environment. A thorough analysis of the on-site operations conducted by the moonwalkers (and drivers) strongly corroborates NASA's earlier disclosure of the revised neutral point distance.

After William Brian's book called attention to the neutral point discrepancy and its implication of a high lunar gravity, NASA spokesmen countered with an argument that scientific writers had correctly noted the revised neutral point for spacecraft journeys, but that in actuality, the gravitational pull between the Earth and Moon was not equal at this point. In other words, a misinterpretation had resulted according to NASA, because the position of the Moon with respect to the spacecraft, along with the relative velocities of the two bodies, had not been taken into consideration. This may have had some validity, except for the fact that other quoted flight characteristics were inconsistent with this explanation. Brian noted that reporters have long tagged NASA, as an abbreviation standing for Never A Straight Answer. He adds that counter arguments and contradictory explanations are standard procedure in order to doubletalk around the inconsistencies. In this case, they do not want to confirm in any way the higher gravity.

Brian did further research and found a NASA document for Apollo 16 that cited a neutral point distance of 60,887 miles, which if taken alone, would indicate an even higher lunar gravity than previous computations. Whenever the space agency is trying to withhold or hide something of monumental importance, research shows that NASA data is inherently contradictory. Not only with the Moon, but with all the space projects on Mars and Venus too.

NASA employed very specialized procedures for relaying filmed activity from the Moon to television viewers. This had been carefully planned, because pictures have an overwhelming effect in conditioning the public. The semi-slowmotion speeds created the illusion of low gravity, which at the same time, reinforced the belief of an airless Moon. This was the lasting impression, despite all the contradictory information in print.

Aside from his careful documentation on the neutral point discrepancy, William Brian analyzed evidence from every aspect of the lunar missions, and concluded that the Moon's gravity lies definitely between 50% to 80% of the Earth's gravity. Since his original calculation of 64% is half way between those two values, I will continue to cite that value for later discussions. Brian's competent research should be studied by serious students of space science, since his book details many other suppressed findings of the U.S. space program.

The confirmed high gravity on the Moon carries major implications. It is time for astronomy to finally take a back seat to space sciences, for conventional physics no longer has its Jeans theory to explain away the lunar atmosphere. Close-mindedness and public deception has had its day, or long night of darkness if you will. New scientific logic will bring out the truth of space sciences and the actual conditions on the Moon, - a planet which can and does support life.

George Adamski frequently emphasized some basic concepts about the Moon, regarding the necessity of an atmosphere. He stated that in order for any planetary form to retain its shape, the inside and outside pressures must be equal. Atmosphere surrounding a body in space furnishes the pressure necessary to keep that form from exploding or disintergrating. Enormous pressures are built up within all planets, yet the atmosphere surrounding them offsets this by exerting a perfect balance of pressure from without. If the Moon did not have an atmosphere, it would have broken up and disintegrated into space long ago.

Being a smaller body, the Moon has a comparatively lighter atmosphere. Yet it is not so light that human beings from Earth and other planets could not acclimate themselves to its environment. This information was confirmed directly to Adamski by the space visitors, and it was explained that they used a process of depressurization requiring 24 hours, if they wished to land and disembark from their ships. Human lungs are able to adjust themselves to very low as well as high pressure, and we would find the lunar air very clean and breatheable.

It was not until 1965 that George Adamski gave a figure for the atmospheric pressure on the Moon. He had been informed by the space people that it was 6 pounds per square inch. This figure is 40% of our sea level pressure of 14.7 pounds per square inch, and appears to be quite proportional to the NASA evidence of 64% surface gravity.

Another very important condition results from the comparatively high density. An atmospheric blanket of that density would greatly moderate the temperatures all around the Moon. The sunlit side would not be as hot as (airless) theories suggested, nor would the nightside be as cold, since the presence of atmosphere would temper the loss of previously trapped heat. Plus there would be constant mixing along the terminator, and general movement of unevenly heated air between the latitudes due to incident angle absorption. Local climatic conditions would generate regional winds.

The abrupt changes in temperature during a lunar eclipse, measured by earth-based thermocouples, can now be reassessed. When the Moon passes into the Earth's shadow, a sudden drop in temperature is recorded over the shadowed portion of the Moon. Astronomers have stated that the surface temperature drops rapidly because they assumed the Moon had no atmosphere. But what they were actually measuring was the abrupt change in molecular kinetic energy of an upper-level atmospheric layer, which was in the Earth's shadow and temporarily shielded from the sun.

This layer is the Moon's ionosphere. Its activity is directly related to illumination by the sun. The layer over the sunlit hemisphere is high in kinetic energy, while the other half facing away from the sun is very low in kinetic energy. The molecular activity in this layer changes rapidly with respect to sun illumination (or lack of), whereas the lunar surface temperature changes gradually due to the dense shielding of the lower atmosphere. The extreme temperature differences thought to exist on the Moon between the day and night hemispheres were erroneous measurements of the Moon's ionosphere. The temperatures at the Apollo sites were distorted in NASA reports, in keeping with the conventional and theoretical Moon taught by astronomy.

This ionosphere was detected with the first successful rocket to the Moon by the Russians in 1959. Aviation Week magazine carried the scientific report, and at that time quoted scientist John Townsend's comment that the discovery of an ionosphere above the Moon was very significant. He stated, "The detection of an ionosphere at a relatively high distance from the Moon means that the Moon has a definite atmosphere, a condition that a few scientists could only guess at before."

In light of all the preceding information, acclimation to the lunar environment by humans can now be discussed. It should be perfectly logical when compared to the Earth. Take for example, the people living in the highlands of Tibet, and those living at 16,000 feet elevation in the Peruvian Andes. Any meteorology textbook will inform us that they are living in an environment of .6 atmospheric density. This is 60% of sea level atmospheric pressure. Gravity on the surface of the Earth is a standard constant of 1 g.

Using the new space findings of 6 lbs atmospheric pressure and 64% gravity on the Moon, the relative values can be shown in a simple chart.

	EARTH (sea level)	ANDES & TIBET (elevation 16,000')	MOON (temperate zone)
Gravity	1 g (100%)	1 g (100%)	.64 g (64%)
Atmospheric Pressure in lbs./in^2	15 (100%)	9 (60%)	6 (40%)

We know that the natives of Tibet and the Andes live comfortably and work normally, in 1 g gravity and the lower air pressure of 9 lbs/in^2. And that if a healthy city traveler were to journey to one of these habitations, he would experience unusual fatigue and some discomfort initially, but within a week or two, the body would naturally acclimate itself to the new environment.

Now consider that people in habitable areas on the Moon would be living in .64 g and 6 lbs air density. Living and working in lower gravity would require less force to oppose gravity, hence less oxygen needed by humans. The lungs will inflate normally, given a proportional balance between gravity and atmosphere pressure. Using the chart, let's compare that relationship for both the Moon and the habitable Andes, using Earth sea level as a standard.

$$\frac{\text{air density (Andes)}}{\text{gravity (Andes)}} = \frac{60\%}{100\%} = .60 \qquad \frac{\text{air density (Moon)}}{\text{gravity (Moon)}} = \frac{40\%}{64\%} = .60$$

It is an established fact on Earth, that human habitations

can extend to an environment that provides 60% of normal sea level pressure with respect to gravity. This same environmental condition of 60% exists on the Moon with respect to its *reduced* gravity.

These simple relationships only provide a reasonable basis for showing that acclimation is feasible. A specialized procedure of depressurization for 24 hours is required according to Adamski's information, since going to the Moon would initially be a more dramatic change to the body, than going to the Andes from 100% sea level Earth conditions. But as our scientists know, the human lungs are able to adjust themselves to very low as well as high pressures, if changes are not done too quickly. An example with which we are most familiar is deep sea divers who must slowly depressurize when returning to the surface. A quick ascent can be fatal.

In fact, the astronauts traveling to the Moon were in an odd combination. The cabin pressure was adjusted to 5 lbs/in^2 of pure oxygen, and when they chose to, they removed their spacesuits. While in space, they were in a zero gravity condition too. So the lungs functioned well at 5 pounds and 0 g. Before they could exit the Lunar Module at the landing site, it was said that the LM cabin was depressurized to .2 psi, in order to safely open the hatch to the lunar "vacuum". But we can properly reinterpret that procedure, and be more specific; pressurizing or depressurizing the cabin to .2 psi *differential* with the Moon's atmospheric pressure.

Life that is indigenous to the Moon, including animal and vegetation, would be naturally adapted to the lunar conditions. Acclimatization is only necessary for people and animal life coming from a planet of higher gravity, and after proper procedures, the same would be comfortably accustomed to the Moon's 40% atmosphere. Naturally, there would be a tendency and a desire to live in the most favorable climatic areas on the Moon also.

Just like the Earth, at any given time half the Moon has daylight from the sun, and the other half is in darkness. At full Moon, the entire front side has daylight, while the far side has a lunar night. At New Moon, the situation is reversed. At a quarter phase, both sides of the Moon are half in day and half in night.

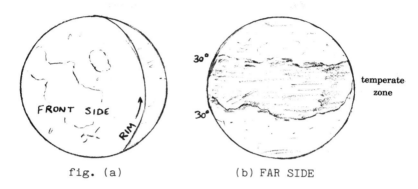

fig. (a)   (b) FAR SIDE

The above drawings can help clarify a little about the differences between the Moon's two hemispheres, or "sides." Because of its synchronous orbit, we on Earth always see the same hemisphere of the Moon. We have called that the front side, or near side. Our six manned missions to the Moon all landed on the front side, so that the astronauts would not be cut off from radio communication with Earth. The Moon's far side is always facing away from the Earth, and has only been seen from spacecraft orbiting the Moon. The circumferential edge between the front and far sides when viewed from the Earth is called the rim.

The front side of the Moon is rugged and covered with vast expanses of desert, as can be seen through earth-based telescopes. It is generally hot when under the direct rays of the sun, but the temperatures are not as extreme as our scientists think. Further away from the equatorial zones, the temperature regularly decreases due to the incident angle of the sun's rays.

Figure (a) is a drawing of a view from space, where most of the front side is seen, and a small portion of the far side. This enables the reader to get a perspective on the two hemispheres relative to the Earth. The temperatures on both sides vary with position of the Sun and with respect to latitude, although we have learned that it is generally cooler on the far side.

The Moon's far side had always been a mystery to man because it cannot be seen from Earth. In 1959 a Russian space probe returned the first few pictures showing the hemisphere's basic image. Later probes by both the U.S. and Russia mapped the broad features of the far side, but because of the controlled way in which space information is given to the public, the far side has still not been fully revealed, if we only consider official sources.

Through his space contacts, George Adamski was able to reveal that the Moon's far side has a very different climate and topography than that seen on the front side. Beyond the rim lies a temperate zone - a part of the Moon that provides a liveable environment. Figure (b) shows the far side and the approximate latitude range of the temperate zone. Now that we are certain of the Moon having an atmosphere, it's quite possible to find an average temperature of 60°- 80° here in the lunar day, and perhaps dropping to 30°- 50° during the lunar night. Highlands would be comparatively cooler all the time.

We should not expect that the temperate zone would be totally uniform. In other words, regional differences in topography would make some portions very habitable, but other territories less so. Just as in California, where only 60 miles separate Death Valley Desert from Sequoia National Park, an area rich in forests and lakes.

The temperate zone of the lunar far side became the final objective of my research on the Moon. The only source material available is the orbital photographs from space missions which have been released to the public by NASA. These of course, were released following complete screening and heavy censoring by the space agency, so few pictures could be considered detailed photographs. And the evidence provided by orbital pictures is hampered by the problems of low resolution and color image, as discussed previously.

Obtaining these pictures required much time and effort, but it was a very interesting part of the research. This resulted in my finding a number of provocative photographs of the lunar far side. Generally, these were oblique shots of areas which lie within the boundaries of the temperate zone. Perhaps the best photograph released was one taken by the first manned trip to the Moon. This Apollo 8 photograph is shown in Plate 21.

Taken of an area near Tsiolovsky crater, the picture gives the startling appearance of green forests and lakes, surrounded by pale golden mountains. The foreground of the picture is a portion of Tsiolovsky Crater. I am not certain what astronomers thought about this photo, or if the general scientific community ever knew it was released and made available. But I feel that the picture provides a substantial hint of real conditions on the far side, something that black and white photography never could do.

Although hundreds of detailed photographs were taken of the lunar far side, few of these have been publicly released. NASA has not provided definitive evidence to support even their own public statements regarding the far side. They have only created an image, and left the orthodox theories intact. However, we know that the official record is full of contradictions, as proven by the books of Firsoff, Steckling, Brian, and others. For me, the rather majestic panorama shown in Plate 21, has a fundamental appearance that hints at the reality of the temperate zone. It would seem certain that this picture mirrors, in its way, the actual conditions NASA found on the far side, which today remains classified evidence.

It is time that the final evidence and truth goes on record. Up to this point, the documented history of telescopic observations has been presented, along with a scientific discussion establishing the Moon's atmosphere, water, vegetation, gravity, and UFO activity. It is in the temperate zone on the lunar far side where the first four factors come together and provide optimal conditions. The 6 lb density atmosphere regulates the sun's energy, providing medium temperatures on the Moon. Along with the Moon's life supporting water, an almost Earthlike environment exists. Adamski's earlier information explained that we from

Earth could live there in the temperate zone - the only necessity was a controlled process of depressurization for acclimation to 40% atmosphere.

George Adamski was shown the Moon's far side, while he was on a Venusian spaceship in August 1954. Again, the Moon's surface was viewed by the use of advanced telescopic instrumentation. After showing Adamski the type of clouds forming near the Moon's rim, his space friend said:

> "Now we are approaching the side never seen from Earth. Look at the surface directly below us. See, there are mountains in this section. You can even see snow on the peaks of the higher ones, and a growth of heavy timber on the lower slopes. On this side of the Moon are a number of mountain lakes and rivers. You can see one of the lakes below. The rivers empty into a very large body of water."

Then it was shown where a number of communities dotted the countryside, both in the valleys and on the mountain slopes. "Preferences of people here, as anywhere else, vary in regard to living at one or another altitude," his friend said. "Here (on the Moon), as elsewhere, the natural activities to support life are very similar to those wherever mankind is found."

The telescopic instrumentation was then used to show a fair sized city. The projection was so close-up, that Adamski could see the central section of the city, and people on the streets. Vehicles similar to buses were serving as conveyances. It was confirmed also, that large ships would often land just outside the city, to bring in supplies to the population, in exchange for minerals mined by the local inhabitants.

This then is the temperate zone - a section around the center of the Moon's far side in which vegetation, trees, and lakes exist. It is an environment where nature, animals, and man co-exist. The Earth and its satellite are really a double planet in this third orbital position from the Sun.

Orthodox thinking had for a long time cast derision upon George Adamski for his published descriptions of the lunar far side. The complete Moon evidence in this book has finally established the validity of Adamski's claims, and it turns out that the Moon is his strongest point! And actually had set him apart from the detractors, false experts, and fraudulent contactees who could not present the astounding truth about the Moon, because they never knew the truth. For years, their lack of knowledge about the Moon seemed to work in their favor, because they did not come into conflict with orthodoxy in this case.

The Earth/Moon system is widely regarded as a double planet because the Moon is so much larger than any other satellite is, in size relation to its parent planet. Its diameter is 2160 miles, and the surface area is 14 million square miles, or about one fourth the actual land area on Earth. Its surface area would equal the combined land areas of Europe, South America, and Australia.

We can see that the Moon is a sizeable habitat, and a fair-sized planet. The space people rightly view it as another mansion, or liveable world, like the other planets in the solar system. Of course, there is open acceptance, communication, and travel between other planets and the Moon. It is only the Earth, in its egotistical rebellion against the thought of life elsewhere, that has a self-imposed separation from this interplanetary cooperation.

NASA discovered what was on the far side, as well as what was on the front side, but could not reveal or even hint at life beyond the Earth. They had to fabricate Moon data and suppress the truth. The whole space program was really a military operation from the start. Not in the sense of conquering the Moon, but by advancing our military technology to the point of ruling the Earth. Before Apollo 8 went to the Moon in 1968, the U.S. had already launched 450 orbiting satellites, and 340 had military purposes.[1] The Soviet Union was doing the same. The public relations image of the Moon adventure was necessary to prop-up public support for the space program, but it was not designed to deliver the truth. NASA's complicity in denying the reality of the Moon was forced by the economic interests which internationally control governments.

The truth is, that the space visitors and the people on the Moon live in peace. Should our governments reveal this, they would also have to inform the public about the propulsion systems of the UFOs. The spacecraft utilize the natural electromagnetic energy that exists in space and in the atmosphere around a planet. By using this free energy, any community could supply all heat, electricity, and transportation needs of its population, without the services of the fuel and electric companies. This is why the truth about UFOs and the Moon has been suppressed. The authorities fear that this information would ruin the stock market system, leading to an economic collapse.

The space visitors' use of free electromagnetic propulsion brings up another point for discussion. Their space craft fly silently using Nature's own forces. They actually operate on pro-gravity principles, by resonating with the natural electromagnetic and gravity fields. This demonstrates real wisdom and knowledge, whereas we fight gravity, by "blasting" off.

Even before the space agency was formed, Adamski had predicted that man would be able to get to the Moon by artificially overcoming gravity with rockets. But, he added, that is as far as man would get. Man couldn't go further, because he wouldn't be able to get back. Not until he could develop a true spaceship that used Nature's forces for propulsion.

Personally, I think that it was good we stopped going to the Moon after the six front-side landings, for two reasons. The first is that we weren't being told the truth anyway. And secondly, we needed to develop a much more efficient method of space flight. To blast a tiny payload of three men towards the Moon, the 36-story Saturn 5 rocket had to develop 7.5 million pounds of thrust at lift-off, creating air shock and sound waves equivalent to nuclear bombs exploding. Birds were knocked dead out of the air. The ground shook like a powerful earthquake, as though a final cataclysm was at hand. Chemical fires and dense smoke covered the launch site. All rocket hardware was used and destroyed in giving one shot towards the Moon. That is not true space travel.

The government may have had information on the Moon's back side before the beginning of the space age. There is a chance that the large observatories got a slight peek of the far side temperate zone, back when they did secret studies of the Moon. Although the same side always faces the Earth, the complexities of the Moon's orbit allows us to see more than 50% of the lunar surface over a period of time. This is due to three major orbital motion effects known as librations. The net result is that 59% of the lunar surface can be seen from the Earth. It is possible that the giant telescopes, such as the 200-inch Palomar, could discern different surface effects beyond the normal eastern and western rims of the Moon. We know that they could resolve the effects of artificial base operations on the front side, but they may have seen hints of habitation beyond the rim also.

George Adamski provided some final details about the Moon during a discussion of space age philosophy in 1955. He stated that the people living on the Moon were originally brought there from other planets ages ago. He added that the Moon had been populated for a long time, and quite naturally, people are born there. The Moon is a regular habitable planet in this system.

From his very first meeting with the interplanetary space visitors, Adamski learned that the human form is universal. People are no different anywhere in the Cosmos, except for mental developments and society growth (scientific). This is equally true on the Moon - a companion world in this third orbit from the Sun.

Some Reflections

I felt a little sadness when this journey of research on the Moon was over. It had been a joyous adventure for four months, as I searched for books and documents, read copious amounts of literature, studied hundreds of Moon pictures, and then sifted out the true evidence. Though I thought that I knew a few things about the Moon in previous years, prior to this research I had seen but a glimpse of her mysteries. But in the pursuit of the puzzle pieces, I quickly grew to love the Moon, and now feel I have come to know her closely.

I am indebted to George Adamski, for without the information in *Inside the Spaceships*, there would have been no impetus to my quest.

- To V.A. Firsoff, for his telescopic genius.
- To all the selenologists and amateur astronomers who got their worthy observations into print.
- To the recent Moon experts, Fred Steckling and William Brian, both of whom pointed out important directions.

I should like to thank NASA too. For although they made it extremely difficult – in the final analysis, it would not have been possible to corroborate George Adamski's experiences, without finding their spurious revelations and scattered hints at reality.

Chapter 9
The Truth about Venus

By the early 1960's, following years of increasing reports on UFO activity in our skies, the idea that Venus had a habitable environment was becoming more and more acceptable in the minds of the public, and in the theories of notable space scientists. Astronomy had always referred to Venus as the twin planet of our Earth, since both planets were nearly equal in size and each had a cloudy atmosphere. But our sister planet was continually covered with a thick blanket of clouds, and the surface conditions on Venus remained a mystery to earth-bound observers. Some scientists reasoned that although the orbit of Venus was closer to the sun, her perpetual cloud cover reflected a large portion of the sun's energy, thus making the surface temperatures very Earth-like.

In November 1959, scientists working for the U.S. Navy and John Hopkins University sent up a stratospheric balloon to an altitude of 16 miles to study Venus. Infra-red readings determined that there was five times more water vapor above the Venusian clouds than above the corresponding high clouds over Earth. In 1960, a spectrographic study by American and Soviet scientists provided further data on the Venusian atmosphere. By observing Venus during its crescent phase, they did a spectrum analysis of the night glow, or "ashen light", which is often very noticeable over the nighttime portion of the hemisphere. The study revealed the presence of both nitrogen and atomic oxygen in the planet's atmosphere. The night glow over the darkened hemisphere was directly attributed to the atomic oxygen. The Earth has the same characteristic element in the upper level of its atmosphere. Normal oxygen (O_2) is disassociated by short-wave solar radiation into single-atom oxygen.

The British space expert V.A. Firsoff remarked that a planetary atmosphere could not retain such an active element as oxygen over a period of time, unless it were constantly replenished from some source such as photosynthesis in green plants. He added that its presence on Venus in apparent abundance constituted strong evidence for life there. Firsoff further reasoned that Venus' magnetic field would tend to keep the bulk of the diatomic oxygen (O_2) in the atmosphere below the clouds, and if there were a permanent inversion of temperatures on Venus, as it seemed likely, carbon dioxide would naturally diffuse upwards across that inversion line, since carbon dioxide is known to be an efficient absorber of radiant energy. With the air being warmer above the clouds than immediately below them, and because the stratosphere around Venus would characteristically lack vertical air currents, the carbon dioxide would be trapped in the upper regions. Firsoff concluded that the air below the clouds of Venus could be much like our own.[1]

Included in the scientific article just referenced, was a descriptive picture showing apparent snow-caps at the poles, based on telescopic observations of Venus with the aid of specialized filters. Although the evidence was tentative, the apparent existence of polar caps was consistent with the recent confirmation of water vapor in the Venusian clouds, and with the explanations for a permanent temperature inversion in the atmosphere. Firsoff summarized his scientific discussion by stating that Venus might well be an "abode of life" at least as comfortable as the Earth.

In 1960 a similar view was given by Dr. Edward G. Pendray, the founder of the American Rocket Society. This scientist stated: "Venus may turn out to be a wonderful place to live. We don't know much about its surface, because we can't see it. But it is about the same size as Earth and nearer to the sun. It may be like Florida all over."

Many space researchers shared these views regarding the Venus environment. However, at the same time, a very different school of thought had developed within the orthodox scientific community. It was based on an astronomical report by Cornell H. Mayer, following a study at the Naval Research Laboratory in 1956. Mayer had made some calculated measurements of the upper atmosphere of Venus, and deduced that the temperature was more than 550 degrees. It was known that the upper atmosphere contained an appreciable amount of carbon dioxide, and conservative scientists predictably envisioned a colossal "green-house" environment for Venus. Their theory provided that the incoming sunlight reaching the surface was converted to longer thermal wavelengths of energy. Then, trapped by the abundant carbon dioxide, these thermal wavelengths could not escape the atmosphere. Therefore, they reasoned, the surface should even be hotter. The orthodox scientists quickly escalated the idea of a hot planet to unprecedented levels, and assigned boiling surface temperatures to Venus. Textbooks were rewritten along these lines.

A school child certainly could not contest this theory that was taught as fact. But for a long time during this period, there was much debate in the scientific community regarding this simple, unproven theory. There were questions as to whether the upper level atmosphere readings had anything to do with temperatures radiating from the surface, or whether they were completely independent from surface conditions. Were the temperature readings actually indicating heat, or were they a measurement of kinetic energy in the upper atmosphere bands due to activation of atomic particles by the solar wind?

Years afterwards, space probes launched around Earth found that our planet had varying temperature bands in our atmosphere. At 100 miles altitude, the temperature was found to be 700°. At 150 miles, 1260°. At 400 miles, 1300°. These thermal bands were identified as regions of kinetic temperatures, and not heat as we commonly understand it. Since it is not "boiling" on the Earth's surface, it is now logical to conclude that the orthodox theory of Venus was based on an inaccurate interpretation of Mayer's ambiguous findings.

Cornell Mayer's report had gotten much of the attention in 1956, but two other important reports on Venus were made that same year following astronomical studies at Ohio State University. Dr. John D. Kraus, considered to be the world's leading authority in radio astronomy, had determined from radio observations that Venus' daily rotation on its axis was nearly the same rate of rotation as the Earth's. His measurements indicated that the length of the Venusian day was about 22.3 hours.[2] Dr. Kraus based his calculation on the observed periodical fluctuation of normal radio "noise" emitted from Venus. These radio waves are perfectly natural in origin.

The Sun and stars emit this long wavelength of energy, as part of their total electromagnetic spectrum that includes visible light, infrared energy, ultraviolet, x-rays, gamma rays, and radio waves. In the case of planets, such as Venus, they absorb a portion of the radio wave energy they receive from the Sun, and then reradiate a smaller portion of that energy at other wavelengths. Thus each planet emits it own unique radio "noise."

But it was during these radio observations to determine the length of the Venusian day, that Dr. Kraus detected other radio signals originating from Venus, which, because of their uniform pattern and amplitude modulation, completely resembled the radio wave broadcast of an earthly radio-telegraph transmitting station. This was such an astounding discovery that Dr. Kraus conducted numerous observations in order to confirm that these signals were originating from Venus. Three scientists working for the U.S. Naval Research Laboratory announced that they had also been receiving these intelligent signals coming from our neighboring planet.[3]

It was then that a news report was carried by the Associated Press. Major Keyhoe's book, *Flying Saucers: Top Secret*, printed a verbatim copy of this press story, which began with the statement - 'An American astronomer thinks there could be a radio telegraph transmitting station on the planet Venus...' The signals received were completely distinct and separate from the common Venus radio noise accompanying the reception.

After the AP story came out, it seems that Dr. Kraus was paid a visit by government men, for he then stopped talking.[4] His subsequent scientific papers written for the American Astronomical Society, though providing descriptive details of measurements, took on a conservative tone that consequently made little impression on scientists. The government had stopped Dr. Kraus from talking, just as it had stopped Dr. Slipher's (Mars Patrol) definitive findings from becoming public press reports, and just the same as it had confined the early Moon observations (of surface changes) to secrecy at the large observatories.

Agencies for the Department of Defense were always at the forefront to intervene, whenever unmistakable findings of life and intelligence in our solar system threatened to emerge in the new adolescent era of sophisticated astronomy. Aided by the heavy minds of orthodoxy, which were always on guard to contradict new thoughts and categorize controversial reports as 'impossible', the government agencies were out to insure that no *incontestable* scientific report (of intelligence on the Moon, Mars, or Venus) became public knowledge. Random anomalies which only lightly suggested possibilities were not a major concern, for throughout the modern history of astronomy, these type of observations never really challenged conventional thinking - and often they were, in part, compatible with orthodox theories.

In the late 1950's, official sources were losing some of their credibility in denying the evidence for UFO sightings around the Earth, and their public censorship was having limited effect. Too many reports were constantly in the press, and too many books had been written documenting the cumulative evidence. A number of scientists were intelligent enough to be aware of the solid UFO evidence behind the official smokescreen. UFOs were known to be real, despite all farfetched arguments to the contrary by hardened skeptics, and intelligent men of science were approaching planetary astronomy with a new perspective. Astronomical distances still left planetary questions at the extreme edge of resolution (and consequent debate), and the orthodox theories about the Moon and Mars still seemed to carry the day, - but no common theories about Venus could be defended without a big question mark in their conclusion.

Therefore in the early 1960's, the debate over the surface conditions on Venus still had two sides - those thinking the planet hot, and those thinking that it had a habitable earth-like environment below the clouds. Fifteen years of UFO sighting reports had stimulated public interest in space, and seemed to parallel the new astronomical probing of the near planets. Discussions varied in opinion, but by 1962, many people in society accepted that UFOs were interplanetary space vehicles. Likewise, Venus was becoming more accepted as the planetary origin of these space vehicles that were being seen and reported world-wide.

And by this time, George Adamski was standing center-stage in the UFO field as far as public recognition. The three books which he authored had been published in many world languages. His clear photographs of Venusian spacecraft had also been published world-wide. During extensive lecture tours around the world, Adamski had been received by several government leaders and officials, which, in its unpretentious way, was respectful recognition that Adamski was our first ambassador to outer space. His public position in the space field was well known, and he had done much to educate the world to the truth behind the flying saucers. Adamski's information on space was the definitive evidence for life in this solar system.

Adamski knew fully well the limitations of our own space knowledge. The saucers were here and man would be arguing for years as to their origin, until the space program had advanced far enough to settle the question. And who was to say, if and when the correct answers would be forthcoming? For with the first true report of another planet's environment - confirmed by the government's own space authorities - the world would not be going back to "business as usual" the next day. And as Adamski emphasized, the space people were here not only to alert us to their existence on other planets, but to help us develop a realistic, scientific, and philosophical knowledge of the Cosmos.

Many people in privileged positions of power and wealth weren't ready to allow that to happen, because it would break down the false social and economic barriers of our society. Their agents in the Silence Group worked overtime to plant stories in the press, so that the public would tend to associate UFOs with psychic claims, fraudulent contactees, and crackpot ideas. That was the interpretation that those behind the coverup wanted to cultivate in the minds of the public.

The Silence Group had prevailed in maintaining the government's tight security lid on UFOs, and because of the new developments in the field of space astronomy, it was equally necessary to censor realistic space findings, while pointedly propping up the theories of hard-bound orthodoxy. These steps had to be rigidly executed until the newly-formed government space agency (NASA) became a functional operation, which could, during its early struggling attempts at space shots, be used as an authoritative vehicle to officially deny the saucer origins. But by the late 1950's, that new stage of censorship was still a few years away.

Throughout the 1950's and early 1960's, the Silence Group and its agents had been able to curtail speculation on Mars and the Moon, by censoring the tentative evidence emerging from studies by a few perceptive astronomers. Conservative science, with its regular orthodox theories, provided a made-to-order case against the UFO origins, despite the increasing public realization that visiting spaceships were here. But cloud-covered Venus was a major problem for the censors. The orthodox theories regarding it were not quite as convincing, or seemingly absolute, and Venus was therefore becoming logically accepted as the planetary origin of the visiting spaceships. After all, tens of thousands of UFO sightings and accounts had been reported world-wide over fifteen years. Like any field, bogus reports and false interpretations had entered the controversy, but despite the added confusion, a sizeable part of society understood UFOs to be real, and Venus the origin of the spaceships.

The government could do nothing to stop this growing acceptance back then, or so it seemed. And all the censors could do was anxiously bide their time, and punctuate their public relations on the "UFO problem" with the viewpoints of selected conservative scientists. But there was not really any major cause for concern. Despite what a growing number may believe (or be perceived as believing), such citizenry is never organized.

The government, like any major institution or corporation, is organized, and could establish orthodox scientific views as official, using the media to indoctrinate the mass public. In due time, the censors knew that they would be able to effectively erode the widening acceptance of UFO reality, once a space probe could be launched out somewhere towards the vicinity of Venus. With a few predetermined results, transformed into "registered readings" by the tiny probe, Venus could be "officially proven" to be uninhabitable. Predictably, conservative scientists would effusively remark on how smart they had been all along, and a certain arrogance in space science thinking would soon set in. (Do you think censors don't understand human psychology?)

By 1962, organized opposition to the truth (regarding UFO reports in general, the reliable accounts of contact with saucers landing on Earth, and all indications of life elsewhere) was now fully positioned to prevent the release of accurate planetary findings. People could talk about flying saucers or spaceships all they wanted, but the opposition would never allow the government's space agency to confirm the reality by announcing habitable conditions on solar planets. The point in fact, was to present a completely opposite picture, in order to undermine the UFO evidence. Powerful economic forces and energy controllers were behind the cryptocracy to falsify the UFO reality and institutionalize confusion regarding space. The confusion about space conditions is now paramount, today. The roots of this situation can be dated to 1962.

It was in that year that the United States launched it's first successful interplanetary probe. Previous probes to the Moon had all failed in their missions, presumably because the (then unknown) high lunar gravity with its bigger gravitational field had thrown off NASA's calculated trajectories for the probes. So the first space shot to successfully send back signals to Earth was the Mariner 2 probe to Venus in late 1962. But it was only a brief flyby that passed Venus at a distance of 21,594 miles.

In February 1963, two months after the Mariner 2 mission, NASA gave a news conference in Washington, D.C., to give a report of the mission's findings. The space agency stated what had to be said to dispel the public belief in spaceships from Venus. After dotting their discussion with some technical and high-sounding jargon, the government spokesmen gave this overriding summary to the newspaper reporters: "The surface temperature on Venus is 800°F. There is no life-supporting water. The planet is intolerably hot, dotted with molten lakes, perpetually darkened by clouds, non-magnetic, and rotating imperceptibly slowly on its axis."

NASA spokesmen were now in the business of conducting the disinformation program for the Silence Group, which was by then, fully positioned to stop the truth behind the flying saucers. The public statements on Venus were a calculated and expedient deception, planned from the beginning. Not only did the mission preclude objectivity from the start, there was no realistic basis for any of the post-mission descriptions about Venus, and that fact was voiced loudly by a few independent scientists. The Mariner 2 probe had very limited capabilities in electronic censoring; as a first, it had to be considered experimental in the unknown zones of space, and the few feeble signals returned from many millions of miles during a momentary flyby were not hardly in the category of definitive findings. The probe did not "see" anything - it only gave a few, limited signals for subjective and debatable interpretations.

The British space expert V.A. Firsoff commented that the NASA report was not a scientific report, but simply "a journalistic hand-out, rather sensational in parts and containing obvious errors...The data (on Venus) remain unknown. We have only interpretations, which appear to be wildly improbable. Interpretations are based on the assumptions made, and if interpretations are improbable one must look for errors in the assumptions, which again are unknown."[5]

Firsoff provided an example of the contradictions in the report. The probe was supposed to distinguish between atmospheric and surface temperatures by means of absorption by water vapor, which stops certain wavelengths of microwave radio emission and transmits others. NASA stated that no water vapor was found, but claimed that surface temperature readings were obtained by using this analytical method in order to differentiate from atmospheric readings.

In the U.S., other noted scientists, such as Dr. John Strong and Dr. Charles Maney, allowed that the first interplanetary probe to reach a destination and send back signals was a remarkable accomplishment, but at the same time, they rejected the interpretations provided by official sources.[6] Studies by astrophysicists had presented reliable evidence to the effect that the atmosphere of Venus was very much like the Earth's, and it had to be taken into consideration that the Mariner 2 probe had passed Venus at a distance of more than 21,000 miles. So the claimed temperature of the surface of Venus was at best, only a speculation. Or in reality, a pre-planned announcement, to extinguish the UFO connection.

The government knew that the public and the general scientific community will always accept the official statements over the more astute investigations of a few experts, in the case that the latter are even heard about. The government can flood the media with its "official" findings. The effect of the Mariner 2 report was catastrophic, and complete. The desired aim had been achieved. The censors had never been able to bury or completely debunk the earthly UFO evidence, but they were now in the driver's seat of a vehicle (NASA) that could discredit the *reality* behind the visiting UFOs, by making Venus appear to be an impossibly inhospitable place. The case was seemingly closed, and for several years the planet was almost ignored as a serious target for space exploration because of the temperature cited in the official report. In fact, 12 years' time would have passed before another U.S. space probe flew by Venus (as an added bonus to the 1974 Mariner probe to Mercury), except for an incidental decision in the mid-1960's.

After launching a flyby probe out towards Mars in 1964, NASA was committed to its program of getting a man to the Moon. Further planetary studies were hampered by budgetary problems, and a future mission to Mars, scheduled for 1969, seemed to be in jeopardy at the time. During this period, the Soviet Union was pursuing a vigorous space exploration program, and had sent four probes out to Venus during the mid-1960's. In November 1965, a Russian probe reached Venus and made an impact landing on the surface. It was the first spacecraft from Earth to impact on another planet.

NASA was now embarrassingly behind, and what was worse, it looked like several years would pass before another interplanetary venture could be fitted into the budget. So within a month after the Russian accomplishment, NASA changed gears in its space exploration program. There was an unused Mariner probe, leftover in storage from the Mars program, and NASA ordered Jet Propulsion Laboratory to take it out of mothballs and re-rig it for a Venus flight. The decision was made to send the probe towards Venus, because it would be easier, cheaper, and quicker than a Mars trip.[7] Launch date was set for June 1967.

In 1966 two first-time photographs of the Earth suddenly renewed the debate about Venus among space scientists. A photo of the Earth, taken for the first time from an interplanetary distance, was made by the Lunar Orbiter 1 space probe while it was flying high above the Moon's surface. The existence of this August 1966 photo was revealed accidentally several months later at a January press conference, and astute reporters were quick to question the significance of it. NASA admitted that the picture was genuinely surprising, because it showed our Earth as an indistinctly featured, cloud-shrouded crescent, that strikingly resembled Venus in telescopic photographs.

The second picture to add surprise was transmitted by the weather-communication satellite ATS-1 in December 1966. The satellite photo was taken from 22,000 miles out, and just as in the Orbiter photograph, the Earth strikingly resembled Venus. Both photographs revealed that Earth from afar looks like Venus from afar, shrouded in clouds. This convinced some scientists to change their minds about cloud cover. The space agency admitted that many of its scientists were then seriously interested in the possibilities of sending a camera-carrying probe close to Venus; perhaps from close range it might be discovered that Venus' seemingly perpetual cloud cover was broken and variable. If this were the case, the greenhouse theory used to explain the unconfirmed Mariner 2 figures (still tentative and still suspect), would certainly lose favor. However, NASA noted that there was no possibility of adding cameras to their next space shot, scheduled for launch in June 1967. In fact, it wasn't until 1974, that a U.S. probe returned the first space pictures of Venus.

The two 1966 photographs of Earth (which were the first taken from space distances) showing our world as a cloud-shrouded planet with indistinguishable features, proved to be a point of confirmation for Adamski. His experiences were reported in his 1955 book *Inside the Spaceships*. While describing a trip into space aboard a scoutship, Adamski gave an identical description of the Earth as seen from space.

"I looked back to Earth to see what our own little globe looks like from that distance out (50,000 miles). And to my surprise, our planet was giving off a white light...a white glow (that) was hazy... There were no identifying markings whatsoever to be seen on our planet. It looked merely like a large ball of light beneath us. From here, one could never have guessed that it was swarming with myriad forms of life."

The later manned Moon missions often presented pictures of the "earth rise" over the lunar horizon. Some of those photographs undoubtedly were shot with sophisticated telescopic cameras, because many show the continents and oceans with clarity. But the early electronic television cameras on the unmanned orbiters showed the Earth as an indistinct globe without any surface detail, just as in the case of Adamski looking with an unaided eye through a porthole from 50,000 miles out in space.

Even after there appeared to be a renewed interest in Venus, the problematic Mariner 2 report was still the basic cornerstone for theoretical models of the Venusian environment. Carl Sagan earned his doctorate by writing his thoughts into a thesis on the "hot-as-hell" planet Venus. As part of his theories, he postulated that the atmospheric pressure on Venus might be "several tens of times" higher than on Earth. Later at Harvard University, he elaborated on the orthodox theories of Mars, writing papers for publication into scientific journals. Not surprisingly, NASA recruited Sagan to head their planetary studies at Jet Propulsion Laboratory when more ambitious projects got underway in the 1970's.

On the other end of the spectrum were the censors with full knowledge of the UFO situation. They had adequately contained the unorthodox findings regarding the Moon and Mars, as was discussed in the previous chapters. As opposed to "officially establishing" a negligible atmosphere around those two bodies (in line with common beliefs), the censor's problem with Venus was to consistently define its atmosphere as insufferably dense, so that in time their definition would become a common belief. Initially there was a glitch in the consistency, because the U.S. and Russia were working independently when pulling the wool over the public eye with their respective space findings.

On October 18, 1967, the Soviets announced that their space probe, Venera 4, reached the Venusian surface and radioed back indications of an atmospheric pressure 18 times greater than the Earth's, along with a temperature reading of 540°F. However, this was unknown in the U.S., when a day later on October 19, the Mariner 5 probe made a flyby pass at the planet, and space officials announced that readings showed an atmospheric pressure 100 times greater than Earth's, and a surface temperature of 800°F. More cooperation was obviously in order.

The United States and the Soviet Union are the only two countries which have the space technology for probing planets. One might incorrectly assume that there would not be any cooperation between these two countries in order to keep the official findings on Venus or Mars consistent. But in fact, there is a high degree of cooperation and agreement in matters of science, and in other sensitive areas. There is a definite collusion between the superpowers for certain mutual interests, the main one being the preservation of the world economy system. The discovery of life, or the suitable conditions for life, on other planetary bodies in our solar system, would topple the corporate power structure of the world. That is because both the capitalistic and communist systems are based on maintaining military tensions, and the attendant armament production and weapons sales, and the control of energy resources. The proof or confirmation of *advanced, peaceful civilizations* that travel through space using *free electromagnetic energy* would be catastrophic to the false money system that is the basis of world power. There are secret intelligence agencies in both governments, whose activities are to insure that the system is not challenged or disrupted.

I can give an excellent example of the collusion in sensitive areas by the superpowers that goes on behind all the public propaganda. The San Diego Evening Tribune won a top award in newspaper journalism in 1975, for printing a report about an underwater collision of two submarines. The U.S. submarine involved was the U.S.S. Pintado (SSN672), and coincidentally, I served for three years on this sub, until my transfer in October, 1972. But the collision occurred in May 1974, when the Pintado was operating inside Russia's territorial waters. The submarines collided head on, and although there was major damage to the bows, both were able to surface and return to home bases for extensive repairs. In this incident, the U.S. was clearly at fault, because our submarine was operating silently, and spying in their internationally-recognized territorial waters. Yet nothing was ever announced publicly by the Russians, and of course not by the United States. Only a few officials in our government and the Pentagon were briefed.

Although it was a top-secret matter, the Evening Tribune learned about the incident a year after it had occurred, and was able to piece the story together from a few high-placed sources, along with a secret photograph of the damaged Pintado submarine sitting in drydock in Guam. The Pentagon refused to confirm the story after it had leaked out, and declined to comment on the cause of damage to the Pintado. Russia never made a formal protest or diplomatic issue out of the incident This is one small example of how they will join forces whenever it is to the mutual advantage of each. I confirmed the story for myself by tracking down a former shipmate who was still attached to the Pintado in May 1974. After seeing the newspaper article and photograph, he told me it was completely true.

One other important thing came out from the submarine incident that will parallel my statements regarding secret space findings. It was brought out by the same newspaper in a follow-up article, that there are two sets of logbooks for military reconnaissance missions. One set is written for the "official" record, and whenever the need arises, for public statements. But the other logbook is the real one. What actually occurs or is learned, gets recorded therein, and that is made available to certain intelligence agencies and the Pentagon.

That there are different "logbooks" for the space missions also, goes without saying. So the public, if it is determined that they deserve any information, gets the false, misleading, or meaningless data. This is a widely-used tool in our society, employed extensively in the guise of public relations.

Around the time of the Mariner 5 probe in 1967, the Silence Group was maintaining full control of planetary space information through the National Security Agency, with NASA providing the official logbook. To dispel any lingering belief that Venus was habitable and the home of the visiting spaceships reported as flying saucers or UFOs, the government and space agency spokesmen were to insist from then on, that all probes and landers to Venus, whether American or Russian, found temperatures exceeding 800°F and atmospheric pressures nearly 90 times that of Earth's. This plan for public reports was coordinated with the Soviet government and space officials as well. Since then those figures have been consistently publicized.

No matter what we were to assume regarding space probe capabilities, it must be admitted that only the top space officials have direct, firsthand access to the registered readings. The regular NASA personnel and project scientists receive relayed information (or secondary information). Space probes transmit their informational data in the form of electronic signals, which are picked up by the government's large radio telescopes. These signals must be converted into meaningful results by decoding their data through programmed computers. The key is to have the correct decoder. The real planetary conditions will only be known if the true computer language and logic circuits are matched with the electronic signals coming from the space probe.

To give an oversimplified, but easy to understand example, let's say that a probe lands on Venus and measures the temperature. The electronic signal is relayed millions of miles back to Earth in the binary code: 1101101001. The equipment in the tight-security control room, using the top-secret, correct decoder, translates this into 70°F. This reading is known only by the top officials. The consoles in regular Mission Control, however, are much further down the line, and can easily be fed modified or programmed information. Their computer equipment displays a reading that is triggered by signals from a modified input, giving a value near 800°F, and this value is then accepted as accurate by the NASA team, the media, and eventually the public.

Everything need not be relayed through decoders with a predetermined range of values. False data can simply be handed down by the top officials, along with a regular batch of ambiguous readings. Detection of the gaseous elements in the Venusian atmosphere, that are expected to be found according to the accepted theories, probably pass unrestricted to computer printouts. It must be understood also, that our probes have very limited capabilities, and they are not even close to being error-free. They can only send back minor information, which is often subjected to much debate. The same scientists will agree on some interpretations of received signals, and widely disagree on others.

If there is anything that seems to be inviolate in planetary sciences, it is the rigid belief in the high surface temperatures and pressures on Venus. No one can prove it, or scientifically explain it, although there has been a lot of theorizing. But the top space officials are the sole authority for these claims. The only way that the surface conditions on another planet can be determined is by a remote lander, and the top space officials in charge of receiving the signals are the only persons who could know absolutely. That being the case, they are the sole authority. Everyone else has been *told*. That is, anyone else claiming to know, is only repeating what he has been told. And there is no way to verify the claimed readings, or to prove otherwise, without having your own personal space probe land there to register the actual conditions.

It follows, that every scientist who teaches, writes, or discusses Venus as a hot and dense atmosphere planet without reservation, must cite the space agency as the authority. Otherwise, he must state that his discussion is theory, since he cannot prove it by any scientific method from earth-based studies. True measurements of surface conditions on any planet can only be obtained by a space probe that has penetrated beneath the ionospheric shell of the atmosphere surrounding that planet. The ionosphere is a region of the atmosphere which contains electrically charged particles, and which extends upward from about the 50 mile level to a height of over 400 miles above the planet's surface.

The reader may be inclined to ask - what is the point of this discussion? To be truthful, the point has been made before in this book. And that is: the government agency that has been withholding and distorting the reality of UFOs in its ongoing public relations, is the same agency that is supplying the planetary space findings to the scientific community and to the public. And each form of censorship is directly related to the other.

The space agency's statements on the Venusian environment have gone unchallenged for two reasons. The first is, that the solid and truthful body of UFO evidence has not been recognized by science, or realized by society. The second being, that there is no way to corroborate or contest the reported probe readings, and society is generally trustful of their officials. The space agency's unchanging statement on these parameters for each and every space mission to Venus has been accepted without question by scientists. It has been accepted as true. It has become a fundamental belief - dogma, if you will. They have not asked for proof. They have been told, and they accept.

Whatever validity there is to other reported parameters on the Venusian atmosphere, all theorizing about Venus has been fundamentally based on the high temperature and pressure belief. I am somewhat sympathetic to the research endeavors of many scientists, since they have been given an impossible puzzle to solve. The acknowledgement that there is a major riddle has been stated many times in science magazines, usually with a rhetorical question asking why a planet that is earthlike in so many ways, is so different with respect to the claimed atmosphere and surface temperature. For the reasons I have already explained regarding the predetermined data and cover-up, I can sympathize with their research complexities, because it *is* an impossible puzzle, given the assumptions. But why aren't researchers questioning those stated parameters?

A colleague of mine suggested one simple analysis to show that there are major discrepancies with the official version of the Venus environment. To begin with, the surface gravity on Venus is nearly the same as the Earth's, and therefore the volume of Venus' atmosphere is about the same as the Earth's. The atmospheric parameters of pressure, volume, mass, and temperature must obey one of the fundamental principles in physics - the general gas law. Knowing that the volume is constant, and approximately equal to the Earth's, the pressure-temperature relationship can be determined from simple mathematical formulas, and by using the Earth as a standard. (The absolute temperature scale, measured in degrees Kelvin, is used in scientific calculations, and is equal to the Celsius temperature plus 273°.)

Pressure of a gas in a constant volume is directly proportional to the absolute temperature. That is, if the temperature doubles, so does the pressure. Let's say that the average surface temperature on Earth is 68°F. This equals 293°K on the absolute temperature scale. If the Earth's temperature were increased to 850°F (728°K), as reported for Venus, the Earth's atmospheric pressure would then be 2.5 times greater than normal.

$$P_2 = \frac{T_2}{T_1}(P_1) = \frac{728°K}{293°K}(P_1) = 2.5 \text{ atm} \qquad (P_1 = 1 \text{ atm})$$

Now let's say that the Earth's atmosphere content of oxygen and nitrogen is replaced with the reportedly major constituent of Venus' atmosphere - carbon dioxide. Changing the molecules to CO_2 would have no effect on atmospheric pressure, even though the molecular weight for CO_2 is approximately 1.5 times the molecular weight of our oxygen-nitrogen air. This is because at a given temperature and volume, the pressure exerted by any single gas molecule does not depend on the type of molecule involved. This is a remarkable property of gases, as compared to liquids or solids.

With the type of gas having no effect, and since the higher temperature of 850°F merely increased the surface pressure 2.5 times, the only way to increase the atmospheric pressure beyond that value would be to change the quantity of gas in the atmosphere, i.e. increase the mass. But this cannot really be done, for the following reason. A planet's gravity establishes the volume and boundary of the planetary atmosphere, but it is not a closed system. If the atmospheric pressure started to increase, by pumping more mass into the system, the kinetic energy of the gaseous molecules would proportionately increase, allowing more molecules to reach escape velocity and be lost into space. It would be impossible for the atmosphere to sustain an increased pressure with the given gravitational field, since the higher energy molecules would escape out into space until the atmospheric parameters returned to their original equilibrium. The inherent properties of a gravitational field makes for a self-regulating system.

Since both Venus and Earth have nearly the same planetary gravity, and also the same atmospheric volume, the natural conclusion is that the Venusian atmosphere cannot be dense because of the self-regulating system of the gravity field. Certainly the official figure of 90 times the Earth's density is a preposterous report, that not only is absurd, - it is impossible. It is a fairytale in the face of scientific logic. Basic scientific principles lead to the conclusion that approximately the same atmospheric pressure would exist on all planetary bodies having similar surface gravities.

It also appears that the real "logbook" of NASA space findings would reveal that Venus' surface temperatures are earth-like. First indications that the high temperatures claimed in the Mariner 2 report were inaccurate, came during the photographic mission of Mariner 10 in 1974. This probe carried two television cameras. The main purpose of the Mariner 10 mission was to study Mercury, but because its trajectory took it on a course that passed Venus, the availablility of getting the first photographic picture of Venus was a big bonus. This is what space scientists had wanted ever since those 1966 satellite photos of Earth had made them reconsider cloud cover.

The Mariner 10 space probe passed within 3,500 miles of Venus on February 5, 1974, but no pictures were reportedly taken. The full planetary picture was made the following day by using 56 photographs recorded by one of the electronic cameras, and computerizing them into the complete picture, shown on Plate 22. It is stated in corresponding NASA write-ups, that this composite photograph of Venus on February 6 was taken from a distance of 450,000 miles, "looking back", long after the probe had flown past the planet on February 5th. It is also stated that the photograph has a resolution of about 4 miles, meaning that any cloud formation with size and shape at least 4 miles across was "seen" by the camera, thus making an accurate image of the atmosphere. What I and others have deduced from this photograph, is that the cloud cover (that for so long had been considered a solid blanket from earth-based observations) proved to be very much broken and variable. It would seem to be a major blow to the old orthodox theories of the Venusian environment.

NASA claimed that the cloud cover only appeared to be broken and variable, because blue filters were used during computer processing in order to enhance the ultraviolet absorption by unknown atmospheric components in an otherwise solid blanket of cloud cover. The space agency was in no hurry to dispel the prevailing beliefs on Venus. In other words, each and every interpretation was fitted to prop up existing theories, and to steer clear of habitability inferences.

On February 7, Mariner 10 took a series of full view pictures from a greater distance, and these pictures showed that the clouds of Venus were constantly changing, while rotating rapidly around the planet. The clouds generally circled around the planet in only four days. This was proved again convincingly by Pioneer probes in 1978. This has created quite a problem for scientists who have long held to the theory that the planet's rotation rate is extremely slow. This old theory states that the planet's spin is retrograde and makes one complete rotation in 243 earth days. There has always been a controversy over the length of the Venusian day, because the surface cannot be seen, even with a space probe.

In the past, various astronomy methods and measurements had "pinpointed" Venus' rotation rate from somewhere between 24 hours to 243 earth days. Spokesmen involved with the NASA cover-up must have been cued to boost the idea of the latter figure, because when they put out all of the other false descriptions of Venus in 1962 from the Mariner 2 shot, they claimed that a radar reading indicated the planet was "rotating imperceptibly slowly on its axis." This was supposedly also confirmed by later space missions.

The officially-claimed rotation rate for Venus cannot be corroborated or refuted by earth-based radar studies, because of the enormous distance involved. Let's say that two radar signals of equal energy are sent out- one to the Moon and one to Venus. The returning radar signal from Venus would be some 10 million times fainter than the radar return from the Moon. In recent years there has been some development with sophisticated radar receivers, but when the 243-day figure was first theorized (1961), it had taken several weeks for scientists to "sort out" a radar return from Venus from all the background radio noise of the heavens.[8]

Then, before the rotational speed could be theorized, an extremely improbable measurement of the Doppler effect had to be determined from this barely discernible return. The theory, like the analysis, was very subjective. In fact, it was simply a project funded through government research contracts, with highly questionable results. The methods were prone to errors and subjective interpretations. Today, unbiased scientists admit that the resolution of earth-based radar is too poor to make any positive determination of the rotation rate, although radar mapping of the planet's surface has achieved some noticeable gains in the last decade.

What we have then, is that the scientifically accepted rotation rate for Venus - listed in all scientific texts as 243 days in a retrograde motion - is actually based on an official "finding" from a space probe mission, just as in the case of the reported surface temperatures and atmospheric pressure. It seems that the "finding" was simply designed to match the earlier theory that had been a favorite in orthodox circles before the Venusian cloud patterns were discovered. In 1974 and 1978, photographic missions by U.S. space probes did determine that the Venusian clouds were broken and variable, and completely circling the planet in about four days' time, but the space agency let the contradictions stand. This left scientists to ponder another impossible puzzle on the Venusian environment.

It is illogical to imagine Venus being the only planet in our solar system to rotate in retrograde, and if Venus were to be practically standing still as NASA claims, then what is causing the great movements throughout its atmosphere to propel the cloud patterns around so rapidly? We know that the earth's rotational spin creates the major wind circulation patterns around our planet, including the westerlies and the trade winds. And the interaction between different air masses causes the weather changes. The "Coriolis effect" of the earth's rotation is also responsible for the surface currents of our oceans. Regarding Venus, logic demands that the clouds are moving rapidly around that planet due to the motive force provided by a higher planetary rotation speed.

Since the 1974 Mariner 10 space mission, a number of probes have been sent out to Venus, through the Russian and American space programs. Newspapers have carried routine reports following the usual press conferences, and science magazines have occasionally elaborated on the theoretical results. The model of the Venusian environment has not significantly changed, because the false parameters (of surface temperature and atmosphere pressure) have been basic to each report. Needless to say, because of those long-standing descriptions, the recent reports on Venus have failed to interest a public bored with space details of supposedly lifeless planets.

This book has explained the reasons why the basic planetary misinformation was initiated, and then perpetuated, by the cryptocracy in control. Intelligence agencies have provided a major role, while the subordinate space agency has played a visible and public role. Space information on planetary conditions that has been passed down through this chain of command, along with their thirty years of public disinformation on UFOs, does not need even a second glance by qualified space researchers, before rejecting it.

This book has also shown why the official descriptions about Venus are either false, unscientific, or contradictory. The theories that are based on those descriptions are pointless exercises. The truth has been denied as a matter of directive, and as a consequence an opposite picture has taken its place. Space science has fallen backwards from the meaningful days of telescopic study, and now become a battleground of meaningless talk.

Chapter 10
Venus - Our Sister Planet

The cloud-shrouded atmosphere of Venus is a firmament. This cloudy formation is not a solid blanket in any atmospheric level or zone. There are several cloud layers, which vary in density and appearance, until there is an abrupt cutoff at 30 miles above the surface of Venus. The firmament does not block the sun's electromagnetic spectrum that manifests as visible light, but it does block the harmful cosmic rays more effectively than the Earth's atmosphere.

Extending to a height of ten miles above the surface is the bottom layer of the atmosphere called the troposphere. Ninety percent of the Venusian air mass is contained in this region, with the same atmospheric content of oxygen and nitrogen that is found in the Earth's troposphere. Carbon dioxide is a very minor constituent in the Venusian troposphere. Normal weather clouds and winds are active in this region, providing an earth-like climate. The surface temperatures and atmospheric pressure are also earth-like. The planet Venus has a rotation period similar to the Earth's, making the Venusian day 26 hours in length, compared to our 24.

The top space officials from both the United States and Russia did determine all or most of this information from landed probes prior to 1980. Direct signals and readings were decoded and kept secret, while only minor information was passed down to regular project scientists, along with the expected instrument readings taken near the top of the Venusian atmosphere. Most of the registered data provided to scientists accurately was irrelevant to surface conditions.

Parameters at the bottom of the troposphere could only be determined by the lander. The true findings on atmospheric pressure and surface temperatures have never been made public. False readings on those conditions have been announced for each space shot - statements, of course, that fit exactly with accepted thinking, which in turn had already been patterned from the beginning.

The top officials realize also, that whatever readings they wish to claim from a landed probe, cannot be proven otherwise. No one else receives those exclusive signals, and not even the project scientists at JPL. Those scientists receive a mixture of announcements, relayed and modified information (secondary), expected data, inconsequential readings, predetermined readouts, and computerized analysis. It's a packaged program in the main.

Since 1975 the Soviet Union has sent six spacecraft probes, and the United States two, to the planet Venus. The remainder of this chapter provides some information on these missions, along with comments. A number of scientific articles and newspaper clippings were reviewed for details. Often, science writers appear to be objective in their reports, but until one can get around the Venusian pressure and temperature discrepancy, the discussions provide little real value.

In June 1975, the Soviet Union launched two spacecraft to Venus. Four months later, both went into orbit around the planet and each sent a descent capsule to the surface. The probes, named Venera 9 and Venera 10, soft-landed 1375 miles apart, and the first two photographs of the Venusian surface were taken and transmitted back to Earth. It was reported that both probes functioned approximately one hour on the surface.

The two landing spots were on the northeastern and southeastern borders of a regional area, now identified as Beta from earth-based radar studies. Both of the transmitted photographs showed that each landing area was "bathed" in sunlight. This provided quite a shock for American scientists, who in particular, had always believed that their theoretical (dense) atmosphere would make it too dark to see anything, and that even if landing craft carried their own lighting, any pictures taken would be grossly distorted and the horizon would appear to bend upward as if looking around from within a huge bowl. But neither was the case, as proved by the Venera pictures.

The spaceprobe mission also disproved the theory that the Venus landscape would be a sand desert caused by wind and heat erosion. What were clearly seen at one location were sharp-edged, angular, young-looking rocks. Boris Nepoklonov, the Soviet mission director stated: "This picture makes us reconsider all our concepts of Venus." Gamma-ray spectroscopy from both landers indicated that the rocky surface contained potassium, thorium, and uranium, - which constitute basalt rocks. From this data, the Soviets stated that the Venusian surface is similar in composition to the Earth's crust. They also added that they learned a good deal of information about the interaction of Venus' upper atmosphere with the solar wind, and that the Venusian cloud cover would appear as only "a slight haze" to an observer in an orbiting spacecraft. The final assessment was that man was only on the threshold of discovering what lies beneath the clouds of Venus.

In 1978, the U.S. space program got its first real opportunity to study the Venus mystery with two Pioneer spacecraft. (It was also the last opportunity for the U.S., since no other missions to Venus have followed that one). The probes for the Pioneer mission were designed to penetrate the Venusian ionosphere and make impact landings. Lacking the technology that allowed Soviet successes with soft-landings, the American probes were destined to impact on the surface and therefore carried no cameras. American hopes were based on obtaining a few instrument readings from below the atmospheric cloud cover. Even with this limited approach to gain some understanding of the Venusian environment, any results would not be really objective or value-free, because by 1978 the dogmatic theories on Venus were very rigid beliefs within the scientific community. Any type of data would be interpreted within the confines of orthodox views. We must keep this in mind when reviewing their reports. And (need it be said again?), any readings on the surface temperatures and pressure were strictly guarded by the officials in control, who then put out the usual false data for the record.

The two Pioneer spacecraft had completely different functions in the mission. Pioneer 1 was an orbiter, and after reaching Venus on December 4, began orbiting the planet at a distance of 40,000 miles. Pioneer 2 was called a transporter "bus", because it carried the descent probes. It reached Venus five days later, on December 9.

From its distant orbit, Pioneer 1 sent back hundreds of photographs, enabling scientists to study the Venusian cloud circulations in its upper atmosphere. The pictures were detailed in showing the changing cloud patterns, and confirmed that Venusian clouds circle the planet in approximately four days time. At some point later in the mission, the spacecraft was directed to a much lower orbit radius by command signals from Earth. This stage of the mission lasted several months, in order to do a comprehensive radar mapping of Venus. At times, the orbiter approached as close as 142 kilometers to the planet. While low in orbit, Pioneer 1 detected that atmospheric lightning was occurring near the planet's surface, similar to storm lightning in our atmosphere. (This was confirmed by a Soviet probe that had landed on the Venusian surface that same month. Readings from that probe indicated the lightning was occurring at an altitude of 3 to 6 miles above the surface, and the probe also registered loud audio signals that were interpreted by Soviet space authorities as thunder).

In February 1979, Pioneer Orbiter 1 was placed in an orbital path to study the region known as Beta. This is where the 1975 Russian probes had set down, and the early landers had shown that this area was composed of volcanic rock. Initial readings by instruments on Pioneer 1 showed detection of sulphur, and sulpheric acid droplets, high in the atmosphere over this region. The only problem, was that scientists were quick to paint a picture of a noxious, sulfuric-acid atmosphere. The impression given was that the whole atmosphere was like that, and public reports for the next five years always conveyed a strong image of a poisonous atmosphere.

Finally, in February 1984, studies presented by NASA's Ames Research Center revealed that a volcano in the Beta region had erupted in 1978 with a force greater than Mount St. Helens, blowing sulfur high into the Venusian atmosphere. This eruption was the real reason why Pioneer 1 had detected those constituents, as the NASA study revealed that the concentration of sulfur dioxide in the high atmosphere over this region had declined steadily for five years. The results of the study determined that it was an exact analogy to volcanic activity on Earth, where large amounts of sulfur-bearing gases are injected into the atmosphere during eruptions, and then slowly dissipate over a few years' time.

There is a lesson to be learned from this, regarding the early 1979 results. It is an illustrating example, of how quick theorizing by scientists without the complete picture, irresponsibly plants a false image in the public's mind for years. Scientists seem unable to acknowledge, or admit, that we have received only the most minor information back from our probes to date, yet they continue to make flat statements on the Venusian environment, based on nothing more than a few slight bits of information. I guess that it goes with the profession. To secure one's place or position in the scientific field, one must continually publish papers, (and stick with the consensus). This is why you will find volumes of theorizing out in the scientific press - much of it, though, going unread. I of course, have had to read a good deal of those type of scientific articles for my research. Indeed, it was an unenviable task, but necessary, in order to learn how opinions are formed, and their derivation - i.e. what is their source. Also, the reasons for their staying-power.

The original radar mapping by Pioneer Venus 1 was completed in 1979, and a geographical relief map of surface altitudes and depressions was drawn up by NASA scientists. This would be analogous to plotting the broad surface features of our ocean floor by sonar. Underwater mountains and valleys on the ocean floor can be located by sonar, without ever physically seeing those features, just as in the case of Pioneer mapping the broad surface features on Venus. One notable discovery on Venus was a 900 mile long canyon near the planet's equator. It was estimated to be several miles deep and 150 miles wide. Its size was comparable to the rift valleys along the Mid-Ocean Ridge on earth, and to an area on Mars called Valles Marineus.

Three years earlier, earth-based radar studies from Goldstone, California, had apparently already discovered this canyon. I have a news clipping on this study, and the following is an excerpt from the 1976 Jet Propulsion Laboratory report.

> "The most startling feature yet seen on Venus is the huge, trough-like depression along the planet's equator that is 850 miles long, 90 miles wide, and more than a mile deep. The valley is strikingly similar to Valles Marineus of Mars, and to the Earth's East African Rift system."

However, scientists conducting the Pioneer orbiter mapping stated that they were absolutely certain that the two studies found different canyons, because their spaceprobe was over the "far" side of Venus that was not in view during the earlier radar study of the "front" side. According to the extremely slow rotation rate theory, the same face of Venus is always in view when the Earth and Venus are in line with the sun and closest together, and that same "front" side remains in view for the duration. Therefore the "far" side could not have been seen during the earth-based radar study, according to the NASA scientists.

I pulled the two reports from my files and checked them against the completed radar map of Venus by the Pioneer Orbiter. This full graphic relief map of Venus is reproduced in the *Science News Magazine* of September 13, 1980. It turns out that both the Goldstone and Pioneer studies had, in fact, discovered the same canyon - and more importantly, because it was the same canyon, that evidence makes a striking blow at the (false) slow-rotation theory. If one does not know the true rotation period of Venus, then he never really knows what "side" he is actually looking at, and that is why the Pioneer scientists thought they had discovered a different canyon initially. But if in fact, the canyon was correctly located on the so-called far side by Pioneer, then that would mean the Goldstone scientists were able to see both sides of Venus during their short observation period in 1976 - something that would be impossible according to the 243-day rotation theory.

For those of you who wish to check on the location of the 900-mile canyon under discussion, it is located on the *Science News* color relief at 170° longitude and 20° south latitude, and designated Dali Chasma. It cannot be confused with any other feature on the map because both radar studies provided details for the location. The Pioneer report stated that the canyon ran roughly east-west in a region about 20 degrees south of the equator. The earlier Goldstone report related that the Canyon was near the equator, and further identified its location by saying that they had found a sharply defined, wide, circular feature to the south. That is labeled on the (Pioneer) graph as Artemis Chasma. When it became apparent that both studies had discovered the same canyon, the old rotation theory should immediately have come under question by scientists. But I have never seen where scientists have admitted that the initial mistake in canyon locations was due to a fundamentally wrong rotation theory. The discrepancy was conveniently forgotten.

Having concluded the discussion of the Pioneer 1 Orbiter, let's review the other half of the 1978 mission. The Pioneer 2 spacecraft reached Venus on December 9th. It was programmed to split up into its five component parts upon approach, in order to penetrate and study the Venusian atmosphere. The 8-foot, drum-shaped transporter "bus" quickly burned upon entering the atmosphere as expected, but the four smaller probes each reached the surface 55 minutes later from a 120-mile altitude, according to the reports. The 4 landing sites were widely separated, and only one of the probes was reportedly able to transmit data from the surface. All had sent back some readings during their quick descent, and according to the San Diego newspaper, "all five probes performed flawlessly." The mechanics and trajectories may have been flawless, but the "scientific interpretations" of the data cannot be accorded the same lofty description, by any means.

Venus was 34 million miles from Earth when Pioneer 2 reached the planet. The transporter bus carried two mass spectrometers and a gas chromatograph, in order to quickly analyze the atmosphere from 300 miles down to the 75 mile altitude during its fiery, 2-minute descent. One spectrometer attempted to measure the densities of atmospheric constituents, and the other was designed to determine physical and chemical processes within the Venusian ionosphere. The processes within the ionosphere are related to the effect of the solar wind - a stream of expanding gases emitted by the sun, that bombards the planets with charged particles. The gas chromatograph gave a reading from a middle zone of the atmosphere, presumably near the 75-mile mark.

The four Pioneer probes that had separated from the transporter bus upon entering the Venusian atmosphere apparently all survived during their 55-minute plunge. The larger one of the four used a parachute for part of its descent, and landed near the planet's equator on the day side. Radio contact immediately ceased upon landing. The three other probes were smaller, and of identical construction. Without parachutes, they also reportedly hit the surface after 55 minutes, one landing near the polar region of the northern hemisphere. The second probe came down in the southern hemisphere on the day side, and the third landed in the southern hemisphere on the night side.

All four probes carried scientific instruments to measure atmospheric structure, cloud particles, and heat distribution. Just how accurately readings could be taken during a speedy, two-mile-per-minute plunge is a matter of conjecture, but

NASA scientists translated the data almost as quickly, into sketches of clouds, winds, and other "features" of Venus. They did admit that the readings may not have been entirely accurate, because cosmic rays bombarding the space probes could have affected the probe's electronics. After giving their initial reports to the media, the scientists stated that no final conclusions about the mission could be drawn until all the data was analyzed.

The four probes were not expected to function after impact. The fact that one probe did, was a surprise development according to NASA. The agency stated that the small day-side probe continued to transmit strong signals for 68 minutes after landing. This "development" apparently gave validity to their latest, (and oft repeated), claims on the surface conditions. It was reported that the other three probes went dead on impact.

Hughes Aircraft Company designed and constructed the Pioneer probes. They used the mission project for big promotional advertising for their company that headlined: Mission Impossible? - Not For Hughes. The task according to their ads, was to construct space probes that could withstand the searing temperatures, crushing pressures, and sulfuric acid clouds of Venus. So the probes were built as pressure vessels with special titanium shells in order that they could withstand 1400 pounds of pressure per square inch. That amount of pressure is equivalent to the pressure at 3000 feet depth in our oceans.

Of course, this was what everyone, including the NASA project personnel, had been led to believe. They would insist on such requirements. And since it was the only U.S. space mission to Venus that was planned to probe beneath the upper clouds, one would expect NASA directors to order this design. How could they order any lesser specifications, and then expect to publicize the usual figures on surface conditions? It doesn't require a lot of sense to figure that one out. And the mission's success would not be hampered by over designed components anyway. In fact, there was a not-to-be-overlooked bonus to their arrangement with Hughes

Aircraft. The corporation's promotional ads that touted its technological engineering in making components that would "survive the Venusian atmosphere," would be a huge assist to public misleading about Venus.

However, it should be quite revealing to consider the Russian successes with their Venusian landers. Their early probes, dating back to the Venera 4 mission in 1967, were not built to such hardy specifications, and yet they were able to transmit some information after reaching the surface. Russia did not need special, over-designed, titanium pressure vessels when they began achieving results eleven years before NASA. In fact, had such harsh conditions actually existed on the surface, their much more fragile probes would not have functioned for a moment. So why did NASA contract for, and promote, the special titanium probes? It seems that the overriding issue was - "to stay with the program."

Two weeks after the Pioneer 2 probes reached Venus, the Soviet's soft-landed two more of their own, that "considerably broadened the body of knowledge about the planet's surface" according to news reports. Venera 11 transmitted back information for 95 minutes, Venera 12 radioed for 110 minutes. The landers carried photographic equipment, but no pictures were made public by the Soviet government.

Both Venera 11 and Venera 12 carried plaques with a bas-relief of Vladimar Lenin, and the U.S.S.R. state symbol. It would be senseless to send such carefully prepared and costly extras if everything would be totally destroyed in the supposedly 90x atmospheric pressure, high temperatures, and corrosive environment publicized by NASA. This would be like paying a great artist to make a beautiful painting, only to throw the picture in an incinerator. The adding of special plaques to their probes strongly suggests the following conclusion: that behind the official statements, there exists within the Soviet space program a real belief that these artifacts will last for a long time, and that their landers will be found by intelligent life on Venus.

While U.S. planetary studies came to a complete halt, the

Soviets continued to study Venus. They are undoubtedly quite motivated to probe the home planet of the visiting UFOs. In March 1982, another Soviet mission completed its journey to Venus with the spacecraft Venera 13 and 14. Their respective landing probes radioed back for more than two hours. (That made a total of twelve Soviet spacecraft to land on the surface, the last eight all being "soft-landings.") The Venera 13 and 14 space probes each carried equipment that could collect and analyze soil samples from the surface. Each lander was also equipped with a pair of cameras that could take color pictures. Reports indicate that many were taken, but that only one picture was released to scientists in the U.S., along with sketchy reports on the mission's preliminary findings.

Lacking real definitive data has never been a problem for scientists in this country. They always hasten to publish volumes of theorizing, and then attend sponsored (and expense-paid) conferences to again discuss their long-held beliefs, following the "latest" report in space science developments. The scientific literature on planetary environments, if analyzed carefully, turns out to be based on theories first, with sparse and inconsequential "developments" fitted in. It appears very authoritative to the uninformed, but only as tedious and unprovable chatter to a knowledgeable space researcher.

From the scientific viewpoint, our space information has come full circle. The probes to Venus have prompted various attention, from the Mariner 2 mission in 1962, to Venera 14 in 1982, a period of twenty years. The UFOs in our skies have gained lasting attention, from 1947 to 1987, a period of forty years. And they are still here. It is left up to the individual to decide for himself, the real truth behind space findings and planetary information. It must be understood that the authorities have had a number of reasons to cloud the truth, all related to the idea that it was politically and economically expedient to prop up the life-denying theories - no matter how wrong, or scientifically incongruous. Until we get a new generation of leadership, at a time when there is nothing to hide, and a new generation of scientists willing to part completely with the theoretical baggage of the past, we will not have a way of securing the knowledge we need to fully understand space conditions.

Since the negative, erroneous image of Venus has been published and repeated so often that it has become an "accepted fact" in the public's thinking pattern, I feel I should repeat a truthful description of Venus at least once in this chapter. And if free to speak out, some people associated with government planetary research could confirm this information very easily.

The upper atmosphere of Venus is a firmament. This cloudy formation is not a solid blanket in any atmospheric level or zone. The firmament does not block the sun's electromagnetic spectrum that manifests as visible light, but it does block the harmful cosmic rays more effectively than the Earth's atmosphere. Closest to the planet's surface is the life-supporting troposphere. Ninety percent of the Venusian air mass is contained in this region, with the same atmospheric content of oxygen and nitrogen that is found in the Earth's troposphere. Carbon dioxide is a very minor constituent in the Venusian troposphere. Normal weather clouds and winds are active in this region, providing an earth-like climate. The surface temperatures and atmospheric pressure are also earth-like. Oceans and numerous lakes exist on the surface. The planet Venus has a rotation period similar to the Earth's, making the Venusian day 26 hours in length. Anyone living on Earth could go to Venus and step out of a spaceship - the conditions are that similar between the two planets.

Chapter 11
An Inhabited Solar System

Venus, Mars, and the Moon are important in that they are our closest neighbors, and the habitability can easily be determined. Our space program of the 1960's and 70's probed and photographed them extensively, since these planets were known to be the homes or bases of the UFOs. Life beyond the Earth should have been published as an established fact years ago. Two things prevented this from becoming our rightful knowledge: the inability, and often the refusal, of the orthodox scientists to go beyond their shared perceptions; and secondly, the absolute secrecy and censorship by the top-level authorities in charge of the space program.

But what about the other planets in our solar system? Are they inhabited also? And are their environments Earthlike, or similar enough, that we could travel to them and step out on their surfaces?

George Adamski stated early on that they were inhabited, for he got his information direct from the space people. Textbook scientists and JPL staff say no, based on the old theories, but they do not have any direct information from scientific instruments. To date, scientists have no way of knowing, because we have not probed beneath the atmospheres of the other planets or landed any instruments. And until they understand the true nature of the sun's energy, gravity, and magnetic fields, their speculations will be way off the mark.

All that has been achieved is some preliminary picture-taking from vast distances during momentary fly-bys. For example, the closest pass to Jupiter by a Voyager probe was at a distance of 166,000 miles. Any so-called measurement from that distance would be purely hypothetical. And until scientists can see the UFO evidence here on Earth, and see the true environments of Venus, Mars, and the Moon, there is no reason to accept their opinions regarding the more distant planets. Their speculations are only extensions of theories that have become scientific dogma. There is simply no data which could prove or disprove the theories. In other words, from a purely scientific standpoint, the planetary conditions on either Mercury, Jupiter, or Saturn is still an open question. The same is true for the planets beyond Saturn.

In order to discuss Mercury, the last of the four inner planets of our system, it is important to first have a true perspective of spatial distances. Diagrams in books and magazines are invariably out of proportion due to an inadequate page size, and Mercury is perceived as being very close to the Sun. In space the planet's actual distance from the Sun is 34 million miles.

The following is an accurate representation that could be laid out in a large yard or playground. If the Sun were the size of a regulation basketball, the Earth would be the size of a small BB placed 90 feet from the basketball. A smaller BB for Mercury would circle the basketball from a distance of 33 feet. To complete this scaled representation, a BB for Venus would be placed at 65 feet, and another for Mars at 132 feet. The actual size of a BB is ●. Try and picture in your mind these sizes and distances for a moment.

Seeing Mercury as a small BB located 33 feet from the basketball, we find that it is not really close when seen at true scale. The planet is usually described as being very similar to the Moon on its surface, and like the Earth on the inside. As early as 1962, radio astronomers found that the night side hemisphere had a warm surface - an effect which would require that an atmosphere be present to carry the heat from the day side to the night side. It was also determined from further studies that Mercury had a thin atmosphere. The methods used were similar to those used for the Moon, (and like the case of the Moon, this means that the density of

Mercury's atmosphere will have to be revised upwards when more accurate methods are employed.) When the atmosphere is accurately determined, we will also learn that the surface temperatures on Mercury are quite moderate.

The U.S. space program has sent only one space probe to Mercury. The spacecraft, Mariner 10, was placed into a precise orbit that allowed three brief fly-by encounters during a one year period from March 1974 to March 1975. These one and a half day encounters were the first close-up views of the planet, and a chance to investigate Mercury's magnetic field and its interaction with the solar wind. The mission was also supposed to check up on the "tenuous" atmosphere determined from radio astronomy, but either the Mariner 10 instrumentation was incapable of registering atmospheric effects, or NASA deliberately denied Mercury's atmosphere, the same as they have denied the Moon's. If Mercury did not have a sufficient atmosphere to offset internal pressures, it would have disintegrated and returned to the elements of space long ago.

The Mariner 10 fly-bys were nightside passes, and therefore photographs could not be taken at the close approach, but only from much greater distances during the orbital pass. In fact, it was the worst trajectory for photographing the planet's illuminated surface, and the end results required complicated imaging back at Jet Propulsion Laboratories. Resolution was compromised also, due to the lack of Congressional funding for a proposed x-band transmitter, designed to top specifications. All of this should be understood when looking at the photos of Mercury taken by Mariner 10.

The pictures are black and white, and look like common pictures of the Moon. Only the daylight half of the planet was observed by Mariner 10 in two hemisphere photographs. The first was taken from 124,000 miles as the probe traveled toward Mercury, and the second from 130,000 miles as it was traveling away from the planet. Broad surface area photographs were transmitted as Mariner's distance decreased to 11,000 miles, and while "looking back" as the spacecraft came out from behind the nightside hemisphere.

The scenes of highest resolution are indistinguishable from pictures taken by the early Ranger spacecraft missions to our Moon.

The spacecraft's orbit brought it to a second pass of Mercury six month later. Its closest approach was 30,000 miles on September 21, 1974. The third and final pass in March 1975 brought it to within 6,000 miles, but only very small areas were picked up with slightly improved detail. The reason given for the much-lessened opportunity was that there was a failure with one of the Earth-based antenna systems. However, a few high resolution transmissions, showing features of 3 kilometer size, discovered water or river channels in an area now dry. Orthodoxers suggested their standard silly interpretation: the features depicted in the photographs had resulted from the flowing of liquid rock. Generally, the other pictures look like the front side of our Moon - plains, craters, and flooded basins.

Space scientists were surprised to find a strong magnetic field at Mercury. This field acts as a protective shield to the sun's energy, and thus creates a bow shock in the solar wind, which was also confirmed by the Mariner probe. Scientists found that the bow shock was comparable and equivalent to the Earth's interaction with the solar wind.

Yet many conclusions came into conflict. The magnetic field at the surface was given as 1% of the Earth's, but it is quite doubtful that our methods can accurately measure things we do not really understand, namely the gravitational and magnetic fields of planetary bodies. It has also been stated that the photographic fly-bys enabled the scientists to confirm the very slow (59 day) rotation rate of Mercury, due to the fact that the same hemisphere was in view at each of the 3 encounters separated by 6-month intervals. This apparently confirmed an earlier theory, that while circling the sun twice, the planet would rotate 3 times on its axis, giving a ratio of 2:3. But any multiple of 3 would present the same exact face at flyby. Since a strong magnetic field is required to create a strong bow shock in the solar wind, and since a strong planetary magnetic field is generally attributed to the fast rotation of a planet, I do not think that we have heard the final answer as to the length of a day on Mercury.

Because the public only sees the end results of a space mission as a series of photographic images in a magazine article, people are very apt to think of a planetary encounter as a live broadcast from space by the spaceprobe. Actually, the probe is exploring in the dark, and its various instruments have uncertain sensitivities to atmospheric frequencies, radar waves, solar intensity, magnetic fields, and cosmic radiations. Photography is nothing more than limited electronic detection of surface illumination contrasts, which must be interpreted by computer imaging back on Earth. The various instruments send their non-absolute indications millions of miles to Earth in the form of very faint radio signals. These signals are barely discernible from the constant radio noise coming to Earth from space itself, and sometimes indistinct from the high frequency noise of the components used to receive the signals.

For example, eight scans by an ultraviolet spectrometer on Mariner 10 were sent back, and initially the signals were interpreted as Mercury having a moon, or satellite. Project scientists thought that they had discovered a moon circling Mercury. The readings were later identified as radio emissions from a 5th magnitude star that was light-years away! And is this not the same type of instrument as the mass spectrometer - that device which has always been the instrument for subjective analysis of planetary atmospheres?

Our space probes operate in unknown zones, pick up some type of frequency, from some type of emission, in a vast and complex planetary field. Something registers, and a feeble signal is transmitted to an Earth-based receiver. Schooled in orthodoxy, project scientists try to interpret the signal. Our space probes are exploring and groping in the dark, so to speak. Their capabilities at present are like looking at a drop of water with a magnifying glass. Compare that with looking at a drop of water with an electron microscope, and you realize what stage of confirmative knowledge we are at in planetary exploration.

A Mariner 10 photograph of Mercury is shown in Plate 26, and first indications reveal that its surface does look like the Moon. In fact, its environment may be very much like the Moon. Readers of this book are aware that there is a lunar civilization and life-supporting conditions on our satellite. When we get the full and correct pictures of the Moon from our space agency, then we can expect to get the correct pictures of Mercury. In other words, since our Moon is inhabited (contrary to the official position of NASA), we may later find that Mercury shows a similarly inhabited environment, if and when we send out better space probes. Mariner 10 did not have the capability of proving or disproving life on Mercury. From a scientific standpoint, it is still an open question. But just as the electron microscope can reveal a whole new world of activity in the drop of water which the magnifying glass cannot see, so too will our probes discover the actual world of Mercury, when their capabilities are increased 10,000-fold. This same analogy can be applied to the present state of knowledge regarding Jupiter, Saturn, and beyond.

W.R. Drake's researches into classical literature and ancient manuscripts found many references to Mercury. One of the suppressed biblical accounts, the Book of Enoch, describes how Enoch was taken into space (the heavens) and transported to various planets, including Mercury. On this celestial journey he was shown the grand design and motions of the solar system. Enoch's ancient account tells of the round shape of the Earth and how our world is inclined on its axis. That knowledge could only be learned from contact with a space civilization.[1] Enoch went on to be an inspired prophet in the cradle of civilization in Sumeria.

Panini, a Sanskrit historian and writer, wrote an account of how he and others had been taken on space trips to Mercury and Venus by the friendly extraterrestrials during the fourth century A.D.[2] The famous philosopher, scientist, and astronomer of the 18th century, Emmanuel Swedenborg, after publishing great works in scientific discoveries and fundamental theories, intimated that his knowledge had come from (telepathic) intuition originating with space people from Mercury.[3] In 1866, three professional astronomers saw an unexplainable light on the nightside half of Mercury. M.K. Jessup attributes this telescopic observation to a brilliant UFO close to the surface of the planet, just as UFOs have been seen over the Moon.[4]

These are a few of the references to Mercury from the records of history. Intelligent men in the past learned, or otherwise gave indication, that Mercury was a living planet. In our recent history of space visitations, this fact has surfaced again. Officials are more certain with Venus and Mars, but the world has a lot of learning to do. On Earth, mankind laughs at the thought of a divine purpose to creation, denies that there is any other life within light years of our little spot in the galaxy, and contemptuously threatens this most beautiful globe with nuclear bombs. His mind is so divorced from cosmic principle and intuition, that we cannot call it intelligent.

Volumes have been written on Jupiter and Saturn, based on nothing but a belief. The theory that these planets are large bodies of swirling gases around a liquid core became a fundamental cornerstone of organized astronomy - forever entrenched, never questioned. The psychology of the situation is almost medieval, because the theory is taught as absolute fact by the theologians of science. And if one is paid as a scientist, one has to write and write, with the result that the original belief now expands into volumes of meaningless, nonsensical concepts. Supposition upon supposition, until natural inquiry is stifled, then suffocated.

It was Einstein who said: "It is, in fact, nothing short of a miracle that the modern methods of instruction have not yet entirely strangled the holy curiosity of inquiry." John Goethe, the great German philosopher, once declared that so-called education was expressly designed to make sensible people stupid.

The theories have not changed, but the present discourses on Jupiter and Saturn are based on the picture-taking flybys of the Pioneer and Voyager probes. The more sophisticated cameras were on the hardy Voyagers, and the closest approach to Jupiter was 166,000 miles by Voyager 1, while Saturn was passed at a 63,000 mile distance by Voyager 2 in August 1981. Most of the photography was taken from much greater distances. The two probes' electronic scanning signals were converted into pictures back on Earth, and in the case of Jupiter, computer-enhanced into false color. We did get a few close-up images of both of the planets' moons, and a more detailed look at Saturn's rings.

The Voyager photos of Jupiter that were released show bright orange and red bands. This was an exaggeration, in order to support the usual description of Jupiter's "storm-wracked atmosphere." The actual colors as seen from space are soft blues and yellow, and blue-green. This was confirmed by California astronomer Andrew Young.[5] The best available photographs of Jupiter and Saturn are reproduced in the illustrations.

In reality, both planets have solid surfaces. Jupiter has atmospheric zones for thousands of miles above its surface, which balance and blend with the sun's energy to make a habitable environment. The earth-like surface of Saturn lies many thousands of miles below its atmospheric firmament. Many advancements in understanding of electromagnetic fields and cosmic science will be required in order to replace the old theories with correct knowledge.

George Adamski gave a complete explanation for the habitability on the more distant planets, and the following is taken from his book, *Flying Saucers Farewell*.

"One of the most frequent problems encountered when giving a lecture on space is the insistence of scientists that the outer planets are devoid of light and heat. Their objection is that radiation from the sun is so weak at these vast distances that Pluto, for instance, would be at absolute zero or close to it, with a frozen atmosphere, and totally incapable of supporting life-forms of any type.

This is the main argument brought against me when doubt is expressed about my meeting human beings from some of these other planets.

The first thing to realize is that the sun does not emit light and heat in the form we observe here on Earth. Radiation from the sun does not manifest itself as light and heat until it penetrates the atmospheres of the planets themselves. Outer space is devoid of light as we know it. The light in outer space is a cold light caused by the phosphorescence of vast clouds of particles and gases responding to the radiation given off by the sun. To a human observer, outer space looks like a dark, vast void, filled with billions upon billions of tiny specks of multicolored light. All of these tiny lights are in a state of continuous motion and activity.

Radiation from the sun is composed of ultra-violet light, hard and soft X-rays, cosmic and gamma rays. The greater portion of these destructive rays are filtered out by a planet's ionosphere and upper atmosphere. The innumerable, infinitesimal particles within a planet's atmosphere emit visible light when excited by the sun's filtered radiation. The earth absorbs these rays, and in return gives off infra-red energy. Energy thus given off activates the atmosphere immediately surrounding the planet, thereby generating heat that keeps the planet warm.

It is easy to see how this energy from the sun can encompass our earth. After all, we are only 93 million miles from the sun. But what about the planets that are more remote from the sun?

According to standard textbooks, the radiation from the sun decreases inversely with the square of the distance. In layman's language, this means that if you double the distance from the sun, the radiation would be only one-fourth as great. If you double the distance again, the radiation would be only one-sixteenth as great, and so on. If the sun's radiation actually decreases at this rate, then the outer planets must indeed be in a state of perpetual coldness.

What, then, is the answer? I know from personal experience that these outer planets have thriving civilizations, with climates and atmospheres similar to our own earth. The larger planets, such as Saturn and Jupiter, have much lower gravity than has been assumed by our scientists. Therefore, our explanation of gravity must be in error in some way.

Our main problem now is not gravity but climate. How do these planets receive enough energy from the sun to exist in a similar state to Earth?

A clue to this answer is found in the vacuum tube; more specifically it is found in the cathode ray tube. This tube, abbreviated CRT, is found in the ordinary home television receiver. In it we have a heater that raises the temperature of a cathode to a point at which it gives off electrons in great quantities. These electrons are negative in nature. High positive voltages are supplied to various grids and anodes in the tube.

There are two types of electricity: positive and negative. The electron is negative and its counterpart, the proton, is positive. Just as the north pole of a magnet will attract the south pole of another magnet, the electrons attract the protons. Similar poles of magnets repel each other and so do similar charges of electricity. Likes repel; unlikes attract.

The high positive voltages on the grids and anodes of the CRT attract the electrons from the cathode. The electrons are pulled toward the anodes with great speed, but, due to the type of construction of these anodes, most electrons rush right on through toward the next one. Theoretically, this could be continued for great distances by use of several different anodes and high positive voltages.

Mercury, Venus, Earth and Mars are close enough to the sun to get good radiation. With the planets beyond Mars it is a different situation. At these distances the sun's radiation has started to diminish. At this time it comes under the influence of the tremendous attracting force generated by the first asteroid belt which totally envelopes the central position of our solar system. The negative charge of the asteroid belt is great enough to attract the particles from the sun and pull them back up to their original speed. Because this belt is grid-like in construction, with thousands of openings and paths, similar to a window screen with air going through, the particles dash on through and enter the influence of the planets beyond.

These, being negative in themselves, as are all planets, attract from space the positive particles they need for light and heat. At the same time infinite numbers of similar particles rush on past and are attracted by a second asteroid belt between Neptune and Pluto, where the process is repeated all over again. This furnishes Pluto and the last three planets with normal light and heat. (Twelve planets in all exist in our system, according to the space travelers.)

A third asteroid belt is beyond the twelfth planet, serving a dual purpose of blending space within our system with that of neighboring systems. At the same time it serves as a protective filter, comparable to the ionosphere encompassing a planet.

We might summarize by saying: The two inner asteroid belts gather rays from the sun and speed them on through space. They equalize, so to speak, conditions within the system from the area of Mercury right on to the outer reaches of our solar system, while the third keeps our system, as a unit, in balance with those beyond. Because of this cosmic activity, of which we on Earth have not previously been aware, we could go to any of our planets and enjoy a climate and atmosphere similar to our own."

Following this discussion, Adamski explains how the asteroid belt acts as a dielectric (as in a capacitor which stores electrical energy) by trapping a portion of the sun's energy, while at the same time imparting energy to particles passing through. This alternating-current action effectively makes the asteroid belt an incubator of electromagnetic energy. This net attraction of the sun's positively charged particles should register as higher kinetic energy (temperature) by a space probe passing through the zone.

Voyager I passed this zone that lies between Mars and

Jupiter in 1978, and found it to be the hottest spot ever measured in the solar system. The temperature was at least 100 times that of the sun's surface.[6] There is no real heat though, since the interplanetary region is a near-vacuum, whereas the plasma fields around the sun are extremely dense. Therefore, the Voyager probe was measuring high kinetic activity of solar particles in the asteroid belt, which is exactly the description given 17 years earlier by Adamski in his book.

The spaceships that Adamski went on were motherships from Venus and Saturn. The people he met on these craft were from Venus and Saturn, along with people from Mars - the three planets most responsible for helping the Earth in its transition towards the space age. But he was told that there was interplanetary cooperation throughout our solar system, and that people of all planets except Earth travel space freely. Every planet except Earth has spaceships.

Although Adamski's main contacts were from the same group, occasionally he met others from our system. While in Mexico in 1957, he had visits by space people who lived and worked in that nation. Two that he met came from different planets, namely Jupiter and Neptune. Adamski related this information in a letter to a European correspondent, and stated simply that having met people from five different planets of our system, he found no more difference between them, than between various nationalities on Earth. Apparently, the information Adamski received was of a universal nature relating to their work on Earth. Adamski had explained in his three published books that the other planets besides Venus, Mars, and Saturn were inhabited, but he indicated that he was not given specific information regarding the other planets.

As related earlier in this chapter, Adamski explained that there were three undiscovered planets beyond the orbit of Pluto, making a total of twelve planets in our solar system. This had first been revealed to him during a discussion on board a Venusian carrier ship, and stated in the book, *Inside The Spaceships* (1955). The simplicity of this statement lay dormant for 28 years.

In January 1983, NASA placed a space telescope, the Infrared Astronomical Satellite (IRAS), in an orbit 560 miles above the Earth. For the first time ever, it revealed the outer reaches of our solar system, which had previously been invisible to astronomers because of the deep layer of atmosphere around our planet. High above the atmospheric interference, this 22.4 inch telescope was so sensitive that it could have detected a 20-watt light bulb on Pluto. For the first few months, astronomers at JPL tested their computers, and by summer, released some sketchy details on the discovery of new comets, asteroids, and mysterious bands of dust circling the sun between Mars and Jupiter. Then the press was given a stunning disclosure in October.

> The orbiting telescope IRAS may have sighted at least one new planet, and more planets may come to light next week when astronomers gather here.
> "There's a very good chance that IRAS will identify a new planet or two circling the sun beyond the orbits of Neptune and Pluto," said Nick Gautier, an infrared astronomer from the University of Arizona.
>
> -USA Today, 10-31-83

The press did not get any more information on that discovery. And NASA was furious that the astronomical community had bypassed JPL in announcing results to the public. Personnel were reprimanded, and NASA prohibited the release of any further data from IRAS. The only proper channel would be JPL, and staff spokesmen were not allowed to say anything until an upcoming press conference in November.

The space agency knew just what had to be told. NASA disavowed any previous "unauthorized" releases, and shifted attention to significant findings way out in the galaxy. Although admitting that scientists had analyzed only 2% of the data delivered by IRAS so far, NASA only emphasized the "steady stream of wonders" beyond our solar system - wispy clouds of interstellar dust and gas, the total energy in the universe, the unknown chemical soup from which stars are born, and the temperature of galaxies.

At the November press conference they redefined the discussion of planetary findings to the "stunning discovery of a possible planetary formation circling Vega, a bright star some 26 light-years away." They added that it would take one of our spaceprobes 200,000 years to get there. "You would have to be made of wood not to be interested," said top JPL spokesman Carl Sagan.

The project director, Nancy Boggess stated, "A lot of chapters in the astronomy books will be rewritten when all the results are in," but she added that it could take another 30 years to plow through all the information received from the year-long IRAS mission.

But the astronomy books are never rewritten to tell the truth about our own solar system. Space discoveries are censored by the agency's top officials. In the case of IRAS, the Kitt Peak Observatory astronomers innocently disclosed the findings of planets beyond Pluto, not knowing the relative significance of the data. NASA of course, did know the significance, and therefore avoided refreshing any reporter's memory at the press conference. As for the general scientific community, it rarely grabs at a lead unless the fact is confirmed over and over, and NASA had conveniently diverted all attention to dull speculation concerning interstellar dust clouds and star systems that are light-years away. In a very short while, the public and the media's interest dies, and all is forgotten.

What is the significance of the discovery by IRAS that was noted by the Arizona astronomers? It confirms the knowledge brought forward by Adamski in 1955. The top officials behind our space developments for the past 25 years have been specifically prepared with information by intelligence agencies of the government. Adamski's relationship to the UFO field is known to be authentic, and his space information regarding our solar system is known to be solid information. He was the only contactee who gave valid and specific space information that could be confirmed later -

be it Venus, Mars, the Moon, or beyond. But for the space agency to confirm anything publicly, would also confirm the truth behind UFOs and our interplanetary space visitors. This they have been instructed not to do, since certain powerful interests are behind the suppression of UFO information.

Given the high uncertainties and unreliability of our space probe instruments, it has been a relatively easy task to leave the state of scientific knowledge about space in doubt, and generally allow the orthodox attitudes to prevail. Only the specific findings on planetary environments have to be carefully controlled, and suppressed. We have thoroughly covered that situation regarding NASA's missions to Mars, Venus, and the Moon. It was top priority policy, by following secret directives, to suppress data and censor findings that would reveal habitability on those planets, and any major findings that would support Adamski's space science information. How else could the authorities keep the UFO reality suppressed?

The image that has been promoted, and carefully nurtured by the bureaucracy, is that our solar system is dead and uninviting - incapable of supporting life, except for the Earth. Of course that image is false, and the space agency knows that completely. But as far as they have gone in exploring our planetary system, NASA is also secretly following Adamski's guidelines, for the authorities know it is the only truths that will be found regarding our solar system. The intelligence agencies of our government have prepared them with that information.

Of course, it is the major findings that would change public and scientific perspective that are carefully controlled, but minor data from space probes that correlate Adamski's statements on space has often surfaced. The latter is usually apparent to only a very discerning reader. The 1978 Voyager probe's measurement of the kinetic energy temperature of the asteroid belt has been discussed already. There has been this type of incidental information from a number of space shots.

For example, in 1960 a Pioneer probe on its journey

toward the Sun registered "magnetic" storms and disturbances three million miles from Earth, and found a gigantic magnetic field with an axis unrelated to the sun. This discovery by the experimental probe closely matched statements made by Adamski in 1955 in *Inside the Spaceships*. In 1976, the structure of the sun's magnetic field was determined for the first time from data returned by the Pioneer 11 spacecraft, which was thrown 100 million miles above the ecliptic plane of the solar system after passing Jupiter. The probe revealed that the sun's magnetic field envelops the entire solar system in an elliptical pattern that is split into northern and southern hemispheres by a thin sheet of electric current. Fifteen years earlier, George Adamski related this description in his book *Flying Saucers Farewell*, and he further explained that these elliptical magnetic fields between planets could be likened to alternating current. These alternating elliptical fields, extending from sun to planet, and from planet to planet, are the invisible bonds which balance the solar system, he added.

There is much more that could be said on this intricate, balanced relationship that pervades and encompasses the whole solar system. To put it simply, a disruption in one part of the system will affect the rest of the solar system. A major disruption in the "magnetic rivers" between neighboring planets could easily be caused by unrestrained nuclear warfare on Earth, thereby unbalancing the cosmic fields of space. Not only would space travel by the space people be endangered, but their own planetary environment could be seriously affected. Now perhaps, we can better understand all the UFO activity by Venus and Mars in observing our Earth "come of age."

It is not generally realized that Adamski published, lectured, and conveyed an extensive amount of information beyond his three well-known books. In this additional material there is many a key for the researcher. It also shows a continual flow of new information from his contacts in the 1960's, as he developed a space education program along philosophical and technological lines. Society's real growth can only be developed from true space information and new applications in science.

In *UFOlogy*, James McCampbell reviewed a case study of an encounter between an Air Force plane and a UFO. The original investigation of this incident was conducted by James McDonald and presented at the December 1969 meeting of the American Association for the Advancement of Science, with his (McDonald's) analysis later being published in a book covering that scientific symposium.[7] Although neither man knew it, their detailed discussions of this incident supplied substantial corroboration of information given by Adamski years earlier, regarding the propulsion of spaceships.

An Air Force B-47 was on a training mission using the military's top ECM (Electronic Countermeasures) equipment, during a flight over the South-Central states in July, 1957. While flying at 35,000 feet, the aircraft commander and the co-pilot visually spotted a UFO, shortly after their navigation radar and two separate ECM receivers had electronically detected a rapidly moving object in the vicinity. The UFO suddenly appeared as an intense bluish-white light as it approached the aircraft. Thinking he might have to take evasive action, the flight commander was startled to see the UFO almost instantaneously change direction "and flash across their flight path from port to starboard at an angular velocity he had never seen matched in all of his twenty years of flying."

The pilot then received permission to ignore his flight plan and chase the object. He increased the B-47's speed to Mach 0.83 before turning to chase, and immediately the UFO pulled ahead. For the next hour and a half, and while covering about 800 miles, the UFO quite literally flew circles around the B-47, by performing extreme maneuvers to show that it could easily outfly and outdistance the military aircraft. During this whole time, the pilot's visual observations of the UFO from the cockpit coincided exactly with the UFO directions and signals detected by the on-board radar and the two ECM receivers, and also by ground control radar from Texas to Oklahoma.

Readings from the ECM equipment were written as part of the official report of the UFO incident as follows.

"...intercepted at approximately Meridian, Mississippi, a signal with the following characteristics; frequency 2995 MC to 3000 MC; pulse width of 2.0 microseconds; pulse repetition frequency of 600 cps; sweep rate of 4 rpm; vertical polarity ...Signal moved rapidly up the D/F scope indicating a rapidly moving signal source; i.e., an airborne source..."

James McCampbell summarized the above data into a single statement, and said,

"This UFO was, in fact, pouring forth large amounts of electromagnetic radiation in a very narrow range of the microwave region and it was pulsed at a low, audio rate."

The following is taken from a transcript of a lecture and discussion given by George Adamski on May 4, 1955. There was a question from the audience asking about the frequencies involved in the running of the spaceships. Giving a general description in layman's terms, Adamski answered:

"The ships themselves carry frequencies from sixty to seventy thousand megacycles in full operation. Static electricity is electrical energy, like a speed that is not in motion. It is in motion, but not what we call motion because it is stillness. Magnetism is already propelling energy. You have to convert static electricity into propulsion, or a pulsating state, in order to use it."

Note that the ECM equipment on board the B-47 measured the UFO's radiating frequency at 3000 MC, which is consistent with the fact that the UFO was simply keeping pace with the 500 mile-per-hour speed of the aircraft. While in full operation, (and they have been tracked on radar flying in excess of 8000 mph in our atmosphere), Adamski says the frequency of the ship's energy would be 60,000 to 70,000 MC. And his description of converting to "a pulsating state," agrees exactly with the ECM receiver detection that the UFO's electromagnetic energy was "pulsed at a low, audio rate."

The conclusions are simple. The highly classified incident did not come to light until McDonalds report in 1969. The case involved the first direct measurement of a UFO's energy field, and it was detected by sophisticated instrumentation on board a military aircraft. Adamski's information preceded McDonald's research, and McCampbell's notable review of the incident, by 14 and 18 years respectively. As Edward Ruppelt, the man in charge of Air Force investigations, once wrote, "What constitutes proof?"

The most significant aspect of this case remains to be discussed. When an investigator for the Condon Committee tried to research the case in 1967, he found that there was a total "security lid" on the incident. No reports could be obtained from Project Blue Book or the Air Defense Command. Details of the incident were finally secured through interviews with the pilot and two other officers of the B-47 flight. The pilot revealed that as soon as he landed following the UFO encounter, AF Intelligence went on board the plane and removed all the electronic countermeasures data and radar scope pictures that had been recorded during the flight. This was followed by intensive interrogation of the crew at the base headquarters by the Intelligence personnel. Lengthy questionnaires were completed, and submitted as part of the intelligence reports. The event and the information was classified in security beyond classification, and the crew was told nothing further regarding the incident.[8] The direct confirmation of the energy associated with UFOs is always kept under the blanket of "national security."

With excursions into space by artificial means, our astronauts have to contend with the experience of weightlessness. Pictures televised back from orbit always show the crew and unsecured objects floating around the cabin. In its harmless banter, media coverage never fails to comment on this accepted, and somewhat amusing, side-effect of "escaping gravity."

But in a related way, what is not laughable to the UFO censors is the description of true space flight given by George Adamski in *Inside the Spaceships*. Adamski and his space friends were not floating around the spacecraft in a weightless condition, because the ships utilize the natural energy forces in providing a gravitational field for the ship. And for the authorities to admit that the UFOs in our skies are interplanetary spaceships, would be to admit that this type of energy is within our immediate grasp. These spaceships are utilizing the natural electromagnetic energy of space for propulsion and for overcoming gravity. We could readily harness this natural energy for all our domestic use, including land transportation, heat, and electricity. It would be as free as the air we breathe. Official acceptance of the authentic reality of UFOs would in turn lead to the acknowledgement of their free energy, and this would break up the economic system of the money changers. So they fight it.

The world's energy controllers have always been the major force in blocking the truth about UFOs from coming out. This cartel is made up of the oil corporations, the power companies, and the nuclear energy industries. And this cartel is actually above - and controls - the international bankers. With their complete dominance of the world's energy resources, the ongoing stability of the world economy is subject to their control, and this forces the many governments, both capitalist and communist, to do their bidding. Those that fear the truth coming out are those in control of the monetary system. Because if the propulsion of these spaceships became known, the energy controllers would be ruined, and their polluting industries obsolete.

The war profiteers are also a major force behind the coverup. The world's military spending now totals $900 billion a year, with the United States and Russia counting for more than half the buildup. The superpowers keep fanning the flames of war around the globe, because international marketing of armaments and nuclear weapons is the basis of the world economy. The U.S. national debt is two trillion dollars (and this debt is placed on the people), while defense corporations are making billions of dollars. There can never be real peace with a system of distorted wealth, because peaceful co-existence would disintegrate the privileged power system of the money changers. The world's population is being kept hostage under poised nuclear weapons, in order to serve a very few money changers. Life is as close as the Moon and planets, but our world will be on the brink of Armageddon and never know that the life is there. The slightest admission that there are peaceful civilizations bringing their visiting spaceships here to our planet would be devastating to the money system of the war profiteers.

So together, the energy cartel and the weapons industries have everything to lose, and therefore they do not want the truth to be known. The truth of UFOs and the truth of space would entirely expose how wrong our global priorities are. These powerful corporations are the force behind the international Silence Group, which has suppressed the truth about UFOs and censored the real knowledge behind planetary findings ever since the 1950's. This Silence Group has an interlocking chain of invisible control working through government intelligence agencies, multinational corporations, and even national institutions.[9] This formidable group is in essence, a secret international government that serves the interests of the energy controllers, weapons producers, and bankers.

They have many ways of shaping events and many areas of influence to control. In their powerful conspiracy of world economics, they have many things to contend with, but we will restrict this discussion only to the issue of UFOs. The cartel has its own clandestine agencies working within the intelligence organizations of world governments. They have used every means to control and conceal the real UFO evidence from the public and scientific bodies. At the same time, this Silence Group insures that regular publicity is given to weird tales and crackpot ideas, thereby keeping the idea of UFOs in a ridiculous light. They even plant obvious hoaxes in the press, and foster false contact claims through the media by paying imposters. The opposition wants the public to associate UFOs with cults, and with psychics claiming to receive bizarre messages from space "entities." Any crackpot scheme is played up to instill a sour impression in the minds of the public.

But the biggest part of the censorship extended into the national space program. Life and living planetary conditions beyond the Earth, which could have been revealed from the earliest probes, was totally suppressed. A lifeless, uninhabitable picture was deceptively documented, and public thinking manipulated, in order to protect the money system of the world. Left in ignorance about space, the masses have been unconsciously led to electing dark leaders who teach hate and revenge, who build more destructive weapons, and who aggressively lay the groundwork for 'wars and threats of war.' The early adventure of space has been replaced with the present militarization of space. We are now marking time. We are closer to biblical prophecy than the other road which could pave the way towards a glorious future.

What is the purpose behind this secret international government? It is to keep the monetary system from changing, despite whatever progress mankind makes socially. The masses will not change their thinking, unless there is a change coming from institutional thinking, or direct information on space from government bodies.

Nuclear weapons and star wars development are promoted today - only to defend our system of money which is a false god. Political leaders and their clever sophists have fully desensitized the common people to the constant talk of wars and arms buildup. Any pretext or propaganda used to fan fires and identify "enemies" is acceptable. The masses have been conditioned to go about their trivial pursuits and directionless lives, and to leave their collective fate to the gambling men of war. Perverse power has been gained by the sudden exponential increase in arms selling in the 1980's by the superpowers. We are Atlantis today, slaves to habits from the past, and worshipping military might. Our fate is being decided by the false prophets of war and commercialism, and the dark forces in political power wield control by keeping the minds of the public confused, uncertain, and in fear.

We know that the space shuttle is for military purposes. It has nothing to do with space exploration or learning, but instead serves as a means to bring our war technology into orbit around the Earth. It will sometimes carry incidental scientific cargo, as part of the public relations hoopla, but the shuttle has really been developed for militarizing space around the Earth. It is not designed to get man into space, but to get man's weapons into space. Therefore it will not contribute to the advancement of man.

If the authorities were to admit the truth about UFOs and space, our whole approach would be forced to change. And rockets would now be outdated. In fact, there is no reason, except for economic ones, that we are still using rockets to artificially overcome gravity. We will never advance in capability, and we will never become a space civilization as long as we are stuck with rocket launching. It is primitive technology, and it opposes everything that this government knows about UFOs and their technology, and the government knows it. So do top scientists and the military.

Rockets are anything but true space machines. They go in one direction, one time, with a tiny crew strapped to tremendous G forces. And they are such an artificial way to overcome gravity, that the tremendous cost is a devastating expenditure.

Often our space visitors have been seen flying in huge formations of ships; occasionally a hundred or more would fly around an area together. Can you imagine seeing a hundred U.S. space shuttles flying together over California? The cost would be a trillion dollars. You would not see them hovering, nor would you see them for very long. They would soon be running out of fuel, be forced to land, then have to be towed to a launching facility. Each would have to be hooked up again to multi-million-dollar booster rockets and external fuel tanks, and 100 earth-shattering blast-offs would be required to put them temporarily back in the sky.

This chapter is perhaps written a bit forcefully, but it is time to shake things up a little. We are out to counteract the insidious coverup regarding space conditions that has been perpetrated on the masses, leaving society lost and hopeless. "When goodness is mocked and good people thrown into despair; when the false, the cruel, and the diabolic are so powerful, it is not surprising that men's minds are stabbed with doubts." - (Paul Brunton) Men can only recover their faith in humanity and in themselves when the truth is known and understood.

Back when the UFO situation was a new and challenging field, there was seemingly a luxury of time to ponder over the information. Thirty years have changed all that. Our present world situation is acutely critical - precariously balanced on the edge of a cliff - and it's imperative that as much information as possible be brought out to the public regarding the truth behind the UFO evidence.

One should readily understand, that the Silence Group does not care if a few people learn the truth about planetary science (Venus, Mars, and the Moon), or if a thousand people learn, or even perhaps ten thousand. But if the common people learn the truth - if they are told - then there *is* a problem for the censors, because the number could soon reach millions. And the energy controllers and the billion-dollar defense industries would no longer have the unquestioned mass support that they always have had.

This is why Adamski's evidence and space information posed such a threat to those in opposition to the truth. His information reached millions of people, and society was waking up to the beauty and splendor of life and space. Adamski always advocated the benefits of our becoming a true space civilization. Mankind would advance in learning and understanding unlike any previous time in history. Our planet is just as important as any other planet, and it is an integral part of the household of life. Any dream one may have, must have benefits here - on Earth. Not somewhere else.

Adamski always emphasized the need for our civilization to shift to a realistic space economy, and have interplanetary spaceships built here on Earth. Then man would be learning all the time, and becoming a true space civilization would lead us to greater cooperation and harmony on Earth. This would steer mankind away from his nuclear experimentation against Nature, and save this civilization. Knowing the truth about space sciences and the truth behind the UFOs, were the things that would advance man's understanding in order to make the Earth a better place to live. That has always been the importance of this field.

It is man's immature idea that the UFOs are an invitation for us to get out in space and we'll just leave the mess on Earth behind. No. It means work with each other and work with Nature here, in peace, so that we will be able to join in the adventure of space. The Earth is our home, and it is time we treat it with respect, and treat out brothers and sisters in every country with respect. Then we will be welcomed and helped to get in space. True space travel and visits to other planets would be our way of life.

The planets in our system are inhabited, and people of all planets except the Earth travel space freely. With their ships utilizing Nature's magnetic fields, the distance between planets can be covered within a few hours to a few days. Most spacecraft seen in our skies are from Venus. Smaller numbers are from Mars and Saturn, followed by visiting craft from other planets in our system. The space visitors are peaceful and friendly, and certainly human, but also very protective of us because we are all one interplanetary family in this solar system. But we on Earth do have to start earning our way a little, because open friendship cannot be extended if we refuse to believe in their existence, and as long as we do not express the will to live peacefully among nations on our own planet.

There is a chasm between knowledge
and ignorance which the arches of
science can never span.

- Thoreau

Chapter 12
Conclusions

Many insights into the remarkable character and
lifetime work of George Adamski have been revealed
through writings and discussions by his former co-workers
and associates. To review all the information which I have
read, and that which I personally learned through contact
with several of his co-workers, would fill the contents of
another book. Adamski also had many meetings with high
government and space officials, and while in Europe he was
received by Queen Juliana and Prince Bernhard of the
Netherlands. In 1963 Pope John XXIII gave him a special
golden medallion, that was only given to very few people for
high humanitarian achievement.

Perhaps the following example of mine will reveal a little
about the nature of the man - a man who had set out on an
extraordinary mission to speak on behalf of the space visitors
coming our way. It was no easy task in the 1950's, with all the
prevailing skepticism, the organized opposition, and the
general insistence of scientists that life on neighboring
planets was impossible. But Adamski faced all the trials and
tribulations of such a mission in a dignified and respectable
manner, to give the message, and to give expression to the
truth by living it.

The example I wish to cite occurred shortly after the
publication of *Flying Saucers Have Landed*. The book itself

was unusual in that its two authors had not met in person until long after initial publication and several reprints of the successful volume. (Desmond Leslie and Adamski had agreed by mail to include Adamski's manuscript and share co-authorship). The event took place in the summer of 1954, when Leslie made a trip to Palomar Gardens, California, to first meet Adamski, his co-author.

One evening, while Leslie and a few others were having a quiet discussion on Adamski's patio just after dark, Leslie recalls that all of a sudden he got a tremendous feeling of being watched. He swung around in time to see a small golden disk not more than fifty feet away, which then shot upward in a trail of light. Leslie was amazed to see a remote scanning disk from a spaceship, yet he relates that Adamski did not alert him to its presence although he knew that it was there all along. Only after the disk had left, did Adamski grin solemnly and say, "I was wondering when you were going to notice that."

Whereas someone else - a lesser character involved in the controversial field of space visitations - would have undoubtedly exclaimed upon noticing the scanning disk: "See that! I want you to see that, which will prove me right, (etc)." George Adamski never worried about so-called proof. Regarding his space contacts, the proof was in the message and knowledge given by the space people. Adamski gave expression of the truth, and presented everything on a practical and understandable level for all people. Following the publication of *Inside the Space Ships*, Adamski was able to develop an international Get Acquainted Program that could bring space science information and space age philosophy to citizens in many countries.

If one looks at the complete record, it becomes apparent that George Adamski was the most qualified person ever, to be contacted. And in retrospect, it can be presently understood that the space visitors did give the full information behind their coming. It was given once. True, there were progressive developments over several years, during the period we began to enter the space age. And the hundreds of thousands of UFO sightings (existent right up to the present) continued to alert the public to the reality of space visitations, and to support that information. But the truth behind the space visitations was given in its entirety once - it will not be repeated. In other words, there will be no new answers to the identity or origin of the spacecraft in our skies. The majority are from Venus, and the other spacecraft that are cooperating in their interplanetary ventures are also originating from planets in this solar system.

This was quite acceptable in the early years, but became more controversial as official announcements regarding space conditions mounted up during the 1960's and 70's. However, this book has examined and reviewed the latter situation thoroughly. The negative image of planetary conditions was based on dogmatic perceptions in orthodox science, that in turn was supported by official announcements regarding space probe missions that were heavily censored. Has officialdom gone beyond the point where it could be straightened out by objective and value-free science?

George Adamski presented the truth of our Venusian space visitors, and he provided actual descriptions of the planetary environment. Soon after his initial contact in 1952, he had been allowed the privilege of a few trips into space aboard their craft, to learn what he could and then give the information to people on Earth. While on a mothership on August 23, 1954, his space friends showed him live scenes of Venus by using a projection system so advanced, Adamski could scarcely describe how it was done. And the pictures and scenes of Venus were vivid and distinct, colorful and dimensional.

Adamski saw magnificent mountains, some rocky and some with snow. Many were thickly timbered, with streams and water cascades running down the mountainsides. He was told that Venus has many lakes and seven oceans, all of which are connected by waterways, both natural and artificial.

They showed him several Venusian cities, that all

followed a circular or oval pattern. People on the streets were going about in the same manner as we do, "except for the absence of rush and worry so noticeable with us." Their clothing was similar to our own. There were conveyances for mass transportation that silently glided down streets bordered with beautiful flowers. Adamski was shown beaches and tropical areas with bird and animal life. He also was informed that people rarely see the stars as we on Earth do, because of the firmament of the Venusian atmosphere.

These descriptions were contained in his book, *Inside the Space Ships*. In a later account, he mentioned that a day on Venus was 26 hours long, and that the atmospheric pressure was identical to that on the Earth.

We know that the Russian and American space programs sent a total of a dozen probes to the planet's surface. Common sense should tell us how the situation was handled on their end (by the Venusian civilization). But perhaps a short discussion given by Adamski in a private report will give a complete understanding to us. The information was included in a special letter by George Adamski to his close co-workers in the spring of 1961. At that time, the very first interplanetary space probe had been launched from Earth and was en route to Venus. The probe was Russia's Venera I, and it had been launched on February 12, 1961. (Earlier probes by the United States and Russia had all been directed towards the Moon).

Adamski's discussion was based on both public press reports and information obtained from meetings with space people at the time. He wrote:

> Russia now has a space probe en route to Venus, although we have been informed that she has lost contact with it. It is for scientific purposes, and since this is the only way we have of securing the knowledge we need, it will be allowed to land on that planet if it is accurately directed... I was told that a large interplanetary ship is following the probe sent out by the Russians, but not interfering with it. Much has already been learned from it (the probe) by our

scientists. For instance, the date on which this space probe was expected to hit Venus was at first set for sometime toward the end of May. Then it was set up to early May, then to mid-April. Later, one of our commentators reported it is nearing Venus. The reason given for these changing dates was that the probe was caught in some unknown force from the sun that was pulling it in faster than anticipated.

This part was verified by my space friends, and pointed out as only one of the infinite number of factors with which we must become familiar regarding outer space to be able to travel it safely. They did not say whether or not this sun's force had drawn the probe sufficiently far off its original trajectory towards Venus. Logically, this could happen. Because we must learn from our own experiences and from our own instruments, the space visitors, while observing and recording the results of our efforts, are not interfering nor passing on to us their information. This is as it should be, because lessons learned from experience are better understood and remembered, as we all know.

If the Russian calculations are accurate enough to enable their probe to enter the pull of Venus, it will be allowed to land there. Should its course be in direct line with a city or community of any kind, it will be slightly diverted to hit in an uninhabited part of the planet, thus protecting life and property. We would do the same if we were in their position. The diversion will be so slight that it will not interfere with the recordings sent to the probe's home base.

Let us say that this space probe lands safely in a desert area - and there are some on Venus similar to those on Earth - its instruments might conceivably send back reports of "no life". We neither know what instruments are enclosed, nor how they might survive such a landing. I strongly suspect there is no camera included that could photograph and send back reports of a person or many persons, who would naturally go to investigate this strange object. You may rest assured that it will be examined, however, with as much interest as we would give to an object under similar conditions. Perhaps even more, because they will have been alerted as to its nature even before it hits.

On the other hand, let us assume there is a camera within the probe that can and does send back photographs of humans, animal life, and various types of vegetation. Such information will not be made world-wide knowledge immediately. There will be reports and contradictions for a long time to come, regardless what nation is successful in reaching another planet first. I would go so far as to say that even when men and women are sent and safely land on another planet, or on our moon, they will be instructed to report and show only so much, should they be hooked up with a world radio or TV chain for reporting. Other information will be noted and given in personal reports to their government on their safe return.

This will probably be due to both the religious and political conditions existing throughout the world, and a fear as to how much could be accepted by the multitudes. Although I believe it may be only a relatively short time before we will have men traveling space in ships of our own making, I doubt that we will soon be given the whole truth of conditions found. So do not be disturbed by conflicting reports, which will be increasing in number as time passes. Remember how important events have been handled in the past (and take all reports in stride). Time will prove, that information given to me and which I have shared with you is true fact.

I had thought naturally along these lines for many years, and only recently did I receive a copy of the complete letter from which this report was taken. With regard to Venus probes, the report provided a logical explanation as to how that planetary civilization would respond to our efforts with remote space vehicles. The situation would not have been any different with probes to Mars and the Moon - the only two other planetary bodies that have been probed by landers. The planetary civilizations would not interfere with our simple devices sent out to check up on surface conditions. Mankind is allowed to follow his own chosen developments, and the interpretation of whatever he can detect in his reach to explore the unknown spaces beyond the Earth. This book has thoroughly reviewed the evidence behind space science research regarding the near planets, and the resulting limitations of our present-day knowledge due to several reasons.

Before my first sighting of spacecraft in 1974 (which was followed by reading the books of George Adamski), I had never studied anything on space science. During the next few years I began to study everything. I have also sighted the ships on several occasions since 1974, and two of those times there were witnesses with me. On one occasion, a scoutship glided down to rooftop level only 100 feet from where we were standing. Another time, I saw a mothership hovering at close range in the daytime sky, then it turned up and shot up into space. I have also seen a scanning disk from a distance of fifteen feet, which then accelerated straight up in a brilliant blue-green flash of light. My other sightings have been of distant scoutcraft.

In 1977 I first began lecturing on UFOs. The following year I founded the Public Interest Space Sciences Center in order to teach and promote the work of George Adamski, along with coordinating the evidence of planetary space science. I lectured at colleges and dozens of organizations, in addition to teaching classes at adult schools. Newspaper and radio interviews followed, along with a program for public television. To share information, I published a newsletter and began extensive correspondence. Through all of this activity, I have met many individuals who have had sightings of ships and a sincere interest in this field. And it was because of my public interest educational efforts, that they had first learned that there was real evidence and solid information to space visitations.

My own research kept me well aware of all the

developments in space science and planetary missions, past and present. When time allowed in my programs, I gave short presentations on up-to-date space sciences to add support to the work of George Adamski, which is the most important evidence in this field. But in past years, I have found that few people, if any, had the time or the inclination to follow through with their own research, nor were they able to analyze the scientific record to their own satisfaction. Those that tried could not find relevant material on the Moon, Mars, and Venus that challenged the conventional presentations and NASA write-ups. Therefore, I decided to write this book in order to present the clear picture - and truthful record - of planetary science in our solar system.

Acknowledgement that there are human civilizations on our neighboring planets, though profound to realize initially, is by itself not going to teach us anything about those space civilizations, or how we are going to achieve that society growth in our own world. It is only a first step. Scientific technology also, is but a small part towards becoming an advanced society. The mere fact that we can use rockets to put a satellite or a military payload into orbit does not make us a space civilization. The mentality of the world must change first. Right thinking must be developed - towards a reverence for all life. We only give lip service to the ideas of peace and brotherhood, all the while supporting the very things that prevent this from being a reality. We will not become a true space civilization until we respect each other as fellow human beings, - recognizing all as equals, brothers and sisters of one planetary home.

Then, properly guided by humanistic thinking, people would actively support true space knowledge, that would advance our civilization and begin to establish a peaceful, productive society on Earth. The mysteries of life would be replaced by the reality of life - the reality which is understood and lived by the space people coming our way. Mankind can presently be alerted to the truth about our neighboring space civilizations, and when our society begins to develop purposefully along these lines, we will be able to go on and become the greatest and only enduring civilization this world has ever known.

In conclusion, I sincerely hope that this book has provided a timely introduction to the subject of UFOs and space science for many people. For those readers interested in furthering their study, I would recommend that they obtain the original accounts of George Adamski's. Information on the current availability of his books is included in the appendix.

Compared to the knowledge that one can learn in this field, the information in this book, by itself, is of minor importance. It merely points out a direction. For personal understanding and individual growth, one must seek to learn self-knowledge, so that he may develop and express his inborn talent, and better serve his fellow-man. "Man know thyself" is the requisite for wisdom that has been handed down through the ages. With this understanding, and above all else in his recognized accomplishments, George Adamski brought out the reality and the truth of life, to the public.

As a society, and in reference to the whole field of flying saucers and space visitations, we are presently at the same point Adamski established in the 1960's. He completed a program which fully presents an understanding of space age philosophy and science, which if applied by society, will go far in establishing a peaceful and advanced civilization on our planet. This program of space knowledge and cosmic science has been carried on by his close associates and former co-workers since 1965.

I would like very much to hear from the readers, as to their interest in this field. Some may wish to send inquiries requesting further information about the work of George Adamski. With the additional reading, one will soon learn the full importance behind the visitations of interplanetary spaceships, and the responsibility of our present-day civilization to bring about true peace. If enough people are informed of the truth regarding space, our society will then make a turn, and this planet Earth will go on to become a true space civilization in our solar system.

Appendix

George Adamski's original hardcover editions (see plate 1) were published as:

Flying Saucers Have Landed (co-authored with
                                    Desmond Leslie)
Inside the Spaceships
Flying Saucers Farewell

The current American editions are as follows:

Inside the Spaceships (1980 reprint includes Adamski's account from *Flying Saucers Have Landed)*

Behind the Flying Saucer Mystery (paperback reprint of *Flying Saucers Farewell)*

These editions, and information on further writings, articles, and publications by George Adamski, may be obtained by writing to the author at:

Public Interest Space Sciences Center
P.O. Box 3033
Walnut Creek, CA 94598

NOTES

Chapter 2

1. *The UFO Controversy In America*, David Jacobs, Indiana University Press, 1975, p. 296.
2. *Our Ancestors Came From Outer Space*, Maurice Chatelain, Doubleday, 1977, p. 18.
3. *Los Angeles Herald Examiner*, Aug. 15, 1976.
4. *Celestial Passengers - UFOs and Space Travel*, Margaret Sachs, Penguin, 1977, pp. 102-105.
5. *Flying Saucers - Fact or Fiction?*, Max Miller, Trend Books, 1957, pp. 97-99.
6. *Flying Saucer Review*, "Remarkable Confirmation for Adamski?", Volume 29 - No.4, 1984, pp. 13-16.
7. *San Francisco Examiner*, Oct. 23, 1973.

Chapter 4

1. *Flying Saucers - Fact or Fiction?*, Max Miller, Trend Books, 1957, p. 54.
2. *Aliens From Space*, Donald Keyhoe, New York: Doubleday, 1973, p. 171.
3. *Flying Saucers - Fact or Fiction?*, Max Miller, Trend Books, 1957, p. 54.
4. Ibid, p. 43.
5. *Life on Mars*, David Chandler, New York: Dutton, 1979, p. 61.
6. *The Flying Saucer Conspiracy*, Major Donald Keyhoe, New York: Holt, 1955, p. 122.
7. Ibid, p. 209.
8. Ibid, pp. 209-211.

Chapter 5

1. *Life On Mars*, David Chandler, New York: Dutton, 1979, p. 110.
2. *Alien Bases On the Moon*, Fred Steckling, GAF International Publishers, 1981, p. 183.
3. *San Diego Evening Tribune*, "New Landing Site Okayed for Viking," July 00, 1976.
4. *Flying Saucer Review*, July-August 1962, p. 10.

Chapter 6

1. *The Expanding Case for the UFO*, M.K. Jessup, New York: Citadel, 1957, p. 180.
2. *The Flying Saucer Conspiracy*, Maj. Donald Keyhoe, New York: Holt, 1955, p. 78.
3. Ibid, p. 264.
4. *Strange World of the Moon*, V.A. Firsoff, New York: Basic Books, 1959, p. 2.
5. *Moongate: Suppressed Findings of the U.S. Space Program*, William Brian, Future Science Research Publishing Co., 1982, p. 100.
6. *The Expanding Case for the UFO*, M.K. Jessup, New York: Citadel, 1957, p. 143.
7. *Science and Mechanics*, "What Is Happening On the Moon?", John Brewer, 1966.
8. *The Flying Saucer Conspiracy*, Maj. Donald Keyhoe, New York: Holt, 1955, p. 74.
9. *The Expanding Case for the UFO*, M.K. Jessup, New York: Citadel, 1957, p. 159.
10. *The Old Moon and the New*, V.A. Firsoff, New Jersey: Barnes, 1969, p. 223.
11. Op. cit., *The Expanding Case For the UFO*, p. 46.

Chapter 7

1. *Our Ancestors Came From Outer Space*, Maurice Chatelain, New York: Doubleday, 1977, p. 17.
2. *Moongate: Suppressed Findings of the U.S. Space Program*, William Brian, Future Science Research Publishing Co., 1982, p. 117.

Chapter 8

1. *Footprints On the Moon*, The Associated Press, American Book-Stratford Press, 1969, p. 135.

246

Chapter 9

1. *Flying Saucer Review*, July-August 1961, "Venus As An Abode of Life", V.A. Firsoff.
2. *Strange World of the Moon*, V.A. Firsoff, New York: Basic Books, 1959, p. 21.
3. *Road In the Sky*, George Hunt Williamson, London: Neville Spearman, 1959, p. 153.
4. *Flying Saucers: Top Secret*, Donald Keyhoe, New York: Putnam, 1960, p. 201.
5. *Flying Saucer Review*, May-June 1963.
6. *Flying Saucer Review*, Sep-Oct 1965, "Is Venus Inhabited?", Charles Maney.
7. *The Washington Evening Star*, Jan. 16, 1967.
8. *The New Astronomies*, Ben Bova, New York: Mentor, 1972, p. 83.

Chapter 11

1. *Gods and Spacemen Throughout History*, W.R. Drake, Chicago: Henry Regnery Co., 1975, p. 41.
2. *Spacemen in the Ancient East*, W.R. Drake, London: Neville Spearman, 1968, p. 65.
3. Op. cit., *Gods and Spacemen Throughout History*, p. 227.
4. *The Expanding Case for the UFO*, M.K. Jessup, New York: Citadel, 1957, p. 136.
5. *Science Digest*, Sept. 1985.
6. *San Francisco Chronicle*, June 11, 1979.
7. *UFOs - A Scientific Debate,"Science in Default"*, James McDonald, edited by Sagan and Page, New York: Norton, 1974, p. 56 ff.
8. *Scientific Study of Unidentified Flying Objects*, University of Colorado, Bantam, 1969, Case 5: pp. 260-266.
9. *Operation Mind Control*, W.H. Bowart, New York: Dell, 1978, p. 24

247

Bibliography

Adamski, George and Leslie, Desmond. *Flying Saucers Have Landed.* Werner Laurie, London, 1953.

Adamski, George. *Inside the Spaceships.* Abelard-Schuman, N. Y., 1955.

Adamski, George. *Flying Saucers Farewell.* Abelard-Schuman, N. Y., 1961.

Allingham, Cedric. *Flying Saucer From Mars.* British Book Center, N. Y., 1955.

Aristophanes. *The Clouds.* Mentor, N. Y., 1962. Originally written in 423 B.C.

Archer, Jules. *Ho Chi Minh - Legend of Hanoi.* Crowell-Collier, N. Y., 1971.

Barnett, Lincoln. *The Universe and Dr. Einstein.* William Morrow, N. Y., 1948.

Blumrich, Josef. *The Spaceships of Ezekiel.* Bantam, N. Y., 1974.

Bova, Ben. *The New Astronomies.* Mentor, N. Y., 1972.

Bowart, W.H. *Operation Mind Control.* Dell, N. Y., 1978.

Brian, William. *Moongate: Suppressed Findings of the U.S. Space Program.* Future Science Research Publishing Co., Portland, 1982.

Brown, Vinson. *Voices of Earth and Sky.* Naturegraph, Happy Camp, CA., 1974.

Brunton, Paul. *A Search In Secret India.* Dutton, N. Y., 1935.

Brunton, Paul. *A Search In Secret Egypt.* Rider, Lond., 1936.

Brunton, Paul. *Hermit In the Himalayas.* Rider, Lond., 1937.

Brunton, Paul. *The Inner Reality.* Rider, Lond., 1939.

Brunton, Paul. *The Spiritual Crisis of Man.* Dutton, N. Y., 1953.

Caldicott, Helen. *Nuclear Madness.* Autumn Press, Brookline, MA., 1978.

Chandler, David. *Life On Mars.* Dutton, N. Y., 1979.

Chatelain, Maurice. *Our Ancestors Came From Outer Space.* Doubleday, N. Y., 1977.

Churchward, James. *The Lost Continent of Mu.* Ives Washburn, N. Y., 1931.

Cousins, Norman. *In Place of Folly.* Harper, N. Y., 1961.

Cramp, Leonard. *Space, Gravity and the Flying Saucer.* British Book Center, N. Y., 1955.

Cramp, Leonard. *Piece For A Jig-saw.* Somerton, Isle of Wight, 1966.

Dickson, Paul. *Out of This World.* American Space Photography. Delta, (Dell), N. Y., 1977.

Downing, Barry. *The Bible and Flying Saucers.* Lippincott, Philadelphia, 1968.

Drake, W.R. *Gods or Spacemen?* Amherst Press, Wisconsin, 1964.

Drake, W.R. *Spacemen in the Ancient East.* Neville Spearman, Lond., 1968.

Drake, W.R. *Gods and Spacemen in Greece and Rome.* Signet, N. Y., 1972.

Drake, W.R. *Gods and Spacemen in the Ancient West.* Signet, N. Y., 1974.

Drake, W.R. *Gods and Spacemen of the Ancient Past.* Signet, N. Y., 1974.

Drake, W.R. *Gods and Spacemen Throughout History.* Henry Regnery, Chicago, 1975.

Firsoff, V.A. *Strange World of the Moon.* Basic Books, N. Y., 1959.

Firsoff, V.A. *The Old Moon and the New.* Barnes, New Jersey, 1969.

Fuller, John. *Aliens in the Skies.* Putnam, N. Y., 1969.

Girvan, Waveney. *Flying Saucers and Common Sense.* Citadel, N. Y., 1955.

Guillaumont, A. *The Gospel According To Thomas.* Harper and Row, N. Y., 1959.

Hansen, L. Taylor. *He Walked The Americas.* Amherst Press, Wisconsin, 1963.

Hayden, Tom. *The Love of Possession Is a Disease With Them.* Holt,

Rinehart, & Winston, San Francisco, 1972.
Hayden, Tom. *The American Future - New Visions Beyond Old Frontiers.* South End Press, Boston, 1980.
Heaps, Leo. *Operation Morning Light.* Paddington Press, N. Y., 1978.
Hefley, James. *Lift-off! - Astronauts and Space Scientists Speak Their Faith.* Zondervan, Grand Rapids, 1970.
Heyerdahl, Thor. *The Ra Expeditions.* Signet, N. Y., 1972.
Hoffmann, Banesh. *Albert Einstein - Creator and Rebel.* Plume, N. Y., 1972.
Homet, Marcel. *Sons of the Sun.* Neville Spearman, Lond., 1963.
Hopana, Ion and Weverbergh, Julien. *UFOs From Behind the Iron Curtain.* Bantam, 1975.
Jessup,M.K. *The Case For The UFO.* Citadel, N. Y., 1955.
Jessup,M.K. *UFO and the Bible.* Citadel, N. Y., 1956.
Jessup,M.K. *The UFO Annual.* Citadel, N. Y., 1956.
Jessup,M.K. *The Expanding Case for the UFO.* Citadel, N. Y., 1957.
Keel, John. *Our Haunted Planet.* Neville Spearman, Lond., 1971.
Keyhoe, Donald. *The Flying Saucers Are Real.* Fawcett, N. Y., 1950.
Keyhoe, Donald. *Flying Saucers From Outer Space.* Holt, N. Y., 1953.
Keyhoe, Donald. *The Flying Saucer Conspiracy.* Holt, N. Y., 1955.
Keyhoe, Donald. *Flying Saucers: Top Secret.* Putnam, N. Y., 1960.
Keyhoe, Donald. *Aliens From Space.* Doubleday, N. Y., 1973.
Landsburg, Alan and Sally. *In Search of Ancient Mysteries.* Bantam, N. Y., 1974.
Larousse. *World Mythology.* Hamlyn, Lond., 1965.
Larousse. *Encyclopedia of Mythology.* Prometheus Press, N. Y., 1959.
le Poer Trench, Brinsley. *Men Among Mankind.* Neville Spearman, Lond., 1962.
Lewis, Richard. *Appointment On The Moon.* Ballantine, N. Y., 1968.
McCampbell, James. *UFOlogy - New Insights from Science and Common Sense.* Jaymac Co., CA., 1973.
McCarry, Charles. *Citizen Nader.* Signet, N. Y., 1972.
Miller, Max. *Flying Saucers - Fact or Fiction?* Trend, Los Angeles, 1957.
Moore, William. *The Philadelphia Experiment: Project Invisibility.* Fawcett, N. Y., 1979.
NASA. *Life Beyond Earth and the Mind of Man.* U.S. Government Printing Office, Washington, D.C. 1973.
National Geographic Society. *Man's Conquest of Space.* By William R. Shelton, 1968.
Neihardt, John. *Black Elk Speaks.* Pocket Books, N. Y., 1972.
Nelson, Earl. *There IS Life On Mars.* Citadel, N. Y., 1956.
O'Leary, Brian. *The Making of an Ex-Astronaut.* Houghton-Mifflin, Boston, 1970.
O'Neill, Gerard. *The High Frontier.* Bantam, N. Y., 1977.
O'Neill, John J. *Prodigal Genius - The Life of Nikola Tesla.* David McKay Co., N. Y., 1944.
Pickthall, Mohammed. *The Meaning of the Glorious Koran.* Mentor, N. Y., 1974.
Potter, Rev. Dr. Charles. *The Lost Years of Jesus Revealed.* Fawcett, Greenwich, CT., 1962.
Reece, Ray. *The Sun Betrayed.* South End Press, Boston, 1979.
Ruppelt, Edward. *The Report on Unidentified Flying Objects.* Doubleday, N. Y., 1977.
Sachs, Margaret. *Celestial Passengers - UFO's and Space Travel.* Penquin, N. Y., 1977.
Sachs, Margaret. *The UFO Encyclopedia.* Perigee, N. Y., 1980.

Saunders, David and Harkins, Roger. *UFOs? Yes! - Where the Condon Committee Went Wrong*. Signet, N. Y., 1968.

Scully, Frank. *Behind the Flying Saucers*. Holt, N. Y., 1950.

Seton, Ernest and Julia. *The Gospel of the Redman*. 1963.

Shearer, Tony. *Lord of the Dawn,* Quetzalcoatl. Naturegraph. Happy Camp, CA., 1971.

Shearer, Tony. *Beneath the Moon and Under the Sun*. SUN Publishing, Albuquerque, N.M., 1975.

Sigma, Rho. *Ether-Technology: A Rational Approach to Gravity-Control.* 1977.

Steckling, Fred. *We Discovered Alien Bases on the Moon*. GAF International, 1981.

Steckling, Fred. *Why Are They Here?* Vantage, N. Y., 1969.

The Associated Press. *Footprints on the Moon*. American Book - Stratford Press, 1969.

Tomas, Andrew. *We Are Not the First*. Putnam, N. Y., 1971.

Tompkins, Peter and Bird, Christopher. *The Secret Life of Plants*. Avon, N. Y., 1973.

Villaseñor, David. *Tapestries In Sand*. Naturegraph, Happy Camp, CA., 1963.

Ward, Theodora. *Men and Angels*. Viking, N. Y., 1969.

Waters, Frank. *Book of the Hopi*. Ballantine, N. Y., 1963.

Wilford, John. *We Reach The Moon*. Bantam, N. Y., 1969.

Williamson, George Hunt. *Road In the Sky*. Neville Spearman, Lond., 1958.

Williamson, George Hunt. *Secret Places of the Lion*. Neville Spearman, Lond., 1958.

Willoya, William and Brown, Vincent. Warriors of the Rainbow. Naturegraph, Happy Camp, CA., 1962.